The Sandino Affair

The Sandino Affair

Neill Macaulay

WACAHOOTA PRESS

MICANOPY • FLORIDA

Fourth Printing
Library of Congress Catalog number 85-20430
Macaulay, Neill
The Sandino Affair
Reprint: Originally published Chicago
Quadrangle Books, 1967.
Bibliography.
Includes index.
1. Sandino, Augusto César, 1895-1934. 2. Nicaragua
—History—1909-1937. 3. Nicaragua—Foreign Relations
—United States. 4. United States—Foreign Relations—
Nicaragua. 5. Guerrillas—Nicaragua—History—20th
century. 6. Revolutionists—Nicaragua—Biography.
1. Title.
FI526.3.S24M33   1998   972.85'05   85-20430
ISBN 0-9653864-4-9 (pbk.)

To Nancy

Preface

THIS BOOK was written at the time of the United States' escalation in Vietnam and was first published on March 3, 1967, eleven months before the Tet offensive. American and allied forces in Vietnam then were making the same basic mistakes that the U.S. Marines and their native collaborators had made in Nicaragua in 1927–32 in their unsuccessful campaign to crush the guerrilla movement led by General Augusto César Sandino—as the final chapter notes. Since that was written, Vietnam was "lost," and by the mid-1980s the government of the United States had developed a new obsession: fear of "losing" Nicaragua. The administration of President Ronald Reagan learned well the military lessons of Vietnam, as the management of the *contra* insurgency in northern Nicaragua demonstrates. U.S.-backed guerrillas are employing tactics long associated with Sandino against the forces of a government that bears his name in an area and among a rural population that had provided the essential friendly environment for the original Sandinistas of the 1920s. The survival of the contras is the measure of their success. The recent history of Nicaragua is loaded with irony.

Twenty years ago there was a liberalizing trend in Nicaragua, with the Somoza family dictatorship easing up on political repression and, for the first time, showing some concern about the country's deplorable social conditions. But this phase ended in the late 1960s with the accession to the presidency, via a fraudulent election, of the unstable Anastasio Somoza Debayle, fol-

lowed by the death of his astute older brother, Luis. In the meantime, the Sandinista National Liberation Front (F.S.L.N) had
been formed by Nicaraguan exiles in Cuba—encouraged and fi-
nanced by the government of Fidel Castro—and was on hand in
Nicaragua to exploit the mistakes of the last member of the
Somoza dynasty. Somoza Debayle's unbridled greed, his near total
moral corruption, alienated virtually every sector of the Nicaraguan population and spelled disaster for the regime that had been
installed four decades earlier by the U.S. Marines.

The Marines had intervened in the Nicaraguan civil war of
1926–27 to prevent the victory of the side that was supported by
revolutionary Mexico, then perceived to be the beachhead of bol-
shevism in the Americas. General Sandino, alone among the leaders of either side, refused to accept American arbitration of the
conflict and led his troops in a guerrilla campaign against the
Marines that lasted until the latter withdrew from the country at
the beginning of 1933. After he had made peace, the man for
whom the present Nicaraguan ruling party is named was murdered by members of the National Guard, the indigenous army
that had been organized by the U.S. Marines, on orders from the
man whom the American government had imposed as its commander, General Anastasio Somoza García. Nicaragua's Sandinistas see themselves engaged with the United States and its puppets
in a war that has been going on for nearly sixty years.

Americans tend to have short historical memories. To most
of us it is incomprehensible that Armenians would still want to
avenge the slaughter of their countrymen seven decades ago.
American citizens—those who are not Jews—are often surprised
to learn that the survivors of the Nazi holocaust and their descendants are unwilling to forget that supreme horror. While no comparable atrocity was committed by U.S. forces in Nicaragua in
1927–33, a proud nation was humiliated, occupied militarily by
insensitive and often bigoted foreigners, who left only after putting into place the elements for a sleazy native tyranny—a historical experience that many, perhaps most, Nicaraguans choose not
to forget. Inspired by the example of the martyred Sandino, the

latter-day Sandinistas remain determined to redeem the honor of their people by continued resistance to the United States. The hostility generated by this affair of more than half a century ago is a major factor in today's confrontation in Central America.

As an officer in Fidel Castro's army in Cuba in 1959, I perceived a similar, though less intense and widespread, antipathy toward the United States among leaders of the Cuban Revolution. Cuba's turn toward the Soviet Union in 1959–60, however, came about not simply because Castro wanted to spite the United States, but because he became convinced that Marxist-Leninist collectivism was far superior to liberal capitalism as a vehicle for economic and social development. That he was wrong seems obvious today, but in 1960 much of the world was dazzled by Soviet space triumphs, impressed by the U.S.S.R.'s recovery from the ravages of World War II, and captivated by the confident, dynamic personality of Chairman Nikita Khrushchev. By contrast, the United States—with its inability to match the Soviet Union in space, its economic recession, the U-2 incident, the humiliation of its president at the Paris summit conference—in 1960 seemed to be a nation in decline. Fidel Castro was hardly alone in believing that communism was the wave of the future. When Castro sponsored the formation of the F.S.L.N. in Havana in 1961, it was inevitable that the Nicaraguan revolutionary front would be Marxist-Leninist as well as Sandinista.

Though the world changed drastically in the eighteen years before they took over the government in Managua, the Sandinistas retained a residual faith in state-directed collectivism and a strong feeling of solidarity with the Cuban regime that has helped to sustain them. They came to power proclaiming "pluralism," which was consistent with the advice of President Castro, who counseled his protégés not to make the mistakes he had made—not to destroy the private sector, not to drive out the middle class, not to provoke a confrontation with the United States.

The administration of President Jimmy Carter was willing to support F.S.L.N. pluralism in Nicaragua if the Sandinistas would refrain from aiding revolutionary movements elsewhere in Central

America—specifically in El Salvador. The Nicaraguans indulged
their anti-Yankee feelings by taking money from Washington
while secretly shipping arms to the Farabundo Martí National
Liberation Front, which the Front then used to launch its "final
offensive" in El Salvador at the beginning of 1981. Within a few
weeks the Sandinistas had to face the consequences of the failure
of their allies in El Salvador and the inauguration of a new president in Washington, one who had far less tolerance than his
predecessor for people who hate the United States. The cutoff of
U.S. aid to Nicaragua, the beginning of the contra campaign, the
mining of Nicaraguan harbors, and the U.S. embargo have followed in a relentless escalation, which the Sandinistas have answered by cracking down on dissent and constricting the forces
of pluralism, and which seems to be leading to the severance of
diplomatic relations and, ultimately, to a new American invasion
of Nicaragua.

That outcome would be costly to the United States and fatal
to the Sandinistas, and both sides would do well to take steps to
avoid it. The Nicaraguans could quietly bury Marxism-Leninism,
resurrect pluralism, and politely ask their Cuban friends to leave,
while the Americans might publicly acknowledge the right of
Nicaragua to be independent and Sandinista, withdraw the demand that its government say "uncle," and do something to honor
the memory of General Sandino—like sending the commandant
of the Marine Corps to Managua to lay a wreath at a monument to
the hero. That would be a gesture comparable to Richard Nixon's
toast to Mao Tse-tung in Peking—one that would do much to ease
deep-seated hostilities and clear the way for a new and mutually
beneficial relationship. Just as rapprochement with China demanded a tribute to the aging Mao, reconciliation with Nicaragua
requires that the United States make peace with the ghost of
Sandino.

A specter haunting the United States in Central America and
the inspiration for the most virulently anti-Yankee government
established on the Western Hemisphere mainland in more than a
century, Sandino was also one of the precursors of modern revo-

lutionary guerrilla warfare. This is the process used to seize political control of an entire country by guerrilla action, without
resort to conventional military operations, except perhaps in the
final stage of the struggle when the guerrilla army has acquired
many of the characteristics of a regular army. This final stage,
which Sandino's forces never attained, is really an anticlimax; the
enemy must be beaten—his will to resist broken—before the guerrillas can employ conventional military procedures for mopping-up
operations. Revolutionary guerrilla warfare is a process of attrition directed against the morale of the target government and its
supporters—military and civilian, native and foreign.

Sandino launched his guerrilla campaign against the U.S.
Marines in Nicaragua in 1927, at almost precisely the same time
that Mao Tse-tung began his long guerrilla struggle against the
government of Chiang Kai-shek in China. That year marked the
end of an era in the evolution of guerrilla warfare: the airplane
and the machine gun mastered the deserts and plains, denying
them to roving columns of guerrilla horsemen. It was in 1927 that
the last of Abdel Krim's Riffs surrendered to the French and
Spanish armies in North Africa and that Luís Carlos Prestes' revolutionary column gave up the struggle in Brazil.

The celebrated guerrillas of the nineteenth and early twentieth centuries—the *gauchos* of the South American pampas, the
llaneros of Venezuela, the *vaqueros* of Mexico, the desert warriors
of the Middle East—had had their day by 1927. The new guerrilla
who emerged that year spurned the horse and the lance and
avoided massed formations in the open, where he could be cut
down by automatic fire or aerial bombardment. The habitat of
the new guerrilla was the forests and the mountains, where he
moved about in small groups, often under cover of dense foliage,
practically secure from observation and attack from the air. To
his arsenal the new guerrilla added that celebrated innovation of
the 1920s, the submachine gun—light, simple, sturdy, and easy to
repair in the field. Like his predecessors, the guerrilla who
emerged in 1927 traveled light, lived off the land, and massed his
forces for the attack. But after the attack he dispersed into small

groups rather than gallop away en masse into the desert or the plains. He struck—usually from ambush—only when the odds were clearly in his favor; otherwise he avoided combat.

More important, the new guerrilla limited his range. His primary concern was to consolidate his control over one limited area from which he could slowly and methodically spread his revolution to other regions of the country. He was not interested in making spectacular raids through enemy territory across half a continent. In the end he might seize half a continent, but first he must make himself secure in one area. His security depended not upon his holding key terrain features, but upon his dominating the population in his zone of operations. The people learned that the guerrilla might withdraw from their village in the face of an advance by regular troops, but also that he would return as soon as the soldiers were gone. By a system of rewards and punishments the guerrilla impressed upon the local population the wisdom of providing him with vital intelligence and supplies and denying these to his enemy.

These were the tactics, recounted and analyzed in this book, that were employed by Sandino in Nicaragua from 1927 to 1933. They are essentially the same as the tactics of the People's Liberation Army in China, the National Liberation Front in Algeria, the 26 of July Movement in Cuba, and the Viet Minh and Vietcong in Vietnam. Sandino lacked the political sophistication of the leaders of the post-World War II liberation movements, but in guerrilla tactics he could have been their teacher. Fidel Castro and Che Guevara did, in fact, learn much from men who had fought with Sandino or had studied his tactics. Politically Sandino provided the Cuban revolutionaries with an object lesson in *what not to do*. Fidel Castro was determined to destroy completely the military machine that had opposed him—something Sandino failed to do, and it cost him his life.

Those whose assistance was acknowledged in the first edition of this book will not be forgotten here. They are John P. Harrison, the late Thomas F. McGann, the late Bernard B. Fall, Richard Millett, Vernon E. Megee, Judy Carroll, Michael O'Quinlivan,

John Marley, my parents, and my wife of twenty-seven years, Nancy Macaulay. Once again I thank them and absolve them of responsibility for any errors of judgment, interpretation, or fact contained herein.

Neill Macaulay
Gainesville, Florida
August 1985

Contents

⊂▤

PREFACE   7

One   Land of Lakes and Volcanos   *19*
Two   The Peace of Tipitapa   *31*
Three   Sandino   *48*
Four   The Battle of Ocotal   *62*
Five   El Chipote: The Illusive Fortress   *83*
Six   1928: The Survival of Sandinismo   *105*
Seven   A Stalemate and a Trip to Mexico   *134*
Eight   The National Guard Offensive   *161*
Nine   Guerrilla Offensives   *186*
Ten   The End of a Banana War   *219*
Eleven   The Death of Caesar   *242*
Postscript   The Ghost of Sandino   *257*

NOTES   *275*

BIBLIOGRAPHICAL NOTE   *307*

INDEX   *311*

The Sandino Affair

I

Land of Lakes and Volcanos

⊂╪

Nicaraguans," wrote General Augusto Sandino, "are intrepid, political, even poets by nature." [1] The poetic nature of Nicaragua has engendered a nation of poets—where Poet is a title of honor, like Doctor or Professor; it produced the incomparable Rubén Darío, the Nicaraguan who became a revolutionary force in Spanish verse. But Nicaragua has achieved less fame for poetry than for political chaos—product of the temerity and fierce partisanship inherent in the nature of her people. Revolution, banditry, civil war, and anarchy became the facts of life in Nicaragua in the century following the end of Spanish rule.

Spain, preoccupied with holding her richer colonies, gave up Central America in 1821 without a fight. After a brief period of Mexican dominance, Nicaragua and the other former colonies—Guatemala, Honduras, El Salvador, and Costa Rica—formed the Federation of Central America in 1824. Within two decades lack of communication among the states of the largely mountainous and jungle-clad isthmus, and local partisanship and the church-state conflict, caused the dissolution of the federation. Thereafter the two political parties of the federation, the Liberals and the Conservatives, developed as national parties in each of the five republics. But they never completely severed the bonds of their common descent from the federation parties. A Liberal from El Salvador could "find more in common with a Liberal from

Nicaragua than with a Conservative from his home town." [2]
In Central America the Conservatives generally represented
the Church and vested economic interests, while the Liberals
were anti-clerical and, sometimes, a bit more friendly to the
lower economic classes.

The Liberal-Conservative conflict in Nicaragua was tied
to the rivalry between the republic's two principal cities,
León and Granada. Both Liberal León and Conservative
Granada lie in the lowlands of the Pacific coastal belt. Here,
where withering heat and stifling humidity seem to conspire
to shorten tempers, the urge to dispatch armies to deal with
troublesome neighbors has been hard to resist. Managua, the
capital and perennial military objective, is situated between
the rival cities, in the same torrid lowlands. This western
region of Nicaragua, home of the vast majority of the people
of this nation, the size of the state of Michigan, is bisected by
a spectacular file of volcanos. Massive, towering cones, rising
in magnificent symmetry, smoldering and, from time to time,
erupting with devastating fury, the volcanos bedevil the
poetic soul of Nicaragua: to settle differences by means not
involving fire and destruction would seem not only prosaic
but unnatural. At times, volcanic dust in the atmosphere
filters out all but the red and orange rays of the setting sun,
and a sunset of violent crimson splashes across the western
sky like a vast flag of mutiny and revolt.

The one natural feature that has had the greatest influence on Nicaragua's history is not a volcano; it is a lake.
Nearly straddling the isthmus, Lake Nicaragua, the largest
lake between Lake Michigan in the U.S. and Lake Titicaca
in South America, made Nicaragua a likely site for an interoceanic canal. The San Juan River, which drifts from Lake
Nicaragua into the Caribbean, was until recent years navigable for fairly large vessels; and the neck of land separating
Lake Managua from the Pacific is only fifteen miles wide at
its narrowest point. The sprawling lake itself can be navi-
gated by the largest ships; except for salt water, it seems to
have all the properties of a sea—including two-hundred-

pound man-eating sharks. Since colonial times an important trans-isthmian trade route has run from San Juan del Norte on the Caribbean up the San Juan River and across Lake Nicaragua to Conservative Granada on its northern shore. From here goods were shipped overland through Managua, Liberal León, and Chinandega to Corinto, Nicaragua's principal port on the Pacific. Managua, the capital, is on the southern shore of the republic's second largest lake, Lake Managua, which can support water-borne commerce but is linked to Lake Nicaragua only by the unnavigable and erratic Tipitapa River.

Both the United States and Great Britain early recognized the strategic importance of Nicaragua. Britain exercised a protectorate over most of Nicaragua's Caribbean shore—the Mosquito Coast—from 1678 to 1894. This low-lying, swampy littoral, with its innumerable coves and inlets, once provided a haven for English pirates and privateers. Separated from the Pacific region by mountains and by the largest tropical rain forest in Central America, and inhabited by Indians of South American extraction, English buccaneers, Jamaican Negroes, and their mixed descendants, the British protectorate had little in common with western Nicaragua, where the population was descended from Spaniards and Indians of the Mexican-Maya family. British interests in Nicaragua collided with American interests in the 1850's, after a group of American financiers led by Cornelius Vanderbilt established the Accessory Transit Company to ferry California-bound freight and passengers across the isthmus. The British tried to extend their Mosquito Coast protectorate to Vanderbilt's Caribbean terminal, San Juan del Norte, but firm American policy forced the British out of this port and eventually caused them to relinquish their entire protectorate.

Meanwhile, Nicaraguan politics followed its turbulent course. In 1855 the Liberals procured the services of William Walker of Tennessee and his band of filibusters in the civil war they were waging that year against the Conservatives. Once in Nicaragua the irrepressible Walker seized control of the government for himself, canceled the charter of Vanderbilt's Transit Company, got himself "elected" President of Nicaragua, threatened the British protectorate on the Mosquito Coast, and legalized slavery in Nicaragua. Such effrontery won Walker the warm support of a few and the relentless opposition of many. Supported by Vanderbilt and the British, armies from the other four Central American republics invaded Nicaragua and in 1857 forced her alien President into exile—but not before Walker's desperados had laid waste the city of Granada. When a comeback attempt failed in 1860, Walker surrendered to the captain of a British man-of-war; the British officer treacherously delivered the hapless Tennessean into the hands of his Honduran enemies who summarily executed him.

The United States did not intervene officially in Nicaragua until the advent of Dollar Diplomacy in the twentieth century. During the first decade of the century, more and more American capital was venturing abroad, encouraged by the government in Washington. President William Howard Taft frankly declared that the foreign policy of his administration was "made to include active intervention to secure for our merchandise and our capitalists opportunity for profitable investment" abroad.[3] Nicaragua was one of the foreign countries attracting American investors. José Santos Zelaya, a Liberal who became President of Nicaragua in 1893, favored foreign investments in his homeland and granted sweeping concessions to U.S. capitalists. By 1909 an American navigation company was operating a transportation monopoly on the rivers running through the banana country west of Bluefields; north of that town another American company was growing bananas on a vast tract of government land near Las Perlas; farther up the east coast an American lumber company was exploiting timber rights on eight thousand square miles of pine lands; other American companies had mineral rights to extensive areas in various parts of the country and were engaged in mining gold; an American firm owned all the port facilities at Corinto, on the Pacific; another American company had the exclusive right to manufacture ice in the republic; individual Americans—with Englishmen, Germans, and other Europeans—owned coffee plantations in the area around Matagalpa. Thus by 1909 the production of coffee, gold, lumber, and bananas—the principal sources of Nicaragua's foreign exchange—was to a large extent in American hands.[4]

But by 1909 President Zelaya, who was in fact a ruthless dictator,[5] had begun granting nationals of other countries concessions that conflicted with those bestowed previously upon American investors. In January 1909 Zelaya gave American banking interests a slap in the face by negotiating a 1,250,000 pounds sterling loan from a London syndicate. At the same time the Nicaraguan dictator was reportedly ready to offer Japan exclusive rights to construct an interoceanic canal across his country. These developments, and Zelaya's constant intermeddling in the affairs of other Central American republics, led Washington to the conclusion that the Nicaraguan dictatorship could no longer be tolerated. On October 10, 1909, some anti-Zelaya Liberals joined the Conservatives in launching a revolt against the dictatorship. Shortly afterward two American soldiers of fortune serving with the rebels were captured and executed by government forces. Reacting supposedly to these executions, American Secretary of State Philander C. Knox indignantly termed Zelaya "a blot on the history of Nicaragua"[6] and broke diplomatic relations. Dictator Zelaya reacted by abandoning the presidency, but the civil war raged on. Marines were landed —ostensibly to protect American property—and became the protectors of the hard-pressed Conservative army on the Caribbean coast. Having occupied Bluefields and proclaimed the neutrality of that port, the Americans then handed the collectorship of customs there to the Conservatives. With such moral and material support from the Yankees, the Conservatives soon crushed their foes and established in Managua a regime amenable to the United States. Their mission accomplished, the Marines were withdrawn in 1910. The next year

President Taft appointed a collector of customs for Nicaragua, and New York bankers made loans to the Nicaraguan government; for security the bankers received a controlling interest in the republic's state railways and national bank.[7]

In 1912 the Liberals, joined by some dissident Conservatives, rose up in arms against the puppet regime. American Marines were landed at the request of Conservative President Adolfo Díaz and took the field against the insurgents. The rebellion was suppressed in short order, but this time the Marines did not withdraw after their victory. To guard against future outbreaks a "legation guard" of at least a hundred men remained in Nicaragua until 1925. During this intervention the Bryan-Chamorro Treaty was negotiated, giving the United States the exclusive right to construct an interoceanic canal across Nicaragua. Not the least of American accomplishments in Nicaragua during this period was the supervision in 1924 of the most nearly honest elections in the history of the country. Carlos Solórzano, a moderate Conservative, was elected President, and Dr. Juan B. Sacasa, a Liberal physician, won the vice-presidency.

The Marines were withdrawn in August 1925, and the inevitable revolt broke out two and a half months later. The uprising was launched in the name of General Emiliano Chamorro, the wily Conservative chieftain who had emerged after the fall of Liberal Dictator Zelaya as Nicaragua's strongest personality. A veteran of three abortive revolts and the revolution of 1909–1910 that deposed Zelaya, Chamorro held high positions in the American-protected Conservative governments that succeeded the Liberal regime. The Bryan-Chamorro Treaty, negotiated while he was Foreign Minister, bears his name. He was President of Nicaragua from 1917 to 1921 and remained the power behind the presidency until the victory of a coalition of anti-Chamorro Conservatives and Liberals in the American-supervised elections of 1924. When the Marines were gone, Chamorro's ultra-Conservative partisans seized Loma Fortress, the military installation dominating Managua, and forced the resignation of President

Solórzano. Both Solórzano and Liberal Vice-President Sacasa prudently fled the country. Chamorro purged Congress of its Liberal members, and a rump session of that body proclaimed him President of Nicaragua in January 1926. The United States made clear its determination not to recognize Chamorro's government, since it had come to power by unconstitutional means.[8]

Despite Washington's professed displeasure with the coup, the American commander of the Nicaraguan constabulary, Major Calvin B. Carter, threw in with the unconstitutional regime, and his four-hundred-man force aided Chamorro's army in its operations against armed opponents of the new government.[9] A Liberal uprising on the east coast was quickly put down in May 1926; during the fighting U.S. Marines and sailors landed at Bluefields to protect American property. The most serious challenge to the Chamorro regime came in August, shortly after the Yankee troops had been withdrawn, when Liberal General José María Moncada took the field on the east coast, pledging loyalty to the exiled Vice-President, Dr. Sacasa. The rebellion spread to other parts of the country; in the southwest, around San Marcos, Liberal General Anastasio Somoza became "Chief of the Revolution." [10] Nicaragua was once more in the grips of civil war, and American sailors and Marines were again landed at Bluefields, on August 27, 1926, for the announced purpose of protecting the property of American and other foreign residents of the city.

The situation was complicated by Mexican support for Sacasa's claims to the presidency. Although committed not to recognize Chamorro, the United States could not permit a Sacasa victory that would boost the prestige and influence of Mexico in Central America. The Mexican Revolution had just taken a leftward turn, with government seizure of American-owned land in Mexico and threats to expropriate American and other foreign oil interests in the republic. The United States government feared that the Mexican revolutionary virus might infect Central America and lead to the formation of a bloc of revolutionary states directed by Mexico and opposed to American interests in the Caribbean. Washington's concern increased as Mexican arms were shipped to the Liberal forces of General Moncada. The immediate protection of American and other foreign property in Nicaragua was no longer of first importance. "The Department of State's policy in Nicaragua after September 1926 was based fundamentally on the assertion of the supremacy of the power of the United States in Central America." [11]

American policy required that both Chamorro and Sacasa be denied the presidency—that the civil war be ended by negotiation and a provisional government installed until after the elections scheduled for 1928. On October 1, 1926, American authorities arranged a truce in the civil war, and Liberal and Conservative representatives were summoned to a peace conference aboard the American warship *Denver*, anchored in Corinto harbor. The presiding officer at the conference was the American *chargé d'affaires* in Nicaragua, Lawrence Dennis—"a dark and saturnine figure from Georgia, who, after an early career as a boy evangelist, abruptly changed his way of life, went to Exeter and Harvard," and served in the infantry in World War I before entering the foreign service.[12] Dennis made it clear that Chamorro was still unacceptable to the United States. The Conservatives proposed that Chamorro resign the presidency in favor of Adolfo Díaz, the American favorite during the 1912 intervention. The Liberals refused to accept Díaz, and the Conservatives rejected a Liberal proposal for a provisional government of "neutrals." The conference ended in failure on October 23. Dennis resigned from the foreign service shortly afterward and went on to become "the 'dean' of American intellectual fascism." [13]

General Chamorro, frustrated in his attempts to win American support, resigned the presidency on October 30, 1926, the day before the thirty-day truce was to end. Subsequently, several Liberal members were reinstated in Congress and Adolfo Díaz was elected President by that body. Díaz

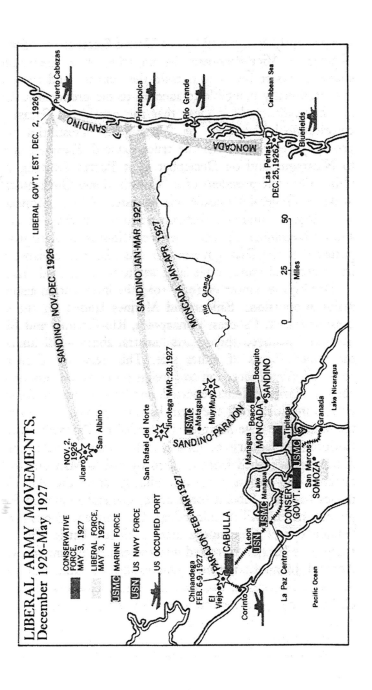

LIBERAL ARMY MOVEMENTS,
December 1926–May 1927

CONSERVATIVE
FORCE,
MAY 3, 1927

LIBERAL FORCE,
MAY 3, 1927

USMC MARINE FORCE

USN US NAVY FORCE

US OCCUPIED PORT

SANDINO NOV.-DEC. 1926

SANDINO JAN.-MAR 1927

MONCADA JAN.-APR. 1927

LIBERAL GOV'T. EST. DEC. 2, 1926

SANDINO

MONCADA

Puerto Cabezas

Prinzapolca

Río Grande

Caribbean Sea

Bluefields

Las Perlas
DEC. 25, 1926

Río Grande

NOV. 2,
1926

Jícaro

San Albino

San Rafael del Norte

Jinotega MAR. 28, 1927

USMC
Matagalpa
Muy Muy

SANDINO-PARAJON

Boaquito

SANDINO

Managua
Boaco
MONCADA

Tipitapa

Granada

Lake Nicaragua

USMC
San Marcos
SOMOZA

Lake
Managua

USMC CONSERV.
GOV'T.

La Paz Centro

PARAJON FEB.-MAR 1927

CABULLA

Chinandega
FEB. 6-9, 1927

El
Viejo

León

USN

Corinto

Pacific Ocean

Miles

0   25   50

was promptly recognized by the United States as President of Nicaragua; Vice-President Sacasa, the State Department claimed, was at the time outside the country and therefore constitutionally ineligible to succeed to the presidency. Mexico, however, made it clear that she considered Sacasa the constitutional President of Nicaragua.[14] Hostilities were promptly resumed when the truce expired. Sacasa returned to Nicaragua and on December 2, at Puerto Cabezas, proclaimed himself president of a "Constitutional Government," in which General Moncada was Minister of War. Moncada's army began winning significant victories on the east coast, and on December 13 the American Minister in Managua reported that the Díaz government was likely to collapse unless it received more active support from the United States.[15]

During the winter of 1926–1927 the intervention assumed major proportions. Sailors and Marines landed on the east coast at Puerto Cabezas, Prinzapolca, Río Grande, and Bluefields and declared these ports "neutral zones"—off-limits to the armed forces of either side. This network of neutral zones afforded protection to foreign property owners on the coast, a Marine colonel reported, and "it seals up the Revolutionists inland so that they can have no communication with the outside."[16] The Marines also landed on the west coast, at Corinto, on January 6. Later in the month a battalion of Marines was rushed from Corinto by rail to Managua to reestablish the Legation Guard. Shortly after the American troops passed, a Liberal force under General Francisco Parajón cut the railroad at Chinandega. Government troops forced Parajón out of Chinandega after a bloody battle. On February 9, as Parajón retreated into the central mountains, Rear Admiral Julian L. Latimer, commander of American naval forces in Nicaragua, declared the entire Granada-Managua-Corinto railroad a neutral zone. An irregular Liberal force under General Francisco Sequeira—better known as "Cabulla"—continued to operate in the vicinity of the railroad, but did not dare attack it. On March 7 Brigadier General

Logan Feland arrived at Corinto to command the two thousand Marines then serving in Nicaragua.

In March 1927 the focus of the war shifted from the coasts to the central mountains. General Moncada had marched up the Río Grande from Pearl Lagoon and was in the vicinity of Muy Muy. On Moncada's right flank during this march was a Liberal force under General Augusto C. Sandino; on March 28 Sandino seized Jinotega.[17] The Liberals were now in a position to threaten both Managua and the highland city of Matagalpa. On April 17 Matagalpa was declared a neutral zone.[18] Marine patrol planes maintained an aerial surveillance of the Liberal forces. On occasions the planes were fired upon, increasing the danger of a major clash between the Marines and Liberal troops.[19]

Responsible Liberal commanders did all they could to avoid war with the Marines. Generals Moncada, Parajón, and Sandino courteously received American officers in their camps. An official party of six Marines headed by Major M. S. Berry visited Sandino in April 1927. As Berry was bidding his host goodbye, Sandino remarked that the Americans' horses looked tired. The Liberal general offered the Marines their choice of any six of his animals, including his personal mount. Berry declined the offer but noted Sandino's friendly attitude in his report. He informed his superiors that Sandino claimed to have three thousand men and that he had personally seen "three hundred well-mounted, well-equipped and well-shod men. They were the highest type I have seen in Nicaragua and all seemed to have the fighting spirit." [20]

The forces of the American-favored government of Adolfo Díaz could not match the Liberals in generalship or fighting spirit. They could not stop the Liberal advance alone. Washington was thus faced with three alternatives: (1) stand aside and let Díaz fall, and suffer a humiliating loss of prestige in what would appear to the world as a Mexican victory; (2) send the Marines into action against the Liberals, a move likely to provoke a strong reaction against the administration in Congress and among the American people; or (3) press for a negotiated settlement between the opposing sides in Nicaragua.[21] The choice was the third alternative. Henry L. Stimson, President Coolidge's personal representative, sailed from New York for Nicaragua on April 9, 1927, to mediate the civil war.

2

The Peace of Tipitapa

W hen Henry L. Stimson left for Nicaragua in April
1927, the second Coolidge administration had reached
its midpoint. It was a time of deteriorating United States–Latin
American relations, a period that Sumner Welles called the
"unhappy four years." [1] When Coolidge was inaugurated
President in his "own right" in 1925, the able Secretary of
State, Charles Evans Hughes, a holdover from the Harding
administration, had been replaced by Frank B. Kellogg. No
aspect of the Coolidge-Kellogg foreign policy was more
roundly denounced in Latin America than the intervention in
Nicaragua. According to *La Nación* of Buenos Aires (January 22, 1927), "never in modern international history has
there been heard such a strenuous and unanimous booing as
that being received by the United States because of her intervention in Nicaragua."

In the United States itself there was strong opposition to
the intervention in the press and in Congress. To Senator
George W. Norris the intervention was "shocking to every
peace-loving citizen in civilization" and a "blot on the national honor." [2] Early in January 1927 the chairman of the
Senate Foreign Relations Committee, William E. Borah, announced that he "personally" opposed the intervention. On
February 20 Senator Borah warned the administration that
he could not support a policy toward Central America "based
solely on mahogany and oil" and executed by "warships and

marines." [3] If Stimson could bring peace to war-torn Nicaragua, he would undercut the critics of the administration at home and abroad.

Stimson and his wife, Mabel White Stimson, sailed from New York on April 9, 1927, aboard the Chilean steamship *Aconcagua*.[4] The American cruiser *Trenton* met the Stimsons at the Pacific end of the Panama Canal and carried them seven hundred miles north to the Nicaraguan port of Corinto—a "neutral zone" under the protection of the United States Navy. There they were met by Admiral Latimer and Charles C. Eberhardt, American Minister to Nicaragua. The Stimson party then boarded the train in Corinto for the hundred-mile journey to Managua.

Stimson was a man of wide governmental experience. Educated at Yale and Harvard, he was a New York lawyer and sometime Republican politician; he had run unsuccessfully for governor of New York in 1910 and the next year was named Secretary of War by President Taft. During World War I he had served as a colonel of field artillery in France. His military background was evident in the erect manner in which he carried his rather lanky frame. Sixty years old when he arrived in Nicaragua, Stimson was an altogether imposing personage: a thin, greying forelock, usually in slight disarray, and a darker brush mustache added distinction to a countenance dominated by dark, pince-nez-framed eyes—eyes that were at once searching and commanding. Stimson was in Nicaragua for the first time and knew nothing of the internal problems of that country. But he clearly understood Nicaragua's strategic importance to the United States. Stimson regarded his ignorance of Nicaraguan affairs as freeing him of prejudice and, perhaps, better enabling him to accomplish his mission as he conceived it: to bring peace and stability to the country.

Shortly after leaving Corinto the narrow-gauge train carrying the Stimson party to Managua passed through Chinandega; from his window Stimson could see that much of the city lay in ruins. Two months before, the Liberal army of

General Francisco Parajón had fought its way into the city only to be driven out three days later by a Conservative column from Managua, supported by two airplanes belonging to Major Carter's constabulary. In the course of the bitter fighting for Chinandega, the city was gutted by fire. Although the fire was probably started by Parajón's soldiers and civilian looters, the Liberals laid the blame for the city's destruction upon the Conservatives—and specifically upon the American pilots of the bombing airplanes. The pilots, in a series of articles one of them wrote for the American press, claimed they never hurt anyone and dropped bombs only for "moral effect." [5] When the ashes cooled at Chinandega, photographs were taken of the grotesquely charred and bloated corpses—some with limbs blown off—which were strewn amidst the rubble. In the hands of skillful radical publicists these photographs of the carnage at Chinandega made potent anti-Yankee propaganda. The American airmen—and their commanding officer, Major Carter—were speedily mustered out of the constabulary, but the damage was already done.

The ruins of Chinandega were not the only evidence of war laid before Stimson on his trip to Managua. In the countryside he noticed farmers going about their business with rifles slung over their shoulders; and though the farmland seemed to him rich and fertile, most of it lay idle. It was pretty country Stimson was traveling through—wide, grassy spaces bounded by avenues of handsome shade trees. Shade was needed in this country, for it was a land of intense heat. Unlike other Central Americans, most Nicaraguans chose to live in the tropical lowlands rather than in the cooler uplands. Despite the heat, Nicaragua's Pacific coastal belt had long been attractive as a rich agricultural area; though heavy, the average rainfall was not excessive, and the rolling country provided ample drainage. Stimson decided that this rich volcanic soil must not be left uncultivated for another year; the war must be ended before the beginning of the planting season in June.

In ancient times the fertility of western Nicaragua at-

tracted settlers and traders from the great nations of Middle
America. The ruler of a tribe that had emigrated from Mexico, Chief Nicarao, gave his name to the country. An Aztec
colony once thrived on the same shore of Lake Managua
along which Stimson's train carried him on his journey from
Corinto. Some years before Stimson's trip another railway
traveler, Rubén Darío, looked across Lake Managua from his
train window and saw the "bald and nude" colossus which
he later enshrined in verse.[6] This was Momotombo, the great
volcano worshiped by the Indians. Stimson was quick to appreciate the influence of Nicaragua's Indian heritage on a
nation nearly three-quarters of whose people had some degree
of Indian blood. He was even tempted to relate the Liberal-
Conservative struggle to the ancient rivalries between the
Indian tribes of the Granada area and those from around
León.

In Managua Stimson was briefed by Admiral Latimer
and Minister Eberhardt. Then, without further delay, he
entered into conversations with prominent Nicaraguan politicians of both parties; on April 22 he began negotiating with
President Adolfo Díaz. Stimson found Díaz conciliatory—as
had other American officials before him. President Díaz was
a rather short, trim, and handsome gentleman of Spanish
extraction; he had a good measure of the dignity and charm
for which his class is noted. The American representative and
the Nicaraguan President quickly came to an agreement:
President Díaz was to continue in office until after the elections of 1928, in which Díaz, as the incumbent, would be
constitutionally ineligible to run for President; in the meantime a general amnesty was to be proclaimed and all troops,
Conservative and Liberal, were to surrender their arms to
American forces; Díaz was to appoint representative Liberals
to important posts in his government; the old Nicaraguan
constabulary was to be disbanded and a new national guard
was to be organized and commanded by American officers;
sufficient American forces would stay in Nicaragua to en-

force these provisions and to supervise the elections of 1928 and succeeding years.

With this peace plan accepted by the President and the responsible elements within the Conservative party, Stimson next undertook to win its acceptance by the Liberals. This he knew would be more difficult. Stimson realized that the government's military position was bad and that the Liberals believed they could win the war unless blocked by American forces. He noted that General Moncada was in a position to threaten crossing the Tipitapa river. If successful, this maneuver would put Managua at Moncada's mercy; the American high command had perfected plans to resist any Liberal attempt to cross the river.[7] Stimson worked diligently to avoid such a clash. He invited the "Constitutional President," Dr. Sacasa, to come to Managua for discussions. Sacasa declined to leave his "capital," Puerto Cabezas, but designated three representatives to meet with Stimson. On April 29 the Sacasa emissaries arrived at Corinto aboard the *USS Preston*, after a record-breaking three-day trip from Puerto Cabezas through the Panama Canal.

Meeting with Stimson, the Liberal representatives were impressed by the American's air of sincerity and integrity. Even Stimson's atrocious mispronunciation of their country's name, "Nicaragew-a," seemed to indicate that here was a great man far removed from their local prejudices and petty quarrels—a powerful man determined that justice be done and peace be restored.[8] Sacasa's representatives were inclined to accept Stimson's terms; only on the question of retaining President Díaz did they hesitate. On this Stimson was adamant. Díaz was a reasonable man and had proven during the 1912 intervention that he could work well with Americans. Furthermore, Stimson believed, there simply was no Nicaraguan who could be considered neutral or impartial and could win the support of both parties. The resignation of Díaz would mean to the United States the loss of a trusted collaborator; the choosing of a replacement, no matter who he might be, would surely add new animosities to those already existing. Faced with Stimson's obduracy on this point, Sacasa's emissaries decided to confer with General Moncada, Sacasa's Minister of War and commander of the Constitutionalist forces in the field.

General Moncada's army was at the time facing government forces in the mountains between Teustepe and Boaco, some fifty miles northeast of Managua. When Sacasa's representatives asked Stimson to put them in touch with General Moncada, Stimson welcomed their request, seeing in it the opportunity to arrange a truce and confer with Moncada himself. Consequently, three American officers were sent through the lines to deliver to Moncada the invitation to confer. Moncada agreed to meet with Stimson and the Sacasa representatives on May 4 at the town of Tipitapa. A forty-eight-hour cease-fire was arranged between the contending armies to facilitate the conference, and Liberal General Anastasio Somoza took advantage of it to come to Managua and confer with Stimson on May 3. Somoza, ambitious and animated, had attended school in the United States and was not above using his familiarity with the American way of life to ingratiate himself with the Yankee intruders. Stimson found Somoza to be a frank and amiable young politician.[9] Shortly before midnight three trucks carrying a platoon of Marines roared out of Managua destined for Tipitapa.

Tipitapa was an unimpressive little town on the south bank of the river of the same name, which, in the rainy season, links Lake Managua with Lake Nicaragua. Fifteen miles from Managua, Tipitapa was one of the outposts of the government army defending the capital. To insure the safety of the conferees, the Marine platoon was ordered into position along the river between the contending armies. Early on the morning of May 4, Stimson, accompanied by the three Sacasa representatives, Admiral Latimer, and Minister Eberhardt, left Managua and drove out to Tipitapa. There he was met by General Moncada and the three American officers who had fetched him; they had traveled most of the preced-

ing night, making the arduous journey down the mountains
from Boaco. After a pleasant round of greetings, Moncada
withdrew with the Sacasa representatives into the local inn—
a dingy, one-story adobe building. Just fifteen minutes later
Moncada emerged, ready to negotiate with Stimson.

José María Moncada, Constitutionalist Minister of War,
was a hard-drinking, sharp-tongued, fifty-six-year-old politician turned general. To some he appeared "cold, antipathetic,
puritanical"—"an introvert like Coolidge"—although he was
capable of writing books loaded with generous ideals.[10] But it
was not Moncada's personality or literary talents that most
impressed Stimson and other foreign observers; it was his
military ability. Moncada had begun his march on Managua
after skillfully out-maneuvering and routing a Conservative
force on the east coast at Las Perlas on Christmas Day, 1926.
He then led his three-thousand-man army up the wild Río
Grande, using Indian canoes where possible, across the continental divide, through unknown jungle-covered mountains,
to the region around Muy Muy. Here Moncada fell upon a
major government force and, after several days of bitter fighting, pushed his enemy back to Teustepe, only forty miles
from the capital. Stimson could admire these achievements:
here was a real leader of men, clearly "the vital force of the
revolution." [11] Stimson felt that a peaceful settlement could
better be arranged by dealing directly with Moncada than by
negotiating with the nebulous "Constitutional government"
the general was supposed to be serving.

Stimson had good reason to believe that he could come to
an understanding with Moncada. The general's political record indicated that he was not a man to be irremediably bound
by abstract principles. Educated in Granada, he began a jour-
nalistic career by writing for a Conservative newspaper there.
Then, under the Liberal dictatorship of Zelaya, he published
a pro-government newspaper. Later he fell out with Zelaya
and fled to Honduras, where in 1906 he became an Under-
Secretary of the Interior of that country. In 1909 he supported the Conservative revolt against Zelaya. From 1910 to

1911 he was Secretary of the Interior in the Conservative government of Nicaragua; in this official capacity Moncada warmly praised the interventionist policies of American Secretary of State Philander C. Knox. But Moncada did not get along with later Conservative governments and was elected to the Nicaraguan Senate as a Liberal in 1924. When General Chamorro effected his *coup d'état* the next year, Senator Moncada stuck by the Liberals; and when the Constitutionalist movement was launched he emerged as the beclouded Dr. Sacasa's Minister of War.

At Tipitapa Moncada sat down with Stimson near the dry river bed under the spreading branches of a huge blackthorn tree. According to Stimson he "spoke English with unusual simplicity and directness." [12] The conversation, as Moncada reported it years later, [13] went like this.

"My government has recognized President Díaz," Stimson announced, "and the United States cannot make an error."

"You have made one," Moncada retorted, "and it will cause the American government to lose much prestige in the public opinion of Hispanic America."

"Peace is imperative," said Stimson. "I have instructions to attain it willingly or by force."

"It is impossible to deal with you," Moncada declared, keeping his temper with difficulty. "My honor is involved. You should call Dr. Sacasa's representatives and repeat to them what you have just said."

"That I will do gladly." Stimson summoned the three representatives and told them of his intention to use force if necessary to achieve peace. He asked them if they were prepared to submit. They all responded negatively. The representatives were dismissed, and Stimson and Moncada resumed their conversation. Moncada admitted that it would be futile for his army to go to war with the United States. He promised Stimson he would do what he could to persuade his commanders to agree to the peace proposals already accepted by President Díaz. Moncada requested and received eight days in which his officers could consider Stimson's terms before announcing their collective decision.

"In less than thirty minutes," Stimson later wrote, "we understood each other and had settled the matter." To help Moncada persuade his commanders to give in, Stimson agreed to send the general a letter stating that United States forces were ready to receive "the arms of all those willing to lay them down, including the government, and to disarm forcibly those who will not do so." [14] The truce remained in effect while Moncada conferred with his officers at Boaco. The day after the Tipitapa meeting President Díaz obliged Stimson by proclaiming a general amnesty and appointing several of Moncada's generals to positions in his government.[15]

As the prospects for peace improved, Stimson learned more about the horrors of Central American warfare. A military hospital he visited on May 10 had a high recovery rate, he was told, but this was because only exceptional cases lived to reach it.[16] The fate of most Nicaraguan wounded was a lingering death where they fell. Towns and cities fiercely contended for were made uninhabitable by the stench of corpses rapidly decomposing in the tropical heat. After the battle of Muy Muy the victorious Liberals had no time to bury or incinerate the dead, but they did shoot a number of pigs that were devouring the remains of their comrades who had fallen in the town plaza—thus producing more carcasses to foul the atmosphere.[17] A few days after the battle of Chinandega an American sailor noted that the bones of some bodies had been picked clean by vultures, while other bodies had "only their abdominal cavities scooped out by the ravaging beaks of the turkey buzzards who gorge themselves to a nauseating stupor, and then awkwardly hop away to perch on some roof top until ready to repeat their disgusting repast." [18] The victims of this carnage were often poor agricultural laborers who were pressed into service by politically minded members of the upper classes. "Dear Colonel," one of these recruiters wrote his superior, "I am sending you herewith forty volunteers who will fight for the cause so dear to us. . . . It will greatly help me, by the way, to secure others if you will make sure to return the ropes." [19]

The disbanding of these conscript armies began in the week following the Tipitapa conference. Admiral Latimer posted a proclamation on May 10 stating that he had orders "to accept the custody of the arms and ammunition of the forces of the Government and to disarm forcibly those who do not peaceably deliver their arms." All "individuals and leaders of groups" not pertaining to the forces of the government were invited to turn in their arms, too. For each serviceable rifle or machine gun delivered to the American forces, "payment of ten córdobas [$10] will be made, in the presence of a Commission of United States officers." [20] Moncada, faced with this invitation to his troops to desert with their weapons, arranged for a second meeting with Stimson at Tipitapa on May 11. This time Stimson gave Moncada written assurances of impartial, American-supervised elections in 1928 and, in the meantime, the appointment of more prominent Liberals to positions in the government. The next day Stimson received a telegram from Boaco by which the Constitutionalist army formally agreed to lay down its arms; the telegram was signed by Moncada and all his generals except Augusto C. Sandino. [21]

The dismantling of the Constitutionalist army began immediately. During the disarmament period which lasted until June 6, 1927, the Liberals turned in 31 machine guns and 3,704 rifles. Government troops delivered 308 machine guns and 10,445 rifles. The bearer of each weapon received the equivalent of $10 from the Nicaraguan treasury. [22] At Puerto Cabezas the helpless Dr. Sacasa, "Constitutional President of Nicaragua," could do no more than halfheartedly suggest that his soldiers not lay down their arms. When the liquidation of his army was an accomplished fact, Sacasa sailed from Puerto Cabezas and arrived in Costa Rica as an exile on May 22. [23]

The disarmament was one of the least complicated aspects of the implementation of the peace agreements. Stimson had

committed his government to a form of intervention unlike
any previously undertaken by American forces in Latin
America. In the past, Marines had landed to guard American
property during revolutions or other disturbances and had
been withdrawn when the danger subsided. On other occasions—in Cuba, Haiti, and the Dominican Republic—United
States forces would occupy a whole country for an extended
period, enforcing the will of an American military government. In Nicaragua, a brigade of Marines was to occupy the
country, but there was to be no American military government. The Marines were to supervise elections and help the
Nicaraguan government to keep order until a new native
constabulary—trained and led by American officers—would
be ready to take over these duties. The American Minister in
Nicaragua was to be the representative of the United States
government there, but the commander of the Marine brigade
held all the power and was responsible not to the Minister but
to the Navy Department. The commander of the constabulary was a Marine officer, but he was supposed to be responsible to the President of Nicaragua and not to the commander
of the Marine brigade. The compliant President of Nicaragua,
of course, was expected to go to the American Minister for
advice. By May 15, according to General Feland, the Marine
commander, Stimson had begun to realize the "great difficulty
of tying together and properly coordinating the different
forms of American control" in Nicaragua; "he has worked
very hard and his mind is somewhat confused with the many
things he has had to consider." [24]

Nevertheless, as Stimson prepared to leave Nicaragua in
mid-May 1927, he had reason to be satisfied. The civil war
was ended; pro-American President Díaz was generally accepted as President of the republic, and Stimson's new-found
friend, General Moncada, was the acknowledged leader of
the Liberal opposition. Both parties supported American
intervention. American Marines were policing the country
and beginning to organize a non-partisan native constabulary;
American property and other interests in Nicaragua seemed

secure. Only a few apparently unimportant guerrilla bands were still under arms.

Among the remaining armed groups was that of Francisco Sequeira—"General Cabulla"—whose headquarters were at El Viejo, north of Chinandega. Cabulla's troops were scattered in "the small villages throughout Chinandega province," and they usually operated along the railroad between León and Chinandega. Although Cabulla's raiders claimed to be a bonafide unit of the Liberal army, their leader had been "repeatedly disowned" by Moncada. Cabulla viewed the coming of peace with concern: if Moncada would not claim him now, he would not only be left out of the division of spoils but might even be declared an outlaw. When Captain Frank A. Hart and four Marines rode up to Cabulla's headquarters on the morning of May 14, the guerrilla chieftain welcomed them and readily agreed to come to Chinandega that afternoon to talk about disarmament.[25]

A little after 12:30 a body of some six hundred riders approached Marine Outpost Number One at Chinandega to the music of a mounted band. About four hundred of the riders were armed with rifles—from single-shot muzzle-loaders to modern repeaters. The Marines watched with interest as the band deployed before their lines. General Cabulla and his headquarters group, escorted by the chieftain's personal bodyguard of sixty well-armed and well-mounted men, rode up to the outpost. Cabulla and an entourage of forty men and five women were allowed to pass into the Marine compound.

For about an hour General Cabulla discussed disarmament with Captain Hart. The Nicaraguan declared that he would not surrender his arms until officially ordered to do so by General Moncada. Cabulla insisted that he or a member of his staff see Moncada personally to receive the order to disarm. A telegram or a letter from Moncada would not do, Cabulla explained, "for I place no faith in signatures." The men finally agreed that Cabulla's secretary would go to Managua with a Marine escort to see Moncada. Since the next day was Sunday and there would be no train service, the trip was scheduled for Monday morning, May 16. Cabulla re-formed his troops shortly before two o'clock and withdrew to El Viejo.

Henry L. Stimson was pleased to learn that Cabulla was willing to lay down his arms. He planned to leave Managua on the morning of the same day Cabulla's representative was due there. When May 16 arrived President Díaz, General Moncada, and a group of Liberal generals, together with other Nicaraguan and American dignitaries, gathered harmoniously at the Managua railroad station to bid farewell to Stimson on his trip home. But the atmosphere of accord surrounding Stimson's departure was clouded by ominous news from La Paz Centro of the first Marine combat fatalities of the intervention.

The town of La Paz Centro was on the railroad, midway between Managua and Chinandega. A Marine detachment was camped across the tracks three hundred yards from the town. Shortly before one o'clock on the morning of May 16, the Marines heard the sound of gunfire coming from the town. Call to arms was sounded and the detachment commander, Captain Richard B. Buchanan, led a platoon of Marines into La Paz Centro to investigate.[26] With bullets whizzing overhead, Buchanan entered the darkened town in the vanguard of his column, a squad of flankers to the right and a half-squad to the left. The main body of the column followed fifty yards behind. Three blocks inside the town, Sergeant Glendell L. Fitzgerald on the left flank spotted a group of about seventy-five men he thought were Conservative soldiers. He called to them and was answered with a hail of bullets. As Fitzgerald's men took cover, Captain Buchanan swung to the left to assist him. Under heavy rifle and machine-gun fire, Buchanan's party advanced to where Fitzgerald's men had taken refuge—under a protruding wooden sidewalk and behind a pile of railroad ties along the town's main street. Lieutenant C. J. Chappell moved his men into line to the left of Buchanan, suffering three casualties in the advance. Corporal Donald L. Truesdale's squad covered the rear of the Marine line.

Looking for a better position, Captain Buchanan tried to cross Main Street and was struck down by fire from the window of a saloon. After recovering the body of their mortally wounded leader, Sergeant Fitzgerald and two privates charged across the darkened street and cleaned out the saloon, killing seven of the enemy. Captain Buchanan and the three other wounded were carried into the saloon, which the Marines made their strong point. At 2:30, as enemy fire from the surrounding houses splattered the saloon, Captain Buchanan died. Private Marvin A. Jackson lingered awhile longer. "That was one boy that didn't want to die," Corporal Truesdale later recalled. "His brains were sticking out of that bullet hole, and he didn't want to die." [27] After three o'clock the enemy began withdrawing from La Paz Centro, leaving fourteen of their dead behind; some of them wore red hatbands, the insignia of the Liberal army. Instead of pursuing the retreating enemy, Lieutenant Chappell reorganized the platoon and carried his casualties to the railroad station.

The closest medical facilities were at the University of León, a traditional center of Liberalism, where a detachment of American sailors was stationed. The León detachment was notified of the impending arrival of the wounded and the bodies of Buchanan and Jackson. It was not long before news of the armed clash reached the inhabitants of León, and a large crowd began to form near the railroad station, where an honor guard of sailors was drawn up, ready to salute the fallen Marines. The natives "gathered around the open square surrounding the railroad station, with the eager anticipation of so many youngsters eagerly awaiting a military parade." [28] A member of the honor guard described the scene:

> After an hour or so had slowly passed, a faint and plaintive sound drifted to our ears. A few minutes later, the faintness of the whistle increased to a shrill blast, and the

nose of the locomotive emerged from around the bend. The men were snapped to attention by the curt order of the commander as the train slowly rolled to a stop. As the first body was lowered from the baggage car, the men came to present arms. Up to this time the natives had remained silent, but the movement of the first box seemed to serve as a cue, for the crowd of casual observers suddenly came to life. Cheers, catcalls and boos were audible from all directions, and as the second body was being lowered and placed into the ambulance, the frenzy of the mob took on diabolical proportions. As the ambulance started, we swung in behind it to serve as an escort.

By this time, the anger of the men had mounted and some of the jeering natives who came within reach of the infuriated gobs in the outer column, received blows to the face. The officers, also enraged at the insulting boos, saw the blows delivered, and much against their will admonished the men to control themselves.[29]

Relations between the people of León and the occupation forces continued to deteriorate. The day after the railroad station incident an American ensign broke up a fight between a Liberal and a Conservative on a city street. The Conservative obeyed the officer's order to leave the scene, but the Liberal, egged on by a crowd of bystanders, refused. Ordered to give up his pistol, the Liberal drew it and pointed it at the ensign. Shouts of "*Viva!*" came from the crowd, whereupon the Nicaraguan fired at the American and missed. "The ensign then shot and killed his antagonist." [30] In another incident the owner of a cantina in León was knocked unconscious as he tried to protect his wife from the advances of four sailors.[31] In León and in the rest of Nicaragua the natural concomitants of military occupation were beginning to appear. Sailors gave fictitious names when charging goods at local stores.[32] Marines married local girls when they already had wives back in the States.[33] American officers and enlisted men were "arrogant and overbearing" in dealing with railroad employees.[34] The American high command tried to

avoid such friction, and those guilty of offenses against Nicaraguans were sometimes punished. But these corrective measures were not enough to dispel the hostility felt toward the
United States in many parts of Nicaragua—especially in the
departments of León and Chinandega, the stomping ground
of General Cabulla.

Although it seemed probable that some of Cabulla's men
were involved in the La Paz Centro attack, the Marine commander in Nicaragua did not order any punitive action
against the guerrilla chieftain. Instead, after the riots in León,
General Feland prepared for trouble in Managua. Before
noon on May 16 Marines took over all police duties in the
capital city and suspended liquor sales there. Later in the day
Feland met with General Moncada, Captain Hart, and Cabulla's secretary to arrange for the disarmament of the Chinandega guerrillas. The next morning Captain Hart and the
secretary returned to Chinandega and met with Cabulla that
afternoon. On May 18 a brigade intelligence report stated
that "no authentic report can be secured regarding the whereabouts of the group that attacked La Paz on the 16th" and
that disarmament of the Chinandega region would begin on
May 19.[35] On that day the U.S. Department of State announced that "the guerrilla band that made the attack [on La
Paz Centro] is at present negotiating with a view to turning
over their arms." [36] Guilty or not, Cabulla's guerrillas turned
in their arms, and their leader retired to his home in El Viejo.

A week later, on the afternoon of May 26, General Cabulla
rode into Chinandega and mistreated a local citizen. Cabulla
was arrested by the Marines and then released after being
"warned that upon repetition of [the] offence he would be
sent to Managua and turned over to civil authorities." [37] After
Cabulla left for his home in El Viejo, Captain William P.
Richards decided to go there himself, "to investigate." Richards and two fully armed squads of Marines reached Cabulla's house at about 9:30 that night. They brushed aside
eight of the general's henchmen and barged into the bedroom
where they encountered Cabulla and his mistress, Concep-

ción Alday. The guerrilla chief sprang from bed and was shot
dead by Captain Richards as he reached for a pistol. Con-
cepción furiously charged the Marines with a machete; she
too was cut down, in a hail of pistol and automatic rifle
bullets.[38]

Cabulla was dead, but a much more serious threat to the
peace of Nicaragua was developing in the northern
mountains. The Marines would soon have to contend with
Sandino.

3

Sandino

Augusto Sandino was a native of the Nicaraguan lowlands. He was born on May 18, 1895, in Niquinohomo,[1] a town of about a thousand inhabitants, some fifteen miles west of Granada. He was the natural son of Don Gregorio Sandino, scion of a moderately wealthy landowning family, and Margarita Calderón, an Indian girl who had been a servant of the Sandino family. According to General Sandino, both his parents were under eighteen when he was born.[2] Until early adolescence the child lived with his mother and bore the name Augusto Calderón. But the father was not unmindful of his responsibilities and contributed generously to the support of his illegitimate son. When Don Gregorio married—taking as his bride a white girl ten years his junior, Doña América—he brought Augusto into his home. In Nicaragua such arrangements were not considered shameful. Despite the circumstances of his birth, Augusto was treated as Don Gregorio's first-born. During his years in the Sandino household Augusto forged lasting bonds of respect and affection with his father and with young Sócrates Sandino, Don Gregorio's son by Doña América. Augusto also had two half-sisters in the Sandino family, Asunción and Zoila América. For the rather simple-minded Margarita Calderón, her complex and assertive son was ever a source of wonderment and perplexity. After Augusto went to live with Don Gregorio, she left town and later had three children by another man.

Niquinohomo, where Augusto was born and spent most of his boyhood, was like many other towns in western Nicaragua. Here a few families of Don Gregorio's status lived in neat adobe houses with red tile roofs built around patios and clustered together in the center of town. The rest of the townspeople, like Margarita Calderón, lived in rectangular huts with walls of cane, or cane and mud, with roofs usually made of thatched palm.[3]

Although class lines existed, there was little social animosity in Niquinohomo during Augusto's boyhood, and life could be quite pleasant. Most of the people engaged in farming or ranching, when they cared to. These were the days of relative stability and prosperity in the Nicaragua of Liberal dictator José Santos Zelaya. Railroads were being built, ports were being improved, and schools were being constructed—Augusto was able to get a primary education without leaving his home town.

When he joined the Sandino household, Augusto Calderón took his father's surname and became Augusto C. Sandino. He found in his father a man of broad interests and an ardent political Liberal. Life with Don Gregorio included a constant exposure to the egalitarian doctrines that were supposed to be the basis of the Liberal party. The father was a voracious reader and collected a sizable library which he put at the disposal of his sons. Like his father, Augusto delighted in the classics. He was thrilled to learn that his first name was the same as that of the first Emperor of Rome; dreams of grandeur eventually led him to redesignate his middle initial: "C." for Calderón became "C." for César.

After a period of study at the commercial high school in Granada, Augusto C. Sandino returned to Niquinohomo to become administrator of part of his father's property. He also became a grain jobber, buying corn and beans from farmers and reselling them on the local markets. During Sandino's youth, his father's Liberal party was ousted from power and a Conservative regime backed by American Marines was firmly established in the country. Two brief but rather bloody wars, in 1909 and 1912, brought this about, but young Sandino apparently took no part in either struggle. The Sandino family fortunes seem not to have suffered greatly from the misfortunes of the Liberal party. According to one source, young Sandino did take an active part in politics: he was almost killed in a political fight in a barroom, after which he swore off alcohol for life.[4]

It was a personal fight—not a political one—that in 1920 marked a major turning point in Sandino's life. The reasons for the fight are obscure: one source says it was caused by an insult to Sandino's mother;[5] another contends that it came as a result of a dispute over a business deal.[6] In any event, Augusto Sandino shot and wounded in the leg one Dagoberto Rivas in the plaza at Niquinohomo and fled the town to avoid arrest.

Sandino's flight took him first to León and then across the border into Honduras. Along the way he worked in gold mines and on sugar and banana plantations. At some point he was joined by his cousin, Santiago Sandino. The two men made their way to the Honduran port of La Ceiba, with Augusto bearing a letter recommending him as a competent mechanic. Bananas were La Ceiba's "main business and *raison d'être*." The town was built around the compound of Vaccaro Brothers and Company—an American firm later to be reorganized as the Standard Fruit Company—with its railroad yard, wharf, shops, offices, and residences. La Ceiba was "a clean, fresh city of wooden houses, many of them two-storied."[7] Augusto found a job as mechanic and warehouseman at the fruit company's Montecristo sugar mill, a few miles outside La Ceiba. When he foiled the attempted theft of the mill's gasoline one day, he was shot at and slightly wounded. He immediately reported the incident to the local police chief, who said he was short of men and could not send anyone after the culprit—whereupon Sandino secured a rifle and went after the assailant himself. He caught up with him at El Porvenir, a couple of miles from the mill. Exactly what Sandino did to him is unclear, but afterward he found it convenient to leave the La Ceiba area and cross the border into Guatemala.

In Guatemala Sandino worked for a while as a mechanic for an American company and then continued his northward march. In 1923 he reached Tampico, Mexico. He found employment with a subsidiary of the South Penn Oil Company and later with the Huasteca Petroleum Company,[8] then controlled by a syndicate dominated by Standard Oil of Indiana. Between jobs in Tampico, Sandino may have crossed into the United States, as he later claimed.[9]

Tampico, when Sandino arrived there in 1923, was a city of about a hundred thousand. Its name was synonymous with oil. Although the post–World War I oil boom had begun to recede, wages in the oil field were still fantastically high. "Tampico and the oil fields were a conglomeration of Mexicans, Americans, millionaires, desperados, military, bandits, go-getters, and adventurers from all over the world." The city itself was bustling and modern. "The two principal hotels were American in name and in fact." Office buildings were "substantial and utilitarian," and there were plenty of bars and cabarets. On the streets peons with thonged sandals and brightly colored serapes jostled with Texans wearing cowboy boots and ten-gallon hats. The American element in this Mexican city clearly predominated. Arriving at Tampico "was like coming upon Pawtucket in the middle of the Sahara." The major oil companies there were American and Tampico was, "next to New York, the busiest port in the world for American shipping." [10] Sandino made his home at Cerro Azul, near the pipe line outside the city. By August 1925 he had acquired a "wife" and an infant daughter. They lived in the house of the head watchman at Cerro Azul.[11]

When Sandino came to Mexico in 1923 the country was gradually becoming stabilized after the violence of the Great Revolution. Gone were Pancho Villa [12] and Emiliano Zapata, Francisco Madero and Venustiano Carranza, the agrarian and bourgeois chieftains who had bloodied the country in ten years of internecine warfare. General Alvaro Obregón, the conqueror of Villa, was President, and his government was recognized by the United States in the same year that Sandino first set foot on Mexican soil. Later that year, when General Adolfo de la Huerta and the Mexican fleet at Veracruz rose in revolt, the United States shipped arms to the government and sent warships to Veracruz and Tampico. Private American interests also supported Obregón: the Huasteca Petroleum Company made a ten-million-pesos loan to the government during the revolt. A rebel plan to strike at Tampico by sea had to be canceled in February 1924 because of the presence there of American naval vessels. When a rebel force tried to take the port by land, it was routed by government troops, and the triumph of the American-backed government was assured. The involvement of the United States in these events could not have surprised Sandino; his observations in Nicaragua and on his trip through Central America to Mexico had given him little reason to doubt Yankee omnipotence.

The oil fields of Tampico supported some fifty thousand workers. Despite high wages, radical social doctrines made numerous converts among them. During and after World War I, socialist, syndicalist, anarchist, and communist organizers and agitators drifted into Tampico, mostly from the United States. The anarchist Industrial Workers of the World dominated the Tampico labor movement until seriously challenged in the 1920's by newly formed communist groups, by purely Mexican radical unions, and by a more conservative, government-backed labor federation. The government often intervened in labor disputes, usually in behalf of its favorite unions. In 1924 the Mexican government temporarily seized the oil refineries and other properties of a struck company in Tampico. During the de la Huerta revolt, anti-government electricians in Tampico briefly took control of the American-owned light plant and street railways—a move that "caused consternation in the United States" and was one of the reasons Yankee warships were dispatched to Tampico in 1924. "This oil region was the scene of a long-

drawn-out struggle between owners and workers. No sooner
was one strike settled than another one began." [13] Sandino
was not oblivious to the social ferment in Tampico, but it is
unlikely that he took any active part in the proletarian struggles there. To his American employer "he was industrious,
sober, apparently of good character, and was in every way a
most satisfactory employee." [14]

Sandino's far-ranging and inquisitive mind and his capitalist background did not predispose him toward the intellectual discipline of any school of radical thought. Rather, his
spirit tended to "mysticism and metaphysics," "inclined more
to intuition than to reason." [15] In Tampico Sandino became a
freemason and associated with theosophical and spiritualist
groups. He also studied ancient history, yoga, and Seventh
Day Adventism. But in the end it was Latin American nationalism that became Sandino's creed.

Sandino found in Tampico a Mexican nationalism that
gloried in Mexico's Indian heritage. Although not a pure
Indian, he could exult that more Indian blood than any other
type coursed his veins. He began to identify himself with a
broad nationality embracing all Americans of Iberian and
Indian descent. But in the meantime, every workday, he dutifully served Latin America's supposed archenemy: Yankee
Imperialism. Sandino had to bear the taunts of the more rabid
Latin nationalists who regarded him, and Nicaraguans in
general, as subservient to the Great Exploiter. He began to
reflect that perhaps the taunters were right. Through his
reading he became acquainted with the lives of great men.
After reading part of a biography of Napoleon, he concluded
that egotism was the prime motivator of the Corsican and
slammed the book to the floor in disgust. But reading the life
of Simón Bolívar made him cry. A vague messianic mysticism
was penetrating the mind of Augusto Sandino. When the
time came he would be prepared to accept his call; he could
carry on the work begun by Bolívar.

After three years in Mexico, Sandino received a communication from his father urging him to come home. It was May

1926, and Mexican newspapers were carrying stories about a Liberal uprising against the Chamorro regime in Nicaragua. On May 14 Sandino resigned as head of the Gasoline Sales Department of Huasteca Petroleum Company in Cerro Azul, "stating that he had urgent business at home in Nicaragua." [16] He gathered up his belongings—mainly $500 that he had saved and a forty-four caliber Smith and Wesson revolver that he had bought—and sailed from Tampico on May 18, his birthday, on the steamship *México*. He disembarked at Veracruz and went overland from there through Guatemala and Honduras to Nicaragua, arriving in his homeland on June 1. Although Sandino had returned to Nicaragua with an acute social and political consciousness, there seemed to be little for him to do. General Chamorro's reactionary regime appeared firmly entrenched in power, having just recently crushed a Liberal revolt on the east coast. After a brief visit to Niquinohomo, Sandino departed for the mountainous Nicaraguan department of Nueva Segovia. There, at the American-owned San Albino gold mine, he was given a job as assistant to the paymaster—"not that he appeared to be especially qualified to fill such a position, but . . . he appeared too well educated to work as a peon." [17]

In conversations with his American bosses at San Albino, Sandino tested their gullibility. He told mine-owner Charles Butters that he had served eleven years in Pancho Villa's army in Mexico. [18] To paymaster Philip Gleason he confided "that he had been with a circus in Mexico, to which country he had gone as a child to act in the capacity of an acrobat." [19] But to the mine workers at San Albino he presented another side. He lectured to them on the injustices of the system under which they worked. He incited them to demand cash wages instead of the usual company-store script. He contrasted labor conditions in Nicaragua with those in Mexico, where social legislation had improved the lot of the workers. Sandino discovered that he had real rabble-rousing ability. His following among the miners grew, and he decided that the time had come to resort to arms.

With the $300 that remained of his savings, Sandino began dealing with Honduran gun runners. In October 1926 he was able to raise and arm a band of twenty-nine men. On November 2 he led this force in an attack on the two-hundred-man government garrison at Jícaro, near San Albino. The Sandinistas killed some of the defenders, but the attack was soon repelled by the garrison. Although none of Sandino's men were killed in the fight, his band was demoralized and began to disintegrate. The failure of the Jícaro attack convinced Sandino that his movement could not succeed alone. He gathered together his few remaining followers and led them down the Coco River to the sea and along the coast to Puerto Cabezas, where he applied for aid from the Constitutionalist government established there on December 2, 1926.[20]

Sandino's reception in Puerto Cabezas was decidedly cool. Neither Constitutionalist President Sacasa nor his Minister of War, General Moncada, were disposed to give this unknown revolutionist the precious war materiel he requested. Moncada later claimed that he immediately distrusted Sandino after hearing him speak of "the necessity for the workers to struggle against the rich and other things that are the principles of communism."[21] The Minister of War suggested that Sandino and his men join an expedition that was being dispatched to the northern mountains. When Moncada left to attack the Conservatives at Las Perlas, Sandino remained in Puerto Cabezas trying to convince the *políticos* that he should be given an independent command. On December 23 American naval forces landed at Puerto Cabezas, declared the port a "neutral zone," and gave Sacasa twenty-four hours to get all his soldiers and military equipment out of town. The President's guard of honor withdrew from Peurto Cabezas in a disorganized manner, and Sandino and six followers, aided by some local prostitutes, helped themselves to the Constitutionalist stores of arms and ammunition left behind. They were able to carry thirty rifles and seven thousand cartridges out of the neutral zone before the twenty-four hours were up. What was left of the Constitutionalist war materiel in

Puerto Cabezas was dumped into the harbor by the Americans when the time limit expired.

From Puerto Cabezas Sandino and his followers proceeded to Prinzapolca, where General Moncada had his headquarters. The Minister of War was fresh from his victory at Las Perlas and was preparing for his march on Managua. He received Sandino "disdainfully" and not only refused his petition for more arms but ordered him to surrender the rifles he had salvaged from the fiasco at Puerto Cabezas. But at least some Constitutionalist leaders appreciated Sandino's resourcefulness: Doctors Arturo Vaca and Onofre Sandoval urged Moncada to let Sandino keep the arms he already had. "Moncada acceded in a depreciatory manner." [22] Sandino's experience at Puerto Cabezas and Prinzapolca left him embittered. He was appalled by the confusion and intrigue that surrounded Sacasa's government, and his relations henceforth with Moncada would be laden with hostility and mistrust. Sandino became convinced that Nicaragua needed new leaders.

During Moncada's march across the mountains to Muy Muy and Boaco, Sandino, now a full-fledged Constitutionalist general, operated more or less independently on the right flank of the main column. As he marched through the northern mountains, he acquired recruits and weapons. In February 1927, after some inconclusive operations in conjunction with Liberal General López Irías, Sandino established himself atop Mount Yucapuca, a flat-topped, treeless peak near San Rafael del Norte. Recruits from the surrounding area increased Sandino's outfit to about one hundred armed men. Government troops attacked Sandino's entrenched Constitutionalists on Yucapuca early in March. In a hard-fought, seven-hour battle, Sandino's men drove off a force of four hundred Conservatives armed with rifles and six machine guns. The attackers suffered heavy losses, including many weapons that fell into Sandino's hands. Sandino then moved his troops into San Rafael del Norte and made his headquarters in the home of Pablo Arauz, which also contained the local telegraph office. Here he communicated with other Liberal-held towns by wire, spending long hours of the day and night in the telegraph office while Pablo Arauz's daughter—Blanca, a pretty girl of nineteen—operated the key. "Thus I fell in love with Blanca and she became my fiancée." [23]

An officer who served with Sandino during this campaign described his chief:

> Sandino is of medium height, very slender, weighs about 115 lbs.; education limited to primary grades; an extreme optimist and possesses unusual ability in convincing others of the feasibility of his most fantastic schemes; extremely energetic; explains his plans in great detail to his lowest subordinates but often keeps his officers in doubt; is far from being cold-blooded and was never known to commit any act of cruelty himself; very religious and believes that for every wrong committed adequate punishment will be meted out to the offender, regardless of steps taken by agents of the law; he has little interest in acquiring money for personal use and rarely has a penny in his pocket; is very vain and sophisticated, fully believing that his wisdom is infallible; he will not tolerate for long a subordinate of outstanding ability; feigns modesty at all times, but in fact is most vain and selfish; his one slogan is "The Welfare of Our Fatherland," always stressing his interest in the peasant class; he has frequently said that if he or one of his close friends ever get into control of the Government that the port of Corinto will be promptly closed and everything diverted to Port Cabo Gracias a Dios [on the Caribbean at the mouth of the Coco River], so that the isolated sections of the Republic may have the greatest advantage in their contact with outside civilization. [24]

In San Rafael del Norte Sandino made plans to attack the government garrison at Jinotega. First he secured his rear by establishing garrisons in key northern towns and villages. He then resumed his southward thrust and, on March 28, attacked Jinotega with two hundred armed men. After a day of fierce fighting, Sandino's troops routed the enemy and entered the city. But the victorious force was badly disorgan-

Attack Jinotega

ized as a result of the action. Discipline crumbled as the troops plundered the town. Sandino acted vigorously to restore his authority: he pulled his forces out of Jinotega and withdrew to San Rafael del Norte where he reorganized them. On April 4 he reoccupied Jinotega and remained there until April 13.

At Jinotega Sandino was joined by the forces of General Francisco Parajón, a Constitutionalist commander who had been driven from his area of operations in the northwestern lowlands. Parajón, leader of the unsuccessful attack on Chinandega in early February, was a small farmer before the War—and a field organizer for the Nicaraguan Federation of Labor. His troops, like those of Sandino, wore the black and red colors of syndicalism in their hatbands. Sandino evidently considered Parajón a worthy ally, one of the "new leaders" the country needed. In mid-April Parajón combined his forces with those of López Irías and followed Sandino's troops southward to aid Moncada, whose advance had been stalled between Muy Muy and Boaco.

Moncada welcomed the arrival of the two-thousand-man Sandino-Parajón-López column. He was not overjoyed to see Sandino, but as he lay in his headquarters hammock the Liberal generalissimo extended his hand to the newly arrived general from the north. The pleasantries over, Moncada issued Sandino a machine gun, a submachine gun, and fifteen thousand rounds of ammunition and ordered him to occupy the town of Boaco—but, according to Sandino, neglected to tell him that a strong Conservative force was entrenched there. While Sandino marched to Boaco, Moncada led the bulk of the army in the turning movement that put the Constitutionalists at Boaquito, a giant step closer to Managua. After reconnoitering his objective, Sandino suspected that Moncada's order to occupy Boaco was motivated more by a desire to rid himself of Sandino than by strategic considerations. Sandino wisely withheld his attack on Boaco and followed Moncada to Boaquito. There Moncada withdrew his order to occupy Boaco and instead sent Sandino to El Común hill, about three miles south of Teustepe. The Conservatives at Boaco were thus cut off from their main force at Teustepe; they evacuated the town during the truce that was called at the time of the Tipitapa conference.

When Moncada met with Henry L. Stimson at Tipitapa on May 4, 1927, Sandino viewed the negotiations with automatic suspicion. "Moncada," Sandino wrote to a friend, "will at the very first opportunity sell out to the Americans." [25] The day after the Tipitapa meeting, Moncada summoned Sandino to his headquarters. This time Moncada got up out of his hammock to greet Sandino; then he lay down again and explained to him the peace terms. Stimson, he said, had promised the Liberals political control of six departments in return for laying down their arms and agreeing to American-supervised elections. Moncada offered Sandino the governor-ship of Jinotega and said that he would receive $10 back pay for each day he had spent in the Constitutionalist army. Furthermore, if Sandino agreed to the terms, all the mules he had requisitioned during the war would be legally his. Sandino indicated his disapproval of these proposals. Moncada urged his subordinate to reconsider and invited him to a council of war that was to be held in Boaco on May 8. Sandino returned to El Común hill to think it over:

> It was not possible for me to be indifferent to the attitude assumed by a traitor [Moncada]. I remembered in those moments the wounding phrases used abroad to characterize us Nicaraguans. So I spent three days on El Común Hill, downcast, sorrowful, without knowing what attitude to take, whether to surrender the arms or defend the country, which was crying for commiseration from her sons. I did not want my soldiers to see me cry, and I sought solitude.[26]

On the day of the council of war, Sandino and his staff proceeded to Boaco. They found Moncada in one of the town's most substantial homes. The generalissimo was in the parlor, sitting in an upholstered rocking chair, talking with a priest. The room was small, but there were curtains and fine furniture and many paintings on the walls. The tiles of the floor formed a mosaic, and there were vases of flowers in the hall and a flower garden in the patio. Moncada no longer wore battle dress; his new uniform was a light Palm Beach suit and shiny shoes. The commander-in-chief asked the priest to excuse him while he conferred with Sandino.

The council of war, Sandino was told, had already been held, and all the other generals—even his close ally, Parajón—had agreed to the disarmament. Moncada had offered to lead the army against the Yankees if his officers chose to resist. Some had been inclined to do so, but their opposition faded when Moncada offered them speedy appointments to important and lucrative positions in the Nicaraguan government. Moncada promised to have these appointments ratified by Stimson at their next meeting, after which he would call the generals together again for final approval of the surrender agreement. Informed of these developments, Sandino told Moncada that he had meditated on the matter and was resolved to accept the decision of the other generals. Sandino said he would bring his troops down from El Común hill and concentrate them at the hacienda El Cacao de los Chavarría, near Teustepe, on the road to Jinotega. Moncada agreed and Sandino returned to his outfit.

The next day, May 9, Sandino wrote Moncada from El Cacao:

> I have found myself in a difficult position . . . my troops having gone to Jinotega, the place from whence they came . . . I have decided to go to Jinotega again to assemble my men, in order to collect all the arms . . . I shall remain there awaiting your orders . . . The disbanding of my men is due to their not finding anything to eat.[27]

Although Moncada must have suspected that his subordinate had other ideas about laying down his arms, he made no attempt to stop Sandino and his men from slipping away to Jinotega. On May 12, 1927, when Moncada and his commanders wired Stimson their acceptance of his terms, Sandino was the only general in Moncada's army not available to sign the telegram. At the time Sandino was gathering up his men in Jinotega and preparing to march to San Rafael del Norte. He did not intend to surrender: "I decided to fight, understanding that I was the one called to protest the betrayal of the Fatherland." [28]

4

The Battle of Ocotal

Augusto Sandino and his troops were welcomed to Jinotega with music and flowers. The Liberals of the town
greeted him as their conquering general, knowing little or
nothing of the events at Tipitapa and Boaco. On May 12,
1927, the day Moncada formally agreed to lay down his arms,
Sandino issued by telegraph a "Circular to the Local Authorities of All Departments." [1] In the message Sandino noted his
services to the Liberal cause in marching to the relief of
Moncada and "breaking the chains that were drowning the
revolution." Just as the Constitutionalists were preparing to
make their final push and march triumphantly into Managua,
Sandino continued, the "Barbaric Colossus of the North, that
is the North Americans," stepped in and saved the day for
the Conservatives by imposing a truce. Sandino explained the
Tipitapa agreement and indicated his opposition to the provision assuring Adolfo Díaz the presidency until after the
1928 elections. He hoped that elections—in which the Liberals were bound to win—could be held before then and
could be supervised by the governments of Argentina, Brazil,
and Chile. In the meantime he was not disposed to lay down
his arms: he would rather die with his few followers, because
"it is preferable to have us die as rebels and not live as
slaves." Finally, Sandino declared that he would "remain here
awaiting the decision of General Stimson in respect to our
matter."

But Sandino did not wait long in Jinotega. He soon learned that the townspeople there lacked enthusiasm for resisting the Yankees. Furthermore, dissension was rife among his troops; Sandino's soldiers were sorely tempted to desert and surrender their arms to the Marines for the promised $10. Had he tarried long in Jinotega, Sandino's whole "army" might have evaporated. After two days there he decided to withdraw with his remaining troops to San Rafael del Norte, his former headquarters, high in the Segovia Mountains.[2] This was a graceful town of adobe and red tile nestled in the grassy folds of a narrow canyon. Here, along-side the sparkling headwaters of the Rio Viejo, more than two thousand *rafaeleños* enjoyed the temperate climate afforded by an altitude of nearly four thousand feet. Near San Rafael del Norte was one of the few wheat-growing regions of tropical Nicaragua. The town was overwhelmingly Liberal in sentiment, and the returning Sandinistas were warmly greeted by many townspeople when they marched in, late in the afternoon of May 15. The general made his headquarters, as before, in the home of Pablo Arauz.

Sandino's fiancée, Blanca Arauz, greeted her betrothed with a kiss and the news that her sister Lucila had promised the Virgin of May a Mass for the troops the day Sandino returned unharmed. The general thanked Lucila for her sentiments and promised to have his troops formed at eight o'clock the next morning to attend the Mass. The priest was a "gentleman of twenty-two years" and the Mass was "magnificent." Although the soldiers behaved "respectfully," Sandino later recalled, "during the celebration of the Mass there were some salvos of rifles and machine guns." [3] Sandino paid the costs of the Mass.

Having attended to these spiritual matters, the general began composing another circular. This message was tele-graphed from San Rafael del Norte on May 18 and was ad-dressed to "All the Authorities of the Segovias." [4] In it Sandino accused Moncada of betraying the Liberal cause and declared his determination to resist the invaders. He had withdrawn his main force to San Rafael del Norte and ordered his supporters in Jinotega and "other places" not to resist the American occupation

> so that the Civil authorities may listen to the pretensions of the Yankees. In the meantime, I will know everything by telegraph, and go to the place of my convenience, and close the Constitutionalist movement with a breach of Yankee blood.
>
> I do not care if the world [turns] against me, but I will comply with my sacred duty . . .
>
> I will protest for my own satisfaction, if there is no one who will second me.

These brave words were issued on Sandino's thirty-second birthday, which also became his wedding day. The ceremony was held before dawn without prior notice to the public. It was two o'clock in the morning and cold and foggy as the wedding party walked through the deserted streets to the church. Sandino was accompanied by six aides and Blanca by her family. The groom wore a uniform of coffee-colored gabardine and tall dark boots; his revolver was at his belt. The bride was dressed in white, with a veil and a crown of orange blossoms. Blanca Arauz was a "very beautiful girl." [5] Her light hair and complexion combined with finely sculptured features supported Sandino's assertion that she was "95 percent white." There was a disarming "air of sweetness about her." [6]

As the wedding party passed from the dreary night into the well-lighted church, Sandino breathed in the pleasant smells. "The odor of the flowers that adorned the church and the different perfumes that filled the air brought me memories of the days of my infancy." The priest invited Sandino to confess. "I confessed. I did it sincerely." Then the general and his aides knelt before the altar and received the sacraments. After the wedding, as he left the church and walked into the street with his bride, Sandino "felt new. It seemed as if I were walking on air." [7] By this time many of his soldiers were awake and had learned of the wedding. They shouted congratulations as the newlyweds passed through the streets. As the general and his bride entered the Arauz home, they could hear the sounds of pistols, rifles, and machine guns being fired into the air in celebration.

The enthusiasm of Sandino's troops for the wedding was somewhat greater than their enthusiasm for fighting the Yankees. New waves of desertion swept his ranks in San Rafael del Norte, and Sandino soon found himself with only thirty men. After a two-day honeymoon he said goodbye to his wife and again retreated—this time seven miles across the lofty Pantasma peaks to the village of Yali. Here he remained in touch with the towns to the south by telegraph.

At this point Sandino's cause looked hopeless—even to him. He began searching for an honorable way out. If he could not save the country from the Marines, maybe he could at least save it from President Díaz. On May 21 he wired General Feland from Yali: "For peace to be durable we propose that the two parties leave the affairs of the Republic in the hands of [an] American governor, until absolutely free elections have been [held]." [8] That same day General Feland ordered the Fifth Marine Regiment into northern Nicaragua, to disarm Sandino or force him across the border into Honduras.[9]

The Marines occupied Jinotega on the afternoon of May 23, and General Moncada came to town early that night. Moncada wired Sandino to come to Jinotega for a conference. Sandino replied the next day, refusing to come but agreeing to lay down his arms "providing the United States takes over the government of Nicaragua, appoints a military Governor, discharges all present Conservative and Liberal office holders, and carefully supervises the next election." [10] In another telegram, to the commander of the Marine detachment in Jinotega, Sandino declared that an American military government was a condition *"sine qua non"* for the disarmament of his forces.[11] This condition, of course, was unacceptable to the United States. Rebuffed, Sandino felt his honor left him no other course but to resist the Marines. Before Sandino took the field against the invaders, General Moncada made one more effort to get him to disarm peacefully: he persuaded Don Gregorio Sandino to go to Yali and try to convince his son of the futility of resistance.

Don Gregorio spent four hours trying to persuade Sandino to lay down his arms. When he refused, as Don Gregorio later described the scene in a personal letter,[12] "his troops applauded him and cheered him." The general declared that his life belonged to his country. What would he have him do, Sandino asked his father rhetorically. After all it had cost him to get the arms, and after all the hardships of a victorious campaign, why should he surrender his weapons? What if he did so and the Yankees did not keep their promise of free elections and "kicked us in the bottom?" Then he would "shoot himself out of rage for not having anything to fight with." Would his father have him do that "or would he prefer him to die fighting?" Don Gregorio answered "that it would be better for him to die fighting than to commit suicide, as God would protect him." After the interview Don Gregorio returned home to Niquinohomo and Sandino withdrew from Yali and retreated into the mountain fortress of Nueva Segovia department to prepare his resistance.

Establishing control over Nueva Segovia was the mission of an expedition of fifty Marines, commanded by Major Harold Clifton Pierce, that left Managua on May 31, 1927.[13] Since Nueva Segovia was traditionally Liberal, the Tipitapa agreements called for the appointment of a Liberal as the department governor. Major Pierce's mission included escorting the appointee, Señor Arnoldo Ramírez Abaunza, to Ocotal, the departmental capital, and installing him in office there. The expedition proceeded from Managua to Matagalpa in trucks, completing this leg of the journey in less than a day. In Matagalpa Major Pierce spent four days out-fitting his expedition for the march overland into Nueva Segovia. He bought fifty riding mules and fifty-six pack mules and hired eleven native mule drivers. Except for Ramírez and his aide, ex-Constitutionalist General Ramón Telles, the mule drivers were the only Nicaraguans to accompany the expedition. On June 5 the party arrived in San Rafael del Norte, the town abandoned by Sandino two weeks earlier and now occupied by a small detachment of Marines under Second Lieutenant Wilbur S. ("Big Foot") Brown.

While the expedition was in San Rafael del Norte, Ramírez visited Blanca de Sandino. Ramírez reported to Major Pierce that Blanca had told him that her husband would not fire on the Marines, "but some of his people, whom he might not be able to control, might do so." [14] As the expedition proceeded from San Rafael del Norte to Ocotal, Major Pierce received several indications that Sandino's men were trailing or flanking his column. At Santa Rosa he was informed that an armed band had passed through there the day before. Pierce soon learned that the Sandinistas were not the only armed band in the department. On June 8 he peacefully disarmed twenty Liberals at Totogalpa. The next day he arrived at Ocotal.

Ocotal lay at two thousand feet in a broad valley, just north of the wide, shallow, east-west arm of the Coco River. The town was founded in 1803, after buccaneers had come up the Coco from the Caribbean and sacked Ciudad Antigua, the former capital of the region. Ocotal was set back from the navigable portions of the Coco to provide protection against such raids. The town was built on the edge of the Río Dipilto, a stream originating in the ridge of mountains to the north, which provided water for washing and drinking. Around Ocotal, on the slopes at the edges of the valley, pine trees grew; the Indian name "Ocotal" means grove of ocote pines. Spaniards settled the area in the sixteenth century and intermarried with the Indian population, but even in the twentieth century blond hair and blue eyes were not uncommon among some of the oldest families of the region.

When Major Pierce arrived at Ocotal he discovered that the town was practically under siege. Of Ocotal's normal population of fourteen hundred, only a few families remained, and these feared attack from a sizable Conservative band lurking on the outskirts of town. The Marines promptly disbanded Ocotal's Liberal garrison and relieved the defenders of their twenty-eight rifles. At the same time Pierce sent a message to the commander of the Conservative forces threatening Ocotal, calling upon him to march his troops into town and surrender his arms.

Meanwhile, Pierce took steps to establish contact with Marine headquarters in Managua. There was telegraph service with some of the nearby towns, but none with the national capital, so other means of communication had to be used. Pierce ordered signal panels laid out in an open field to be read by the two-plane air patrol covering the expedition. In addition, the major had two fourteen-foot poles erected seventy-five feet apart in the field, each marked by a white flag on top. A message was placed in a leather pouch and loosely suspended between the poles on a string, the ends of which were looped over headless nails driven into each pole. When the expected DeHaviland biplanes appeared over the town, the airmen read the panels and one plane swooped down between the poles dangling a weight on a twenty-five- to fifty-foot line, which caught the message string and slipped it off the poles. As the pilot climbed the plane to a safe altitude, the observer reeled in the line and retrieved the message, which was then flown to Marine headquarters in Managua. Major Pierce's first message from Ocotal contained a request for an American flag and for money to pay for the weapons he was confiscating.

After several conferences with Pierce, the commander of the Conservative forces besieging Ocotal decided to lay down his arms. With their flags flying and their trumpets blaring,

168 Conservatives—some cavalry, some infantry—marched into Ocotal. "Pretty good-looking little army for Nicaragua," Pierce remarked.[15] The little army surrendered ninety-eight rifles to the Americans. In the meantime the Marines were busily constructing an airfield on the outskirts of town, a job they completed in three days.

While this was being done, Governor Ramírez was corresponding with Sandino—presumably trying to persuade him to surrender. Other reports on Sandino filtered into Ocotal: when Major Pierce heard that Sandino was holding two storekeepers for ransom in Telpaneca, he relayed this information to Managua. Subsequently, Marine headquarters ordered Pierce to march to Telpaneca and investigate. Señor Ramírez said that he would tag along with the Marines rather than remain in Ocotal without protection. Pierce agreed that the town needed a permanent garrison, so when he departed for Telpaneca on June 13, he left Captain Gilbert D. Hatfield and ten Marines in Ocotal to protect the town and the governor.

The rainy season had set in and it took Pierce two days to cover the thirty miles of muddy trail from Ocotal to Telpaneca. When he got there he discovered that the kidnaping story was false but that Sandino had been there; he had appropriated $325 in cash and $395 in merchandise from a local store. Pierce found the inhabitants of Telpaneca reluctant to talk about Sandino. About all he learned was that Sandino had his headquarters on top of a mountain which they called "El Chipote," believed to be about nine miles northwest of Quilali. Major Pierce left Telpaneca for Matagalpa on June 16, considering his mission to Nueva Segovia accomplished. The next day Marine intelligence reported what it thought the commanding general wanted to hear:

> According to reports [Sandino's] band is not large and is scattered over a considerable area along the Rio Coco. He has three machine guns and in all probability his entire force is armed with rifles. He has plenty of ammunition and explosives. He is not a strong leader and his band is probably com-

posed of foreigners and fugitives from justice. It is improb-
able that he will be able to hold this band together through
the adverse weather conditions approaching. All places of
importance are denied him by the Marines, so there is a limit
to the amount of pillaging he can do. It would take a man
with unusual leadership qualities to augment such a group,
or even to keep their numbers intact, and it is believed that
he has no such qualities. His arms and ammunition should be
useless from improper care in a month or so, and . . . he will
not be able to cause any serious trouble.[16]

For awhile General Feland was willing to wait and let
the weather disarm Sandino. He successfully opposed Henry
Stimson's plan to send an Army cavalry regiment to Nicaragua to operate in the countryside. "Admiral Latimer," he
informed the Marine Corps Commandant on June 6, "stood
with me because he didn't want any of the Army down
here." But the admiral wanted the Marines to buy a few
thousand horses "and send a lot of Marines careering all over
the country." Such unwarranted charging about would bring
resistance, just at the time when Sandino had "about petered
out." [17] These encouraging words reached General Lejeune
when the Marine Commandant's chief concern was beefing
up his brigade in China. There, the anti-imperialist Kuomintang had seized Shanghai and then split into left and right
wings, thus threatening a civil war within a civil war—with
American and other foreign interests hanging in the balance.
In Nicaragua the Marine brigade had grown to 2,800 by the
first of June; during this month one thousand officers and
men were withdrawn from Nicaragua to satisfy the demand
for Marines in China. By the end of the month Feland was
warning Lejeune that the Marine force should not be reduced
below twelve hundred until after the elections. "The rebel-
lious chief Sandino," he reported, "is still carrying on." [18]
    In Nueva Segovia Sandino wrote Governor Ramírez on
June 14 that he would respect the governor's authority in
the town of Ocotal, but not in San Fernando, Ciudad Antigua, Telpaneca, Quilali, Murra, Jalapa, or Jícaro. His forces

controlled the area in which these towns were located, Sandino declared, and they would not withdraw nor "surrender
one single rifle" until the government Ramírez was serving
"is replaced by an honorable Liberal government." The general requested that these sentiments be communicated to
Managua and that the Yankees be informed that "if they want
to disarm us, we shall know how to kill them." [19] Four days
later Sandino named one of his officers, Francisco Estrada,
governor of the Department of Nueva Segovia, with its capital in Jícaro, which was to be renamed Sandino City.[20]

At San Fernando the Sandinistas controlled the telegraph
office and could communicate with Ocotal, ten miles away.
On June 25 Sandino wired the commander of the Marine
detachment at Ocotal that he had arrived in San Fernando
with a force of mountaineers and learned that the Marines
were arming Conservatives to send against him. "Shall I wait
here for you or shall I go to you?" Sandino asked. A reply
came the same day: [21]

> It is not true that I am arming Conservatives to attack
> you . . . as I need no other help than that of the Marines. . . .
> What I do need are quick running horses to be able to take
> you in your mountains. You have never wanted to attack us
> although we are small in number, nor have you ever shown
> intentions of such. For this I am giving you the idea of com-
> ing here, assuring you that we shall not run away. . . . I
> thank you for your letter, and trusting that you will soon
> come and salute me personally, I am yours respectfully,
>   G. D. HATFIELD, Capt., USMC

The Sandinistas did not attack. Hatfield waited until June
27 and then wired Sandino again.

> Dear General:
>   Since there seems to be no opportunity to meet you on
> the field of battle, it has occurred to me that if you are
> honest in your desire to defend the rights and insure the
> happiness of your people, you might be willing to come in
> and talk with me. Your safety both coming and leaving us is

guaranteed, and you may bring a reasonable number of men as a bodyguard, say 25, to insure your safety while on the road.

I believe that I can convince you that we do not desire the country of Nicaragua, that you will have an honest election and that you, yourself, are the only obstacle to a permanent peace.

This offer is made on the supposition that you are doing what you think best for your people, even though you are mistaken in method.

If, however, you are merely trying to glorify yourself and to collect tribute from helpless persons, then a talk with you is useless.

Hoping that you are a patriot and not a robber, and that you will talk to me soon, I am,

G. D. HATFIELD, Capt., USMC

Sandino replied on June 29, from "El Chipote via San Fernando." It was no fault of his, Sandino claimed, that there had been no battle. "You and yours ran away from Telpaneca the day I expected to assault you with only machetes, because I have no arms with which to fight." He invited the Marines to come and get him; he would not come in for a conference and fall like a dove deceived by "a few grains of rice at the door of a trap." He might be in the woods, he said, but he was no woodenhead. "I will allow you to come for the conference that you want, and I also allow you to come with a guard of 500 men." And when "you come to my mountains," Sandino advised, "make your wills beforehand." Until then, the general concluded, "I remain your most obedient servant, who ardently desires to put you in a handsome tomb with beautiful bouquets of flowers."

"Bravo! General," Hatfield replied. "If words were bullets and phrases were soldiers, you would be a field marshal instead of a mule thief." He advised Sandino to wire him again "when you have something more than the ravings of a conceited maniac."

General Feland finally decided something would have to

be done about this upstart in the north. On June 30 he wrote General Lejeune that "I am not planning a campaign, in the usual sense of the word, but I am trying to force him out of the country by successively occupying the towns which he claims." [22] A key role in this operation was intended for the Nicaraguan National Guard, the permanent, non-partisan, native constabulary the Marines had been organizing and training since May 12, 1927. On July 1 the first company of the National Guard, forty-eight Nicaraguans under two American officers, departed Managua for Ocotal to reinforce Hatfield, whose Marine command was being increased to forty-one officers and men.[23]

As these National Guardsmen prepared to assume their new duties in the north, Feland's leisurely "non-campaign" received a jolt. On June 30 Managua learned that Sandino had seized the American-owned San Albino gold mine. He had approached the mine with fifty armed men and demanded of Charles Butters, his former employer, five hundred pounds of dynamite with fuses and caps. After getting this equipment Sandino was "reported to have forcibly taken over the mine, driving off all foreigners, and to be running the mine to its ruin." [24] On July 2 Admiral Latimer ordered General Feland to begin operations to disarm Sandino as soon as possible. Feland, in turn, designated Major Oliver Floyd to command a force of seventy-five Marines and 150 Nicaraguan volunteers and assigned him the mission of disarming Sandino.[25] The Nicaraguan troops were to be recruited in Matagalpa and sworn in as Provisional Guardsmen, to serve only for the duration of the expedition.

General Feland originally intended the Nueva Segovia expedition to be primarily a Nicaraguan effort. The Marines accompanying Major Floyd were "principally to look after him and the Marine officers with him, and to give a little backbone to the outfit." [26] Major Floyd, however, had other ideas. He believed the Marines would have to bear the brunt of the fighting, and he thought the purpose of the native troops was merely to furnish a token involvement of Nica-

raguans in the campaign against their countrymen under Sandino. He looked upon the Nicaraguans as more of a hin-
drance than a help; in Matagalpa he decided to recruit only
one company of Provisional Guardsmen. The Nicaraguans
were placed under the command of Marine Captain Victor
F. Bleasdale, a man who "literally ate cold steel and fire, and
enjoyed it." [27] Second in command was another Marine captain; the company's other six officers were Nicaraguans, three
of whom were ex-Conservative colonels and one, the mess
officer, a former Conservative general. On July 15 Major
Floyd's column of seventy-five Marines and seventy-four
Provisional Guardsmen departed Matagalpa for Nueva Segovia to disarm Sandino. But Sandino had learned of these
preparations. He decided to strike against the Marines at
Ocotal before this new force could enter his area.

From the San Albino mine Sandino issued his first manifesto [28] on July 1, 1927. To the people of Nicaragua and
Latin America he announced that the "bonds of nationality"
gave him the right to act upon the problems of Nicaragua—
which were also those of "Central America and all the continent that speaks our language." Although he was only an
urban working man, Sandino admitted, "my ideals sprout
upon a wide horizon of internationalism." He did not care if
the oligarchs called him a plebian: "my greatest honor is having been issued from the womb of the oppressed." He denounced Nicaragua's Conservative leaders and declared that
"the Liberal Revolution is on the march. There are some
people who have not committed treason, who did not falter
or sell their rifles to satisfy the ambition of Moncada." As for
the invaders, "I am accepting the invitation to combat and
I, myself, am provoking it." Sandino wanted to show Nicaragua, Central America, "and the Indo-Hispanic race that in
a spur of the Andean mountain range there is a group of
patriots who know how to fight and die as men." The
Yankees were a "bunch of dope fiends" who had come "to
murder us in our own land." The United States wanted to
build a canal across his country, Sandino continued, and

"civilization demands that the Nicaraguan Canal be constructed." Let the canal be built, he said, "but let it be done with capital from everyone," with at least half the costs borne by Latin American capital and the rest by "the other countries of the world." Sandino urged Nicaraguans of both parties to join his ranks.

Sandino's flamboyant defiance of the Yankees attracted scores of recruits to his band. Loot from the Telpaneca and San Albino raids had solved most of his logistical problems and whetted the appetite of his troops for further operations. At the same time, their American antagonists were encountering some logistical and personnel difficulties. A pack train bearing supplies for Ocotal was forced to halt at Condega when two Marine guards deserted.[29] The two Marines, complete with weapons and individual equipment, appeared at San Fernando on July 7 and told Sandinista Colonel Rufo Marín that they had come "to present themselves to Sandino, because they had been traitors to the United States forces." [30] These developments boosted the morale of the Sandinistas, who began firing regularly on Marine aircraft.[31] The fire was sometimes returned, but this seems to have done little to dampen the spirits of the Nicaraguans.

The chances for peace were not bright when Captain Hatfield in Ocotal wired Sandino [32] in San Fernando on July 11, telling the general that "in spite of your insolent replies in the past, I am giving you another opportunity to surrender with honor." He warned Sandino that the Marines were prepared to hunt him to his stronghold and destroy him. Hatfield urged the Nicaraguan to follow the example of Philippine insurrectionist Emilio Aguinaldo, who had laid down his arms twenty-five years before. He gave Sandino two more days to consider the matter, announcing that he would expect Sandino "in Ocotal at eight o'clock in the morning of July 14, 1927. Please advise me of your intentions in one word, either yes or no."

General Sandino's answer was "no," but he required somewhat more than one word to express it. "Your threats seem very pale to me," he declared. "If you are determined in this . . . you may come, and . . . I shall have the honor of sprinkling the soil of my native country with the blood of traitors and invaders." Furthermore, "if the United States wants peace in Nicaragua they will have to turn the presidency over to a true Liberal, and only then will I put down my arms peacefully."

In Ocotal Captain Hatfield sensed that attack was imminent. The townspeople began hiding their valuables. But despite their fear of looting, the people of Ocotal were largely pro-Sandino and kept their distance from the Marines. The American commander suspected even the local priest of being a Sandinista.[33] July 14 came and Hatfield's deadline for Sandino's surrender passed without incident. Hatfield's thirty-nine enlisted Marines were billeted in the city hall, a two-story adobe building facing the town plaza; the forty-eight Nicaraguan Guardsmen, commanded by National Guard Captain G. C. Darnall (a Marine first lieutenant), had their barracks across the plaza from the city hall and a few yards down a side street. The Marine and National Guard officers' quarters were in another building facing the plaza. On the night of July 15 Captain Hatfield and the other three officers took turns on watch while their men slept with their clothes on and their weapons at hand.[34]

During the day Sandino had concentrated his forces at San Fernando. The general's "army" was formed around a hard core of about sixty officers and men, many of whom had served with him in the Constitutionalist campaign. These soldiers were responsible for the distribution and employment of the band's weapons: about 120 rifles, at least two machine guns, and numerous dynamite bombs. Around this nucleus Sandino had rallied perhaps as many as eight hundred local peasants—most armed with machetes or *cutaches* (short, double-edged swords) and licensed to pillage any Conservative property falling within their grasp. The general issued an attack order,[35] and shortly after dusk on July 15 his men began infiltrating the town of Ocotal. Paragraph seven of

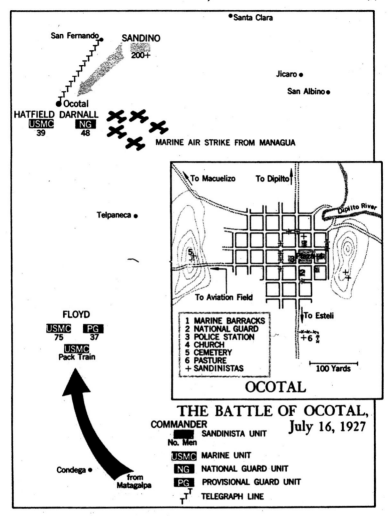

Santa Clara

San Fernando

SANDINO
200+

Jicaro
San Albino

Ocotal

HATFIELD   DARNALL
USMC   NG
39   48

MARINE AIR STRIKE FROM MANAGUA

To Macuelizo   To Dipilto

Dipilto River

Telpaneca

To Aviation Field

To Esteli

FLOYD

USMC   PG
75   37

USMC
Pack Train

1 MARINE BARRACKS
2 NATIONAL GUARD
3 POLICE STATION
4 CHURCH
5 CEMETERY
6 PASTURE
+ SANDINISTAS

+6

100 Yards

OCOTAL

THE BATTLE OF OCOTAL,
July 16, 1927

COMMANDER
⬛ SANDINISTA UNIT
No. Men

USMC   MARINE UNIT
NG   NATIONAL GUARD UNIT
PG   PROVISIONAL GUARD UNIT
T   TELEGRAPH LINE

Condega

from
Matagalpa

Sandino's order read: "It is prohibited to drink liquor and the one who does so I shall receive as if it were an outrage to our country." This was a flagrant departure from the traditional military doctrine of Central America—where a soldier is expected to charge into battle in a drunken stupor.

Sandino's plan was carefully executed. By one o'clock on the morning of July 16 most of Sandino's regulars were inside Ocotal and arms had been distributed to local collaborators; a detachment of Sandinistas was at the unguarded airstrip, preparing to blow five craters in it with dynamite; Sandino had his command post just outside town, on a rise behind the church, where he could best observe and direct the action. His right-hand man, Rufo Marín, was stationed on the opposite side of town, on the road to Macueliza. Within the town there were three companies of Sandinistas: one to attack the Marines in city hall, one to attack the National Guard barracks, and one for "driving out of the houses all the responsible people who may be hidden." [36]

At 1:15 A.M. a Marine sentry noticed a suspicious movement down the street from city hall and went to investigate. Suddenly the night was shattered by a Sandinista fusillade. But the fury was without effect, and the unscathed sentry scurried back to city hall. Within three minutes all Marines were at their battle stations and receiving fire from all directions. The street in front of city hall was swept by a Sandinista machine gun firing from an elevated position at the end of the street. Another Sandinista machine gun opened up from Governor Ramírez' office, diagonally across the plaza from city hall. The Sandinista attack was punctuated with dynamite explosions and shouts of *"Viva Sandino!"* and "Death to the Yankees!"

The National Guard wasted no time going into action. While the men fired from their battle stations, Guard First Lieutenant Thomas G. Bruce (a Marine first sergeant) hauled a machine gun into the street in front of the barracks and began firing from an unprotected prone position at the gun in the governor's office. Marine and Guard officers, who had been sleeping in the officers' quarters across the plaza, came dashing through the crossfire to join their units. After the initial scrambling for positions, neither side moved against the other. While Sandinista snipers and machine gunners maintained a steady fire against the Marines and Guardsmen, Sandino's foragers went to work pillaging Conservative property. At three o'clock bugles sounded assembly, and Sandino and

Marín appeared in town to reorganize their troops. Two Marine automatic riflemen and some sharpshooters kept up a desultory fire while their comrades steeled themselves for the expected enemy assault.

The attack, led by handsome Rufo Marín, came within an hour. Maintaining a heavy volume of fire, Sandinistas advanced from the church into the tree-studded plaza in front of city hall; others worked their way into buildings and behind walls adjoining the city hall and the National Guard barracks. Marine rifles and automatic weapons took a heavy toll of the Sandinistas. In three headlong rushes the attackers vainly threw themselves against the adobe walls of city hall. Dawn revealed seven Sandinistas lying dead on one corner. Rufo Marín, trying to rally his troops, appeared on that corner and was shot down, mortally wounded. Confusion followed the loss of Marín; Sandinista firing slackened and the attack fizzled. Part of the attacking force slunk from the plaza and began rummaging for any property that might have been overlooked in the earlier looting; but Sandino's officers soon had most of their men back on the firing line.

At 8:10 the Sandinista firing halted abruptly and a messenger bearing a flag of truce appeared before city hall. The Marines held their fire as the messenger delivered two notes —one from Sandino and one from his chief of staff, Porfirio Sánchez—to Captain Hatfield. The notes acknowledged that the Marines had put up a brave fight and suggested that now they must be low on water. The notes promised Hatfield and his men that they would not be harmed if they would throw their weapons in the street and surrender within sixty minutes—otherwise the town would be put to the torch and the Marines and Guardsmen would be caught in "an amount of rifle fire . . . never dreamed of before." Captain Hatfield, who had enough water in his tanks to last two weeks, replied "that Marines did not know how to surrender" and regardless of the water situation, they "would stick it out until killed or captured, and that firing would be resumed as soon

as the flag bearer turned the nearest corner." [37] The fighting was promptly resumed. Although no all-out Sandinista assault developed, snipers began to work closer to the strongholds of the Marines and Guardsmen. A Sandinista machine gun began raking the city hall from the church belfry. A Marine was killed by a Sandinista who had scaled the wall adjoining the courtyard of city hall. A Marine sergeant fired at the sniper with a pistol and he tumbled lifeless from the wall.

At 10:15 two Marine patrol planes appeared over Ocotal. One plane—piloted by Lieutenant Hayne D. ("Cuckoo") Boyden—briefly touched down on the crater-pocked airfield and was greeted by Sandinista gunfire, while the other—flown by Gunnery Sergeant Michael Wodarczyk—circled over town and read the signal panels laid out in the courtyard at the city hall. Both were quickly aware of the seriousness of the situation in Ocotal. "Cuckoo" Boyden turned and flew away toward Managua while Gunner Wodarczyk stayed behind, making strafing runs against the Sandinistas until eleven o'clock. Fear spread among the Sandinistas and the townspeople that the planes would return shortly in greater numbers and with bombs. A delegation of local citizens urged Governor Ramírez to intercede with Sandino and get him to call off his attack. Sandino refused to withdraw his forces, and at 2:35 P.M. a flight of five DeHavilands appeared over Ocotal.

The Marine biplanes, led by Major Ross E. Rowell, each carried four bombs and twelve hundred rounds of machine-gun ammunition. Each was armed with two machine guns: a forward gun was in a fixed position and was fired by the pilot; the rear gun was on a swivel mount and was operated by the observer. Flying these flimsy machines over the Segovia Mountains, with their misty peaks and treacherous air currents, would have been perilous even if there had been no danger from ground fire. The hazards of flight were increased with the rainy season; detouring around bad weather delayed the arrival of the planes at Ocotal and consumed much precious gasoline. Although the action of the planes at Ocotal had to be brief, it was nonetheless highly effective.

On arriving at Ocotal the planes formed a column and made their reconnaissance. The airmen read the panels in the courtyard of the city hall and learned that one Marine was dead and that the enemy was employing machine guns. They located a concentration of Sandinistas in an open area and began their attack. Major Rowell led off, diving out of the column from fifteen hundred feet. One after another the planes dived at the Sandinistas, each opening fire with the fixed machine gun on the way down and loosing a bomb at the end of the dive. As the planes climbed away the observers manning the free guns mowed down the Sandinistas as they scrambled for cover. As the Sandinistas dispersed, many of them darting crazily through the open fields that surrounded the town, some planes attacked with only machine guns, saving their bombs for the larger concentrations. Toward the end of the action the planes were plunging to within three hundred feet of the ground before pulling out of their dives. Through it all, the Marine airmen scrupulously avoided bombing civilian residences. Within forty-five minutes the air attack was over and the aircraft were heading for Managua. They had made the first organized dive-bombing attack in history—long before the Nazi Luftwaffe was popularly credited with the "innovation."

The action of the planes put an end to the Sandinista attack; with the first air strikes the Sandinistas had begun withdrawing from town. By 5:25 they were all gone, except for seven snipers who gamely kept banging away from behind a wall in front of the church. After one of these snipers was killed and the other six were bluffed into surrendering by Lieutenant Bruce, the firing stopped and the Marines and Guardsmen ventured out from behind their barricades. Captain Hatfield sent out patrols to count the enemy dead, and they found "more than fifty in the street alone, to say nothing of those that had died in houses and along the river," [38] where the planes were believed to have taken a heavy toll of the fleeing Sandinistas. Hatfield decided that it was too near dark to search the town. Four days after the attack he wrote in his report:

> From the number of dead seen, the number of funerals held daily since then and the increased size of the cemetery, I believe there were at least 300 [Sandinista] dead from all causes . . . Sandino's forces, I believe, amounted to about 400 and were augmented by about 100 here in town, a fact evidenced by practically every Liberal family in town being in mourning. All Conservative homes and business places were looted and several Conservative personal enemies were killed by the invaders.

The Marine losses were one dead and one wounded; the National Guard lost three wounded and four captured.

The Marines at Ocotal held their ground masterfully. They fought with all the tenacity, courage, and skill for which the Corps was famous. Sandino's scrawny brown peasants fought less skillfully, but no less bravely. If nothing else, they showed they knew how to die. Eventually they would develop their own unique and effective style of warfare and prove themselves worthy opponents of the United States Marines.

5

El Chipote: The Illusive Fortress

Patrick Henry

After the battle of Ocotal, Sandino led his depleted forces back to San Fernando. There, on July 20, 1927, he issued a proclamation listing his reasons for the attack: first, to protest the arrangement by which Díaz remained in the presidency and to defend "the constitutionality of Dr. Juan Sacasa"; second, to disprove "the idea that we are bandits"; and third, "to prove that we prefer death to slavery." Sandino's proclamation went on to declare that the peace obtained by Moncada at Tipitapa "is not the peace that can give liberty to men, but a peace that puts men under the domination of others." The blame for the affair at Ocotal, he charged, lay with President Calvin Coolidge of the United States. "Whoever believes we are downcast by the heavy casualties misjudges my army," he warned. "Today we are more impatient than ever to seek out the traitors of our country, determined to die if we cannot secure complete liberty for all men."[1]

With the attack on Ocotal, Augusto Sandino became a continental figure. To American Secretary of State Frank B. Kellogg, Sandino's "activities cannot be considered to have any political significance whatsoever," and his forces were "in effect nothing more than common outlaws."[2] In the

U.S. underestimates

official terminology of Washington, Sandino was a bandit, but to countless Latin Americans the Nicaraguan general was their David battling the Goliath of "Yankee Imperialism." Some of the leading artists and intellectuals of the hemisphere —including José Vasconcelos, Víctor Raúl Haya de la Torre, and Gabriela Mistral—declared their support for Sandino.[3]

In the United States itself Sandino was not without his admirers. His attack on the Marines thrust him before the American public in the midst of a gaudy summer—the apogee of the Roaring Twenties. Charles Lindbergh was being wildly acclaimed for his epoch-making flight; Sacco and Vanzetti were on their way to the electric chair; and Babe Ruth was on his way to hitting sixty home runs. But the American public's appetite for heroes and potential martyrs was still unsatiated; many were eager to idolize Sandino, caring little that he was a foreigner and performed his acts of defiance against their own countrymen. In Washington opponents of the administration echoed Sandino's demands for the withdrawal of the Marines from Nicaragua. During the months ahead the Marines would be referred to in the American Congress as their country's "ambassadors of death";[4] Senator Burton K. Wheeler of Montana would suggest that if the business of the Marines was to fight bandits, they could be put to better use in Chicago.[5] This activity on the home front irritated the apolitical Marines, but it did not affect their determination to carry out their mission: to capture or destroy Sandino and his bandit gang.

The day after the attack on Ocotal, July 17, 1927, Marine planes flew ammunition to Captain Hatfield's garrison and evacuated the wounded.[6] On July 21 the supply convoy that had been stalled at Condega arrived in Ocotal, escorted by fifty mounted Marines from Major Floyd's column. The next day the rest of Floyd's expedition arrived, minus half of the Provisional Guardsmen—twenty had been left on garrison duty and seventeen had deserted along the way from Matagalpa. Early in the morning of July 25 Major Floyd's mounted column of seventy-eight Marines and thirty-seven Provisional Guardsmen departed Ocotal for San Fernando, to put down Sandino's rebellion.[7]

Sandino planned to ambush the Marines as they entered San Fernando, a town perched on a hilltop only ten miles from Ocotal. He posted a sentry on a knoll just outside San Fernando to alert his forces in town when the enemy approached. The sentry, however, abandoned his post on that hot afternoon of July 25 to play with an Indian girl in a nearby shack. Unknown to the forty-odd Sandinistas lounging in the houses of San Fernando, the point of Major Floyd's column slipped into town at three o'clock. To the Marines the town looked deserted; only a harmless old man and an old woman appeared on the streets. When the old man caught sight of the Marines, he headed for a nearby house. The intrepid Captain Bleasdale, riding just behind the point, wanted to question the old man; he and his interpreter, Marine Private Rafael Toro, galloped across the open, grassy plaza in the direction of the elderly native. The hoofbeats alerted the Sandinistas and they opened fire on Bleasdale and Toro as they rode across the plaza, mortally wounding Toro. But the Sandinistas had lost the element of surprise, and the entire Marine-Guard column was quickly upon them. The would-be ambushers fled in disorder, leaving behind eleven of their dead. Sandino considered himself lucky to have escaped from San Fernando with his life.[8] The day after the encounter, Major Floyd reported:

> After my observations yesterday, I am convinced that my further progress will be accomplished only as follows under present conditions:
> a) I will have to wage a real blood and thunder campaign and I will have casualties every day.
> b) I will be involved in a small real war.
> c) These people will shoot it out with small arms opposition for at least a while.
> d) All people encountered are unquestionably strong for Sandino.

e) Nothing can be pressured from the country.

f) Arms will be received only from dead and wounded.[9]

The events of the next day, when Floyd resumed his march into Sandinista territory, seemed to bear out the major's forecast. On the morning of July 27 two Marine patrol planes covering Floyd's column spotted a group of forty men lying in ambush along the major's route of march, just south of the Honduran border. The Sandinistas fired on the planes with a machine gun and the aircraft reacted with dive-bombing and strafing attacks. After dropping three bombs and counting six enemy "dead or seriously wounded," the planes flew away. "Later, one of the planes returned to the scene and dropped another bomb to disperse any of the enemy still remaining."[10] Major Floyd's column entered the area early that afternoon. The Marines and Provisional Guardsmen were ambushed one mile southeast of Santa Clara by a force of from sixty to 120 riflemen supported by two machine guns. The fight lasted from 2:30 until four o'clock when the Sandinistas fled the scene leaving five of their dead behind. The Marines did not suffer a single casualty. Four years later Sandino described the day's action:

> They attacked with tactics . . . and it was a moment in which military schooling dominated the primitive tactics of the Sandinistas. We tried to defend the position by intrenching ourselves . . . and the invader attacked us on the flanks. Also, the aviators took part in the attacks and we defenders of the position had to retreat in disorder, losing more than sixty men, counting dead and wounded.[11]

His defeats at Ocotal, San Fernando, and Santa Clara impressed upon Sandino the folly of accepting battle on the enemy's terms. Henceforth he would attack only when the odds were heavily in his favor—when he clearly had the advantages of surprise, cover, and superior firepower. Never again would he foolishly "stand his ground," nor would he try to redeem an attack that had hopelessly bogged down. Major Floyd might wage a "blood and thunder campaign," but Sandino would adopt the hit-and-run tactics of guerrilla warfare.

From Santa Clara Sandino retreated into the jungles around El Chipote mountain, his base of operations. This was ideal country for guerrilla warfare: a remote, almost trackless, sparsely settled mountain wilderness. The terrain was as varied as it was wild. The valleys were humid and reeking, sheltered from the sun by a canopy of leaves and branches and twisted vines, supported by the trunks of great trees— the smooth-skinned ceiba, the dark mahogany, the silvery matapalo. Through the canopy ranged herds of scampering tree mice and troops of screaming, white-faced monkeys. Here the coarse cry of the macaw and the roar of the jaguar were familiar sounds. Up the slopes at the edge of the valleys the air became drier, the vegetation thinner, the tropical forms fewer. This was the realm of the ocote pine, the mountain partridge and the bluebird, the road runner and the woodpecker. Higher up, beginning at about four thousand feet, the underbrush was heavier and the pines bigger. Here clouds brushed against the mountainsides, providing ample moisture for the orchids and bromeliads that enveloped the limbs and trunks of the pines, sometimes almost concealing them. On the mile-high plateaus, where there was enough ground water, groves of stately oak and sweetgum were interspersed with the pine. This was the cloud forest—the top of the mountain range—the home of the jeweled quetzal, one of the world's most beautiful birds. Here the air was fresh and cool, but never freezing.

This mountainous region was inhabited by a sturdy border people. On the north was the Republic of Honduras and to the east, on the other side of the north-south arm of the Coco River, the Spanish language and culture faded and the domain of the Indian began. The people of the area had little respect for boundaries or for laws. They had been alternately neglected and persecuted by the governments of Honduras and Nicaragua, and their region had become a spawning ground for bandits and smugglers. But there were also those who kept a few cattle and tended patches of corn and beans that were planted with primitive digging sticks in the clearings. The natives of the region were immediately attracted to the flamboyant Sandino and willingly shared with him their food and other resources. While the forest shielded the Sandinistas from the eyes of Marine aviators, Sandino's local admirers consistently supplied him with accurate information about the movement of enemy troops.[12]

While Sandino was regrouping his forces on El Chipote mountain, Major Floyd met only token resistance as he pushed into the area and occupied Jícaro—"Sandino City"— and the San Albino gold mine. At San Albino Floyd learned that Sandino had extracted much ore from the mine and had even minted gold coins. The general had not driven away all foreigners, for two British subjects were still living at the mine—one George Williams and a Mr. Mattison. Floyd persuaded Mattison to cut the main drive-belt and hide the mercury supply, so that the mine would be inoperative should the Sandinistas return. As a further precaution, Floyd destroyed all the mine's explosives and cyanide. It was a curious operation for Marines who had come to Nicaragua "to protect American and foreign property."

At San Albino George Williams—who lived with his native wife and family in a solidly built log house under the protection of a huge Union Jack fluttering overhead—told Floyd that Sandino had retired to his stronghold at El Chipote. But Floyd had little respect for Williams or for the natives of the area whom he questioned:

> Everyone talks about El Chipote. No one who talks has ever been there; ask any man where El Chipote is and he will give you an answer, then upon further questioning it will develop that he has not been there and that even his informant never was there. Sandino is a notorious prevaricator; Sandino is out for the money, and nothing else; there was never in this country a place known as El Chipote until Sandino's recent regime; El Chipote is a semi-slang term meaning a bump raised by a blow on the head; Nicaraguans love

the sensational and among their hundred rumors there will always be one truth, yet nobody has been to El Chipote.[13]

Captain Bleasdale wanted to take a patrol out of San Albino to check on some of these rumors, but Major Floyd, "who was somewhat of a student of classic war," declared, "I will never divide my force in the presence of the enemy." [14] Besides, he had already won the war: he had occupied Sandino's capital, Jícaro, and destroyed his source of wealth, the San Albino mine. The Sandinistas now could only fold up their tents and steal away. After posting a small garrison at Jícaro under First Lieutenant George J. O'Shea, Floyd left for Matagalpa on August 14, convinced that he had ended forever the menace of Sandino. Floyd had applied the criteria of conventional warfare to a revolutionary guerrilla situation. He was among the first of a long line of twentieth-century American military thinkers to make this mistake.

Major Floyd's optimistic reports on the situation in Nueva Segovia dispelled any misgivings there might have been about the steady reduction of Marine forces in Nicaragua. "Sandino's power is broken," brigade intelligence declared on August 8. "There should be no further trouble of any nature in the entire republic." [15] The last of the Eleventh Regiment departed on September 6, leaving only the Fifth Marines and one aircraft squadron to enforce the will of Washington in Nicaragua. Brigadier General Logan Feland left for the United States after turning over command of the depleted Second Brigade to Colonel Louis M. Gulick on August 24. About the same time there was a change in the command of the brigade's parent organization. At his own request, Rear Admiral Julian L. Latimer was relieved as commander of the Special Service Squadron and was replaced by Rear Admiral David F. Sellers.[16]

While general and field-grade officers congratulated themselves on eliminating banditry in Nicaragua, Lieutenant O'Shea of the Jícaro garrison was not so sure that Sandino had been crushed, or that El Chipote was a myth. Early in September O'Shea led a patrol into the surrounding countryside to gather intelligence: he questioned natives, he was fired upon, he captured Sandinista documents. Everything indicated that Sandino was massing his forces on a mountain northeast of Quilali, preparing for further operations.[17]

On September 2, 1927, as O'Shea probed nearby, Sandino and hundreds of his followers gathered on El Chipote mountain to sign the "Articles of Incorporation of the Defending Army of the National Sovereignty of Nicaragua." [18] The document listed fourteen points:

1) The army was composed of Nicaraguan and Hispanic-American Liberal volunteers and was dedicated to defend the liberty of Nicaragua. The Supreme Chief of the army was General Augusto César Sandino. The army would be guided in its acts by "the most elevated spirit of patriotism and discipline" and would be governed by the Military Code of the Republic of Nicaragua.

2) The army did not recognize the authority of the "traitorous interventionist government of Nicaragua" nor that of the Yankee invaders.

3) The army was not a faction of the Liberal party but rather "the soul and nerves of the Fatherland and the Race."

4) "Every guerrilla who hereafter [joins] the Defending Army of the National Sovereignty of Nicaragua is obliged to report to the Supreme Chief . . . who will enlist him with due formality and select the zone in which he will have to operate."

5) The Department of Nueva Segovia would be divided into four zones—Pueblo Nuevo, Quilali, Somoto, and Ocotal. Each zone would be assigned as an area of operations to an expeditionary chief named by the Supreme Chief of the Revolution.

6) Expeditionary chiefs were "strictly forbidden to molest peaceful peasants, but they may collect forced loans from native and foreign capitalists" to maintain the war effort. All sums thus collected were to be duly accounted for, and any

abuse of this provision would lead to "proceedings in conformity with our Military Code."

7) Officers of the army were "strictly forbidden to make secret pacts with the enemy, nor may they make pacts of any kind." Offenders would be court-martialed.

8) The "powers of the Revolution" resided in the army's General Headquarters.

9) All orders from the Supreme Chief of the revolution were to be complied with.

10) The army would not pay any salaries, "because every worthy Nicaraguan is obligated to defend voluntarily the dignity of the Nation."

11) All official army correspondence was to close with the words "Fatherland and Liberty."

12) "The Defending Army of the National Sovereignty of Nicaragua is in active communication with the Indo-Hispanic nations" and had already named its representatives to these countries.

13) The military rank awarded by the General Headquarters was to be recognized "upon the triumph of our cause," and to facilitate this, each officer would be given a written commission.

14) The Supreme Chief of the revolution swore "before the Fatherland and the Army" that he was without "political commitments to anyone and that his acts conform to the most elevated patriotism," and that he was "assuming responsibility for [these acts] before the Fatherland and History."

The first test of the reconstituted Sandinista army came before dawn on September 19, 1927. During this dark, foggy night, about 140 Sandinistas led by Carlos Salgado infiltrated the town of Telpaneca, a village located on a bend in the Coco River. Salgado was a "cunning and experienced" guerrilla chieftain who could be recognized anywhere: "he was an exact counterpart of the Indian head on our American five-cent piece." [19] Salgado's men slipped by the Marine sentries and were at the doors and windows of the Marine and National Guard barracks before they were discovered. The

Sandinistas attacked with rifles, dynamite bombs, machetes, two Lewis machine guns, and three Thompson submachine guns. The fog rising from the river made the darkness almost complete and afforded few targets for the defenders—twenty Marines and twenty-five Guardsmen commanded by Guard Captain H. S. Keimling (a Marine first lieutenant). Captain Keimling, an "extremely popular and efficient" officer,[20] had his troops barricade themselves in their barracks and mess hall. The Marines fought doggedly and with good humor—joking and drinking coffee as they beat back three waves of attackers. The National Guardsmen gave a fine account of themselves—firing with cool discipline, smiling enigmatic Indian smiles, and tossing sputtering dynamite bombs back at the attackers who threw them. The Sandinistas fought well, too. "Several bandit groups fired by command and did some pretty good shooting." [21] They showed good spirit, yelling "*Viva Sandino!*" and "Death to the United States!" Some clattered their machetes against adobe walls and shouted "This is for Marines!"

The fog began to lift at 2:30 A.M., and at three o'clock the Sandinistas were evacuating their dead and wounded. They split into two groups and started an orderly withdrawal as the sun began to rise. By five o'clock all was quiet in Telpaneca. Although only two Marines had been killed, Sandino convinced his men that they had inflicted much heavier casualties on the enemy, that they had won a great victory. By taking their dead with them, the Sandinistas deprived the Marines of any concrete evidence of the casualties they had inflicted. In the future the Sandinistas would follow this practice whenever possible, leaving the Marines with nothing but their estimates of enemy losses—estimates which were sometimes as wildly exaggerated as the figures published by Sandino on Marine losses.

After the attack on Telpaneca, Marine headquarters no longer doubted the existence of a Sandinista base of operations. Marine aircraft began scanning the area around Quilali for evidences of El Chipote. On the morning of October 8

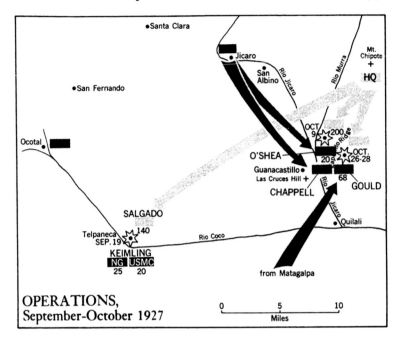

OPERATIONS,
September-October 1927

a two-plane patrol spotted a Sandinista pack train and swooped down upon it with machine guns blazing. The Sandinistas fired back with rifles and hit one of the planes. The wounded plane limped through the air for a few minutes and then crash-landed on Zapotillo ridge. The other plane flew low over the wreckage and dropped a map to the downed aviators, Second Lieutenant Earl A. Thomas and Sergeant Frank E. Dowdell. The airmen took their bearings and then set out on foot for Jícaro, the town garrisoned by the troops of the energetic Lieutenant O'Shea. But the hapless aviators were overtaken and captured by a band of guerrillas. That same day the two Marines were tried before a Sandinista court-martial and shot. The body of Lieutenant Thomas was hanged from a tree and photographed.[22] Then the Sandinistas set up an ambush for the expected rescue party.

Within four hours of the crash the garrison at Jícaro had been notified and a patrol of nine Marines, ten National Guardsmen, and a Navy surgeon was headed for the scene under the command of Lieutenant O'Shea.[23] The men traveled on foot, leading five pack animals, and reached the area of the crash early the next morning. An air patrol flew over and indicated to O'Shea the exact location of the wreckage, three miles distant—in a straight line. Three and a quarter hours later O'Shea was at last marching along a trail at the top of Zapotillo ridge, but his air cover had flown away because of lack of gasoline. Unknown to the lieutenant, he was being stealthily flanked by a group of Sandinistas on a parallel trail. As O'Shea's men moved through a dip in the trail, they were fired upon by a large force of guerrillas well positioned ahead. The smaller flanking party swung into position behind O'Shea, and the Americans and the Guardsmen were caught in a well-sprung trap. O'Shea quickly decided to attack the smaller force, and his men blasted their way out of the trap with well-placed hand and rifle grenades, dispersing the guerrillas with fire and maneuver. Dr. John B. O'Neill, the Navy surgeon, lagged behind with O'Shea's rear guard and broke up a Sandinista rush with an expertly tossed hand grenade.

O'Shea's breakthrough did not put him out of danger. His native guides had deserted and he had lost his compass; he had no time to ponder which way to go, because groups of Sandinistas were running and yelling at him from several directions. For two and a half hours the lieutenant's little band battled its way back down the trail, pushing against a force of about a hundred guerrillas while another hundred bore down on its rear. For awhile O'Shea would lead the patrol, throwing hand grenades as he went; then O'Neill would take over, firing a rifle he had picked up from a dead Guardsman. The patrol's Thompson submachine gunner laid down a deadly fire and the rifle grenadier knocked out a Sandinista machine gun, demonstrating the high value of these two weapons in close-range bush warfare. As night began to fall the patrol veered off the trail and descended into a ravine, slipping out between the two groups of Sandinistas. The men groped their way through the jungle during much of the night, and the next morning they made contact with an air patrol. Late that afternoon they "arrived in Jícaro, suffering from exposure and complete exhaustion, bruised, cut up by thorns and bitten by insects." [24] Of the twenty men who had left Jícaro, four were killed on Zapotillo ridge; the casualties, inexplicably, were all members of the National Guard.

About a week later another Marine–National Guard effort to search the area of the crash was begun. The plan called for a two-pronged drive on Zapotillo ridge. One force, twenty-eight Marines and forty Guardsmen, under First Lieutenant Moses J. Gould, left Matagalpa on October 18 and marched north, while a somewhat smaller patrol, under Second Lieutenant C. J. Chappell, followed O'Shea's route south from Jícaro. Chappell reached the area first, on October 26, and was immediately surrounded and forced into a defensive position by a superior force of guerrillas. The guerrilla siege was lifted two days later when Gould arrived on the scene and, with air support, put the Sandinistas to flight. After a fruitless search for the missing aviators, the combined patrols began the march to Jícaro. Along the way Gould and Chappell were attacked by an "estimated" force of 250 guerrillas, which they repelled, losing only one Marine wounded and two Guardsmen killed—the only casualties sustained by either patrol during the entire week. Lieutenant Gould guessed that sixty guerrillas had been killed or wounded.[25] Sandino, however, claimed his forces suffered "hardly a casualty." [26]

General Sandino's version of his battles reached the world press through two able collaborators. One was Dr. Pedro José Zepeda, a hefty, wavy-haired Nicaraguan physician residing in Mexico City. "Doc" Zepeda was articulate and personable, a man with many connections; Will Rogers claimed him as his "good friend." [27] Zepeda furnished the wire services in Mexico City with Sandinista communiqués he received from Froylán Turcios in Tegucigalpa, Honduras. Turcios, a Honduran poet, was the official foreign representative of Sandino's Defending Army of the National Sovereignty of

Nicaragua. In Tegucigalpa he received dispatches by courier direct from Sandino's headquarters at El Chipote. Sandino's letters to Turcios, together with his manifestos and communiqués, were printed in *Ariel,* a fortnightly review Turcios published in Tegucigalpa. Turcios stressed an analogy suggested a quarter-century before by the great Uruguayan essayist, José Enrique Rodó: Sandino was Ariel, the airy spirit of Shakespeare's *Tempest,* symbol and ideal of the Hispanic race, battling Caliban, the brutalizing materialism of the United States, represented in Nicaragua by the Madines. Froylán Turcios was "a middle-aged man of charming simplicity" with "just a hint of politician along with the poet." [28]

The longer Sandino eluded the Marines, the more embarrassing his movement became to Washington. In November 1927 a number of inconclusive patrol actions were fought. Finally, on November 23 Marine aircraft located and bombed El Chipote. With their target now pinpointed on their maps, the Marine aviators began a stepped-up bombing offensive designed to destroy Sandino's troublemaking capacity once and for all. The results of the offensive were not those forecast. The slaughter of Sandinistas in the open fields around Ocotal was not repeated at El Chipote—a heavily wooded, five-thousand-foot mountain, where the guerrillas were well dug in. The aircraft squadron raided El Chipote almost daily after November 23. "Each airplane carried ten seventeen-pound fragmentation bombs on external wing racks, releasable by the pilot singly or in salvo," a Marine aviator noted. "These bombs had a very small lethal radius, and were practically innocuous in heavily wooded areas." [29] The Sandinistas were not driven off El Chipote by the air raids. They fired back at the planes with rifles and machine guns and scored a number of hits, though none were vital.

While the air offensive against Sandino was under way, two attempts were made to settle the Nicaraguan conflict by peaceful means. On December 2 Roy Johnson, a civilian employee of the Marine garrison at Telpaneca, wrote a letter to Sandino and persuaded two local *señoritas* to carry the message to the general at El Chipote.

> Señor General Augusto C. Sandino,
>   Wherever he may be.
> Dear sir: I ask an audience with you whenever you may deem best. It is quite possible to have an arrangement convenient for you and rather good for the tranquility of the country. We shall handle the conditions for the arrangement properly. As you know, I have fought in revolutions in Central America and it is possible that I know some of the men of your army.
>   Awaiting your valued reply, I am your most devoted servant,
>
> ROY A. JOHNSON [30]

After reading the letter and talking with the girls who brought it, Sandino notified his outposts of the impending visit, explaining that "the individual who asks for the conference is English and says he is coming from the King of England and he wants to treat with matters which will be for the good of the country." [31] The same day, December 6, Sandino replied to Johnson, giving him instructions on how to reach his headquarters, but warning

> that if you are coming with the intention of buying our patriotism, imposing indecent conditions upon us, you should make your will beforehand, and then you will see how the true sons of my country defend the sovereignty of Nicaragua. There are persons in my army who know you too well and who well know your activities in the revolutions to which you refer.[32]

The intrepid Johnson went anyway; his body was found a month later by a Marine patrol near Quilali.[33]

The next attempt to negotiate with Sandino was made by a group of American Quakers acting jointly with the Fellowship of Reconciliation, a pacifist organization based in New York. The peace delegation, headed by Professor Elbert Russel of Duke University, arrived in Nicaragua on December 10 and later met with the American *chargé d'affaires*, Dr. Dana G. Munro. The pacifists said they intended to persuade Sandino to end his armed rebellion and asked permission to communicate with the guerrilla chieftain. Munro referred them to Colonel Gulick, who gave them permission to go to San Rafael del Norte and talk with Sandino's wife. Robert Cuba Jones and John Nevin Sayre made the trip and interviewed Blanca on December 27. At the insistence of Jones and Sayre, Blanca wrote Sandino asking if he would lay down his arms if the Marines promised to withdraw from the country immediately afterward. Sandino replied directly to Jones and Sayre five days later, demanding that the Marines withdraw first.[34] But by this time a Marine ground-air offensive against Sandino was in full swing.

Early in December, when it had become clear that air power alone could not drive Sandino off El Chipote, Brigade Commander Gulick conceived a simple strategy: two combat patrols of one hundred men each would converge upon Sandino's hideout and put an end to his bandit career before the year was out.[35] But widespread harassing actions by the Sandinistas delayed the Marines in putting their forces together, and it was not until December 19 that the grand offensive got under way. On that day a potent force of 114 Marines and Guardsmen under Marine Captain Richard Livingston left Jinotega, and a second heavily armed column of forty Marines and twenty Guardsmen under National Guard First Lieutenant Merton A. Richal departed Telpaneca.[36] The two forces were to rendezvous at Quilali and coordinate their attack on El Chipote. Marine garrisons in other parts of Nicaragua were weakened to allow for this concentration of forces in the far north. Little heed was paid to "a persistent rumor on the streets of Matagalpa that as soon as Captain Livingston starts north, Sandino will start south via back trails and attack Matagalpa." According to the rumor, Sandino had informed a friend in Matagalpa that his troops would not "make any fight at El Chipote." When the Marines took El Chipote, Sandino allegedly told his friend, "he would have Matagalpa." [37] Sandino may have already decided not to make a stand at El Chipote, but he could not pass up the opportunity to do some damage to the columns marching through his territory on their way to their objective.

At 9:30 on the morning of December 30, Captain Livingston's 114-man column was moving single-file along the Camino Real, a narrow trail beside the Jícaro River, within a mile of Quilali. Here the men walked into an expertly laid ambush. Their entire right flank was covered by a line of Sandinista riflemen and bomb throwers intrenched and concealed in heavy foliage along a steep slope just above the trail. On Livingston's left flank was the two-hundred-foot wide Jícaro River, and on a rise across the river a Sandinista machine gun heaped more flanking fire upon the column. Just ahead of Livingston's column another Sandinista machine gun had been set up to enfilade the column, but it had been laid slightly off to the right and did not achieve the intended effect. The Sandinistas made no attempt to rush Livingston, and after eighty minutes they retired in the face of a vigorous Marine counterattack. Marine planes then appeared and strafed the vacated guerrilla positions. Five Marines were killed in the ambush on the Camino Real, and twenty-three were wounded, including Captain Livingston; two Guardsmen were killed and two were wounded. After the wounding of Livingston, First Lieutenant Moses J. Gould took command of the column and, when the Sandinistas had withdrawn, led the battered column into Quilali. The next day Gould wrote in his report:

> The discipline maintained, the morale, and the accuracy of the fire of the bandits, as well as the tactical disposition of their troops were far above anything displayed by them in any of their actions heretofore in this section and leads to the belief that they are receiving training instructions from sources other than Nicaraguans because of the up-to-dateness of their tactics.

Sandino's tactics were certainly up to date, but in some

respects they were as old as those employed by Hannibal at Cannae. In all probability, the Carthaginian general was one of those "sources other than Nicaraguans" furnishing "training instructions" to the men of classics-minded Augusto César Sandino. Some people suspected that the two Marine deserters who joined Sandino in July had a hand in the ambush—although this was later publicly denied by Marine headquarters in Washington.[38]

Meanwhile, Lieutenant Richal's sixty-man column was attacked by a smaller force of guerrillas at Guanacastillo on the day of the Camino Real encounter. This proved to be only a harassing action, and the attackers quickly withdrew after wounding one Marine. Early in the afternoon of New Year's Day, 1928, a much more serious attack hit Richal as his column approached Las Cruces hill, six miles northwest of Quilali. As Richal's point, led by National Guard Lieutenant Bruce (of Ocotal fame), approached the base of the hill, a shower of bombs and bullets rained down from the heights. Bruce was instantly killed and most of the Guardsmen comprising the point fled in panic as the Sandinistas charged down upon them; one Guardsman, Policarpo Gutiérrez, abandoned his fallen chief only after receiving a shower of machete blows—wounds that later required the amputation of his left arm. The attackers fell upon Bruce's lifeless body and viciously mutilated it with their machetes, after grabbing his two pistols, field glasses, map case, compass, and an American flag. Richal quickly deployed his main body in a skirmish line and advanced against his enemy. His machine gun jammed, but his Stokes mortar and thirty-seven millimeter mountain gun blasted the Sandinistas out of their positions on Las Cruces hill. Richal's men took the hill, but their gallant leader was seriously wounded in the attack. A sergeant took command and intrenched his men on the crest of the hill, where they soon found themselves surrounded.

Meanwhile, a force of forty-four men from Livingston's column was dispatched from Quilali to the relief of Richal. Marine planes appeared and bombed and strafed the Sandin-

istas as the relief column fought its way through the encirclement to the top of Las Cruces hill. There they spent the night
with Richal's men. Early the next morning the combined
forces advanced under heavy air cover from Las Cruces hill
into Quilali, without drawing enemy fire. The guerrillas then
closed in around Quilali and laid siege to the town. It was a
sad situation for the proud force that had been sent to crush
Sandino. Eight of the 174 officers and men had been killed.
Worse yet, from a tactical standpoint, thirty-one of their
number had been wounded—eighteen seriously. Only by air
could the wounded be evacuated and reinforcements brought
in early enough to avert disaster.

The Marines and Guardsmen set about constructing an
airfield in the middle of Quilali—"an aggregation of
shacks" [39] near the Jícaro River. They battered down buildings and converted the town's grass-grown main street into
a runway. Marine First Lieutenant Christian F. Schilt volun-
teered to fly the hazardous missions into beleaguered Quilali.
Between January 6 and January 8 Schilt made ten flights in
and out of Quilali under heavy enemy fire, delivering a total
of fourteen hundred pounds of medicine and supplies and
evacuating eighteen wounded. He also brought in a relief
commander, Captain Roger W. Peard. Each time Schilt's
Vought Corsair touched down in Quilali, Marines had to run
out and grab the wings in order to slow the plane down and
keep it from smashing off the end of the abbreviated runway. Schilt's takeoffs "were equally spectacular and uncon-
ventional," one authority wrote. "Marines held the plane in
place while Schilt checked his engine, then released him as
the engine roared full throttle to jump the plane into the
air." [40] For these daring flights Lieutenant Schilt was awarded
the Congressional Medal of Honor. Sandino's siege subsided
with Schilt's flights into Quilali. Captain Peard was able to
withdraw his troops on January 10 to San Albino, where he
made contact with Marine patrols from Ocotal and
Matagalpa.

The withdrawal from Quilali came on the heels of a National Guard mutiny at Somotillo. Nine Guardsmen, incited by Sandinista sympathizers among the local populace, had attacked the Marine contingent of the Somotillo garrison on January 8. Four of the mutineers were killed and the rest fled across the border into Honduras.[41] These embarrassing events occurred just as delegates from the nations of the hemisphere were gathering in Havana for a Pan American Conference. President Coolidge considered the meeting so important that he accompanied the American representative, Charles Evans Hughes, to the conference. Coolidge's presence did not prevent a show of sympathy for Sandino by some delegates. During the conference the *Heraldo de Cuba* regularly printed Sandino's dispatches to Froylán Turcios.

President Coolidge's concern for Latin American opinion did not interfere with a rapid build-up of Marine strength in Nicaragua. The Eleventh Regiment was reactivated and placed under the command of the able Colonel Robert H. Dunlap, who was ordered to sail with his 1,148-man command for Nicaragua on January 9, 1928, to augment the 1,415 Marines on duty there. On January 15 Colonel Gulick was relieved as brigade commander and Brigadier General Feland resumed command of the Marines in Nicaragua.[42] While General Feland was reorganizing the brigade, his superior, Rear Admiral David F. Sellers, wrote to Sandino:

> Fully realizing the solemn obligation to preserve order in Nicaragua . . . the forces under my command have recently been very largely augmented with men and munitions. . . . It is superfluous for me to point out that the energetic and intensive campaign that our forces are shortly to inaugurate can have but one final result. . . . It has occurred to me that . . . you might now be willing to consider the advisability of discontinuing the present armed resistance to the United States forces. . . . I do not feel justified at this time in halting any of the preparations . . . now going forward energetically unless you see fit to notify me immediately and in writing that you are willing to discuss ways and means for [your] acceptance . . . of the Stimson Agreement.[43]

Meanwhile, new ground-air operations against El Chipote had gotten under way. As a force of more than three hundred Marines was being massed at San Albino for the final drive on Sandino's stronghold, Marine aircraft relentlessly pounded El Chipote. The air raids were now more effective, for the creaky old DeHaviland planes had been replaced by sturdy new Vought Corsairs and Curtiss Falcons, which had much greater bomb-carrying capacities.[44] On January 14 one of Major Rowell's aviators scored a direct hit with a fifty-pound bomb, demolishing a Sandinista building on the mountainside. After the bomb burst about forty persons ran from a nearby house and the plane dropped another bomb, making a direct hit in the middle of the group. The aviators reported that they saw approximately forty-five dead in and around the shacks on El Chipote after that day's work. The Marine fliers had little pity for the Sandinistas, especially after photographs of Lieutenant Thomas' body hanging from a tree were published in Honduran and Mexican newspapers.

Not all the air raid casualties on El Chipote were combatants. Soldiers and professional revolutionaries from all over Central America were drawn to Sandino's mountain fortress, and so were their women. Troops of camp followers, some with children, crossed the Honduran border and made their way to El Chipote, where they washed clothes, cooked, and provided female companionship for the guerrillas. General Sandino became attracted to Teresa Villatoro, a vivacious young woman from El Salvador, who was accompanied by her five-year-old son. While Blanca de Sandino tended the telegraph office in San Rafael del Norte, Teresa became General Sandino's mistress on El Chipote mountain. During an aerial bombardment, Teresa was hit in the forehead by a piece of shrapnel. The injury was not serious, but a small piece of Teresa's skull was removed when the wound was cleaned. Sandino had this bone fragment mounted in a ring of San Albino gold which he wore thereafter as a token of their relationship.[45]

Sandino denied losing many personnel in the air raids, but he conceded that two hundred of his horses and mules were killed. According to the guerrilla general, the stench of decomposing animal flesh made further occupancy of El Chipote impossible. On January 19 Marine aviators reported El Chipote "completely deserted." Sandino had withdrawn most of his troops, but he still maintained a camp at the very top of the mountain. On January 20 the general circulated a memorandum [46] among his officers, recommending that the last troops withdraw and that straw dummies be placed in the positions they occupied; all officers agreeing with the recommendation were asked to sign the memorandum. The next day Marine aviators discovered that there were still some Sandinistas on El Chipote, although they saw no large concentrations.

The commander of the Marine ground troops in the area, Major Archibald Young—who had been informed by brigade intelligence that "there is practically no doubt that Sandino has planned to make a determined stand at Chipote" [47]—decided to play it safe. He advanced cautiously up the face of El Chipote, blasting with mortars and rifle grenades every conceivable ambush site in his path. Young met with no serious resistance, although three of his men were wounded by desultory fire. It took the Marine battalion six days to cover the three miles from the base of El Chipote, on the Murra River, to its summit. When the Marines got there, on January 26, they caught no "bandits," but they did find some stores of food to destroy. As his troops occupied Sandino's "fortress," the Commandant of the United States Marine Corps expressed the hope that the bloodshed in Nicaragua was now at an end.[48] The hope was premature.

6

1928: The Survival of Sandinismo

After Sandino's "defeat" at El Chipote, the Marines expected him to flee across the Honduran border or to retreat further into the wilderness of Nueva Segovia and Jinotega departments. Instead, Sandino marched south toward the more settled mountain areas, in the direction of the sizable towns of Jinotega and Matagalpa—an area left virtually defenseless by the concentration of Marines on a deserted mountain top in Nueva Segovia. There was no one to oppose Sandino's entry into San Rafael del Norte, and early in February 1928 his troops once again occupied that town.[1] There Sandino and his chiefs made their plans to raid the rich coffee-producing area around Matagalpa. Other areas of Nicaragua were already feeling the effects of Sandinismo. The general's sympathizers were tying up the port of Corinto with a dock strike, and his Peruvian admirer, Haya de la Torre, was agitating among the proletariat of León.[2]

While Sandino was in San Rafael del Norte, he received an important foreign visitor, Carleton Beals. This American journalist and energetic exponent of liberal causes had gone to Honduras and contacted Froylán Turcios, who furnished him the necessary escort for his trip overland into Nicaragua to interview Sandino. Through a series of articles in *The*

Nation,[3] Beals gave the American public an intimate glimpse of the Nicaraguan chieftain who was making life difficult for American Marines and diplomats. The picture that emerges from Beals's articles is that of a fierce and austere idealist, a resourceful and imaginative commander with a gift for order and discipline rare among his race.

> He is short, probably not more than five feet. . . . He was dressed in a new uniform of almost black khaki, and wore puttees, immaculately polished. A silk red and black handkerchief was knotted about his throat. His broad-brimmed Stetson, low over his forehead, was pinched into a shovel-like shape. Occasionally, as we conversed, he shoved his sombrero far back on his head and hitched his chair forward. The gesture revealed his straight black hair and full forehead. His face is straight-lined from temple to sharp-angled jawbone, which slants to an even, firm jaw. His regular, curved eyebrows are high above liquid black eyes without visible pupils, eyes of remarkable mobility and refraction to light— quick intense eyes. He is a man utterly without vices, with an unequivocal sense of justice, a keen eye for the welfare of the humblest soldier.

Beals was impressed by the inspirational, almost hypnotic, quality of Sandino's leadership. Unlettered soldiers were entranced by a repetitious flow of epigrams:

> Many battles have made our hearts hard, but our souls strong. . . .
> Death is but one little moment of discomfort; it is not to be taken too seriously. . . .
> Death most quickly singles out him who is afraid of death. . . .
> God and our mountains fight for us.

As Carleton Beals talked with Sandino before dawn on February 3, 1928, the general's wife served coffee and pastries. Later in the morning Marine planes roared low over San Rafael del Norte and saw that the town was occupied by about 150 Sandinistas, mostly mounted. The aviators were under orders not to fire upon civilian dwellings, and Sandino's men were instructed not to fire unless fired upon, so Beals was spared a dangerous involvement in the war he was reporting.[4]

Beals's articles contributed mightily to the pro-Sandino campaign being waged by liberals and radicals in the United States. But this was not the only service Beals rendered Sandino: when the journalist left San Rafael del Norte for Managua, he carried Sandino's reply to Admiral Sellers' letter of January 20.

San Rafael, February 3, 1928

Mr. D. F. Sellers
Representative of Imperialism in Nicaragua, Managua:

I had formulated a reply, in which I answered concretely, point for point, your letter of January 20th, but special circumstances prevent me from delivering it directly.

I refer to the final point of your letter. Don't believe that the present struggle has for an origin or base, the revolution just passed. Today this is a struggle of the Nicaraguan people in general, to expel the foreign invasion of my country. Regarding the Stimson–Moncada treaties, we have reiterated a thousand times our [disregard for] them.

The only way to put an end to this struggle is the immediate withdrawal of the invading forces from our territory, at the same time replacing the present president by one who is a Nicaraguan citizen and who is not running as a candidate for the Presidency, and supervising the coming elections by representatives of Latin America instead of by American Marines.

Country and Liberty,
A. C. SANDINO[5]

The day after this letter was written, Sandino marched to the outskirts of Jinotega, and that night his troops enjoyed a fiesta only a few hundred yards from the unsuspecting Marine garrison. Two nights later Sandino had driven to within twelve miles of Matagalpa. In this region perhaps as much as 80 percent of the rural population was pure Indian.

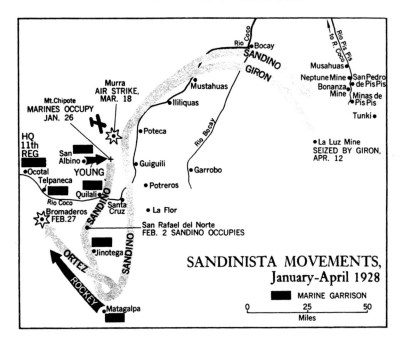

SANDINISTA MOVEMENTS,
January-April 1928

■ MARINE GARRISON

0   25   50
Miles

On the cool slopes of the mountains ringing the little city of
Matagalpa were some forty rich coffee plantations. Most of
the steady workers on the plantations were *mestizos*, but during the coffee-picking season great numbers of Indians were
hired and housed in plantation dormitories. Americans owned
about a dozen of these plantations, and Europeans of various
nationalities owned most of the remainder. Here a cosmopol-
itan gentry enjoyed life in their pretty little manors, conduct-
ing "a pleasant and cultivated social life in company with
their charming Nicaraguan neighbors of the higher class,"
and at times meeting "in Matagalpa for dinner-coated recep-
tions and dances." [6] Sandino appeared on the scene shortly
after the 1927–1928 harvest, and his first victims were one
English and two German plantation owners. With good
humor the general relieved these proprietors of their cash,
mules, and miscellaneous equipment, giving receipts for
everything he took. While deploring their losses, some ur-
bane residents of the coffee region saw fit to commend San-

dino for his courtesy and for the good order of his troops. One planter expressed these sentiments in a letter to the editor of a Managua newspaper.

After the first few incursions, Sandino dropped out of action, leaving a strong raiding party under Miguel Angel Ortez y Guillén to keep the Matagalpa region in turmoil for the next two weeks. Ortez, a native of Ocotal who sometimes used the *nom de guerre* "General Ferrara," was one of Sandino's most aggressive young lieutenants. He was a dashing figure—rather short, but trim and muscular, with flowing blond hair accenting his distinct caucasian features. Ortez was highly popular with his men, and his courage and military ability won him the respect of his Marine and National Guard adversaries.[7]

The Marines threw the newly arrived Eleventh Regiment into action against Sandino and Ortez. "The combat efficiency of the regiment," its operations section reported, "is as good as could be expected under the circumstances." [8] About 65 percent of the men were recruits who had received only six weeks of training before being shipped to Nicaragua. Although some of the recruits had "never seen a horse," a force of two hundred Marines was organized in Matagalpa and mounted on native horses. This outfit, commanded by Major Keller Rockey, rode out of Matagalpa on February 15 accompanied by a supply train of oxcarts and pack animals.[9]

As the mounted column pressed northward, the Sandinistas fell back, seemingly in full retreat toward the wilderness of Nueva Segovia. Then, on February 27, Ortez struck, at Bromaderos in the department of Estelí. There he ambushed an empty convoy of ninety-five mules proceeding westward on the Yali-Condega trail and escorted by thirty-five Marines under First Lieutenant Edward F. O'Day. At 1:30 P.M. Sandinistas on the right flank opened fire on the train along its entire length as it passed across a flat space between two ranges of hills. Other Sandinistas sealed off the trail to the front and rear of the convoy. Lieutenant O'Day "estimated beyond doubt that the bandit forces had a minimum of four machine guns, at least 600 rifles, and a large quantity of dynamite bombs." [10] The convoy was hopelessly dispersed, and the Marines scrambled for positions on a ridge to the left of the trail, leaving three of their dead behind. At 2:30 a skirmish line of Sandinistas advanced to the trail to collect the spoils while their machine guns maintained a steady fire upon the Marines on the ridge above the trail. The skirmishers split the skulls of the dead Marines with their machetes and looted the remnants of the convoy; then most of them fell back to their original positions with their booty—weapons, saddles, and other equipment.

About dusk another Sandinista line of skirmishers advanced to the trail but did not attempt to assault the Marine position. Early in the night the Marines on the ridge listened as Ortez's tenor voice across the trail commended his troops for their "good work." The guerrilla commander's commendations were repeated all down the line, and three tremendous cheers rang out: *"Viva Sandino!" "Viva Nicaragua!" "Viva el general Ferrara!"* Each cheer was punctuated with the detonation of several dynamite bombs. About 8:30 some of the guerrillas began to withdraw, and the Marines could hear shouted farewells as mules and oxcarts rumbled away. The Marines stayed on the ridge all night and were subjected to the sporadic fire of about two hundred Sandinistas who remained behind. Meanwhile, a runner from O'Day's detachment slipped past the guerrillas and at 10:30 P.M. reported the ambush to Captain William K. MacNulty, who was patrolling the area with a force of eighty-eight Marines. At about dawn MacNulty appeared at the ambush site and attacked the remaining Sandinistas, who quickly dispersed in the face of his advance. The guerrillas, as usual, left no casualties on the field. Three Marines were killed in the ambush and two died of wounds the next day; eight Marines and four native mule drivers were wounded. A third of Lieutenant O'Day's mules were killed, wounded, or captured.

A large part of the Sandinista force at Bromaderos had been recruited from the nearby towns and villages only shortly before the encounter. After the fight most of these recruits returned to their homes and resumed their normal occupations, awaiting the next call to arms. This pointed up one of the most vexing problems faced by the Marines in trying to pacify Nicaragua—the problem of the "part-time bandit." Although a "good citizen" most of the time, the "part-time bandit" was "always ready to furnish food and information or to join the regulars for an opportunity to loot, or for an especially important raid." [11] Often "bandit suspects" would be rounded up by the Marines and National Guardsmen, only to be released on writs of habeas corpus. As early as January 1928 the American *chargé d'affaires* in Nicaragua wired his superiors in Washington to protest that "even prisoners of war" were being released on writs of habeas corpus.[12]

This was no way to fight a war, but according to the U.S. Department of State, no war existed, so there could be no "prisoners of war"; civil criminal procedure had to be complied with. The United States would not permit President Díaz's government to declare a state of war in the mountain departments. Washington legalists thought such a declaration would raise Sandino's status from that of ordinary bandit to "leader of an organized rebellion with the possibilities of a recognition of his belligerency by any nation." [13] In 1928 Secretary of State Frank B. Kellogg would not even assent to a proclamation of martial law, for this would have put American officers in the "embarrassing" position of court-martialing Nicaraguan citizens. The co-author of the Kellogg-Briand Peace Pact did not like to be reminded that the armed forces of his country were involved in something resembling a war. When a representative of Cecil B. DeMille called at the State Department to discuss filming the Marines in action in Nicaragua, Kellogg termed the project "inadvisable" and the matter was dropped.[14]

The Marines dutifully maintained the fiction that Sandino was only a bandit. But they recognized that he was a bandit with a distinction, quite different from the ordinary bandit encountered in the West Indies and Central America, who avoids contact with the forces of law and order and fights only when combat is unavoidable; and who can usually be persuaded to cease operations with an offer of amnesty accompanied with some sort of financial inducement.[15]

Shortly after the fight at Bromaderos, the Marine Corps officially classified Sandino as a "guerrilla." But the promotion was only temporary, and Sandino soon reverted to the grade of "bandit." When questioned about Sandino's status as a "bandit" by the Senate Foreign Relations Committee, General Lejeune conceded that Sandino and his followers were "called bandits for the lack of some other word."[16] In Nicaragua General Feland explained to Carleton Beals that military men "use the word 'bandit' in a technical sense, meaning the member of a band." Beals wondered how the Marines would classify John Philip Sousa.[17]

While Washington denounced Sandino as a bandit, the forces of the Communist International (Comintern) rallied to his defense. Sandino was warmly applauded by the Anti-Imperialist League, an organization with branches operating in various parts of the Western hemisphere by early 1928, all supervised by the South American Bureau of the Comintern. The New York affiliate of this communist front, the All American Anti-Imperialist League, conducted a vigorous propaganda campaign against American intervention in Nicaragua. One of the most effective spokesmen for the New York branch was Sandino's half-brother, Sócrates Sandino, a mild-mannered carpenter who had been living quietly in Brooklyn since 1926. The communists "exhibited him as if he were a circus personality."[18] Sócrates addressed rallies and signed his name to a series of articles distributed by the North American Newspaper Alliance. The author of these articles contended that the fight of General Sandino and the League was not against the American people but only against certain policies of the American government. At League rallies in New York, collections were taken up to send "medical supplies" to Sandino's army. This activity infuriated organizations like the American Legion, but little could be done legally to restrict the activities of Sócrates Sandino and the League, since the United States was supposedly not at war.[19]

In Mexico a chapter of the Anti-Imperialist League was organized by Gustavo Machado, an exiled Venezuelan communist. Machado worked closely with Sandino's representative in Mexico City, Pedro José Zepeda, during the spring of 1928. Machado appeared with Zepeda at fund-raising rallies and exhibited the American flag that had been taken from the body of Lieutenant Bruce.[20] Sandino was pleased with this communist support. "When you feel nervous because of sleepiness and hunger," the general told two of his officers, "think of the things that Dr. Machado is doing in Mexico." [21] In other parts of the continent intellectuals declared their support for General Sandino. The Chilean poetress Gabriela Mistral was obsessed with the "spectacular concept of a clash of races"; she urged the formation of a Hispanic League to fight in Nicaragua.[22] Joaquín García Monge, editor of the widely read Costa Rican magazine *Repertorio Americano*, welcomed articles in defense of Sandino and even helped organize a "Pro-Sandino Committee" in San José to raise money for the Nicaraguan general.[23] In Peru articles from *Ariel* were faithfully reproduced in *Amauta*, a review edited by the renowned Marxist José Carlos Mariátegui.

In faraway Moscow the Sixth World Congress of the Comintern, meeting in the summer of 1928, sent "fraternal greetings to the workers and peasants of Nicaragua, and the heroic army of national emancipation of General Sandino." [24] While the Comintern met in Moscow, "The First International Anti-Imperialist Congress" got under way in Frankfurt, Germany, with a Sandinista delegation in attendance. These delegates were drawn from the general's supporters then residing in Mexico, and their passage to Germany was probably paid by the Comintern. Sandino took a personal interest in the Congress, writing to Henri Barbusse, one of its leaders, that "although at the present historical moment our struggle is national and racial, it will become international as the colonial and semi-colonial peoples unite with the peoples of the imperialistic nations." [25] On the podium at the Frankfurt Congress a Sandinista unfurled the captured American banner while Jawaharlal Nehru, Katayama Sen, and Madame Sun Yat-sen looked on approvingly. But indications of dissensions within the Sandinista-communist alliance also began to appear: the general's chief representative at Frankfurt, José Constantino González, refused to support a communist move to expel Haya de la Torre's APRA delegation from the congress.

In China that year anti-imperialist troops of the Kuomintang marched victoriously into Peking carrying a huge portrait of Augusto C. Sandino. One of the units of the Kuomintang Army, American Marines in China noted, was called the "Sandino Division." [26] The protests of "the natives" against the presence of American Marines in China and Nicaragua were noted in the United States, but the American public was preoccupied with other things, and intervention abroad did not become a major issue of public debate in the election year of 1928. "I suppose that it is inevitable that nations interfere with one another and influence each other," New York lawyer John Foster Dulles observed philosophically. "If so, I submit, there may well be situations where intervention by military forces is the most humane procedure." [27]

In Nicaragua the Marines gradually consolidated their control over most of the country in 1928. Early in the year General Feland divided the republic into three operating areas: the eastern, the southern, and the northern. The eastern and southern areas were occupied by Marines of the Fifth Regiment and troops of the National Guard, while the northern area, the northwest corner of the country where the Sandinista threat was judged to be greatest, was assigned to Colonel Robert H. Dunlap's Eleventh Regiment. Before Dunlap assumed command in the north there had been "too much uninspired direction from the comparatively comfortable brigade headquarters in Managua," a Marine officer wrote. "Few of the senior commanders had troubled to visit the outlying garrisons or to familiarize themselves with the formidable obstacles to movement and supply with which the field commanders had to cope." Colonel Dunlap made his headquarters at Ocotal and changed all this. Early in the spring he personally led a patrol over "some 250 miles of the most dangerous trails in his area." He also sent his staff officers into the field with patrols "in order to familiarize themselves with the combat situation." [28]

Sandino evidently underestimated the reinvigorating influence of the new Marine leadership. On March 22, 1928, he wrote a curious letter to the commanders of the American forces in Jinotega and Matagalpa. In it Sandino alluded to the democratic ideals of the United States and expressed his belief that the Marine officers and men were not in accord with President Coolidge's imperialistic policy in Nicaragua. Furthermore, he said he had a little over $2,000,000 which he would give to them if they would "protest to your government about the occupation of our territory, and then evacuate the towns occupied by you and concentrate in Managua." [29] The offer was ignored.

As Colonel Dunlap's troops pressed forward on the ground, Marine aircraft cruised the skies of the northern area in a relentless search for the enemy. On March 18 a two-plane patrol led by Gunnery Sergeant Wodarczyk located a large force of Sandinistas at Murra, near the Honduran border. The next day the two planes shuttled back and forth from Ocotal, bombing and strafing at least eight separate bands of guerrillas near Murra. The aviators claimed their attacks inflicted heavy casualties upon the enemy; ground fire wounded one airman in the foot. On March 20 careful aerial reconnaissance revealed that the Sandinistas had abandoned the Murra area; only a flock of vultures remained to greet the aviators. [30]

In the weeks after Murra the planes located no sizable enemy concentrations, but they did find other targets. On

April 3 "a plane attacked five men of suspicious looking character at Espino, firing into the house into which they fled." [31] The next day a two-plane patrol noticed "about 25 men standing in front of the doorways" at a village near Matagalpa. "As the planes approached they ran into a house. The house was strafed with machine-gun fire, but nothing was developed. The houses were not bombed due to the number of women and children present." [32] (The women and children were presumably not endangered by the machine-gun fire.) Later the same day several men ran out of a house near Ojoche as the planes approached; "six bombs were dropped in and around the vicinity." The next day the aviators noticed something suspicious at Naranjo: "the population did not appear to be afraid of the planes. A short burst was fired into the mountainside nearby but nothing developed." [33] On April 12 "a group of about six horses were observed around three small houses" near Murra. "Three men were seen to run into the brush and hide. Four bombs were dropped in and around the houses, two making direct hits." [34] In June a two-plane patrol led by Major Rowell

> noted a large house at Quiboto in which some horses were concealed. The leading plane dropped a bomb in the yard and a second one through the roof of the house. The escort plane dropped a bomb in the yard. At this point someone ran from the rear of the house to a grove near the house. A bomb was dropped in the center of the grove and the place was strafed with machine-gun fire. Casualties inflicted: unknown.[35]

Major Rowell apparently did not question the effectiveness of this aerial terrorism. He complained about "restrictions of a political nature" that hurt the morale and efficiency of his unit. He was ordered not to bomb towns, and these became sanctuaries for the enemy. Rowell deplored newspapers that played up the abuses of his airmen while overlooking the savagery of the guerrillas.[36] Like the German soldiers confronted by Belgian and French *francs-tireurs* in

World War I, Rowell was shocked by the atrocities per- petrated by local resistance fighters against his comrades and the natives who collaborated with them. Why much of the world should excuse the excesses of the partisans while con- demning the countermeasures taken by the occupying forces was as incomprehensible to the Marine aviators as it was to the German high command. The guerrilla would personally confront his helpless victim, torture and kill him with de- liberation, and then put his mutilated body on display. The death of this unfortunate person was quite unlike that of the non-combatants who perished in the air raids, who were de- stroyed incidentally and without malice by men who prob- ably never saw them; they were not the intended victims of their assailants but were caught in the regrettable, though ever-present, margin of error of a modern military machine. Such thoughts may have assuaged the consciences of some Americans, but there were many other people, especially out- side the Anglo-Germanic world, who found this kind of im- personal, mechanized violence more abhorrent than the most brutal and deliberate face-to-face killing.

By mid-1928 the Sandinistas had become very air-con- scious. "They move almost entirely at hours when the planes cannot reach them," Major Rowell noted. "They camouflage their camps and stables and confine their operations to ter- rain offering the best cover from aerial observation and never fire on the planes unless they find themselves discovered and attacked." The airmen scanned farm houses and villages for signs of the enemy, taking into account the proportion of men to women visible, the amount of wash on clotheslines, the number of animals present, and the general bearing of the people. The Marines seldom used more than two planes on reconnaissance missions. They would throttle their en- gines and glide in over suspicious places from behind hills or mountains, flying low enough to look into windows and doors. There was always the problem of distinguishing guer- rillas from "ignorant but innocent people who run from the planes through fright." [37] The Marines learned that by flying in at low altitudes they muffled their sound—but also forfeited their chance for a dive-bombing attack. Once guerrillas had been spotted, it was sometimes better to withhold fire and fly over them regularly for several days in formation at high altitude. When the guerrillas became accustomed to the sight of the planes and became careless, the Marines would swoop down on them.

The Marines had twelve Falcon and Corsair observation-bomber aircraft in Nicaragua, all based at Managua. For operations in the northern area, the planes could refuel and take on ammunition at the auxiliary airfield at Ocotal. Each plane was originally equipped with a 110-pound radio set with a range of fifty miles. These radios proved impractical and were removed from most of the planes. Besides the Falcons and Corsairs, the Marines had seven Loening amphibian observation-bombers based at Managua; these planes operated mostly in the eastern area, and in the spring of 1928 two of them were transferred to an airfield at Puerto Cabezas. The amphibians were equipped with serviceable radio sets, as were the Marine transport aircraft: five trimotor Fokkers based in Managua. Each of the Fokkers could carry two thousand pounds of cargo or eight fully equipped fighting men in one trip to any of five landing fields in the combat zone. Even where the planes could not land, they could drop supplies. For accuracy and economy, free-fall drops proved more satisfactory than parachute drops. Even pay was delivered to troops in the field by air drop.

After the aerial bombardment of Murra, on March 19, 1928, the main body of Sandinistas headed eastward. Of the major Sandinista chiefs, only Ortez remained in the west, in Colonel Dunlap's northern area. While the Marines chased Ortez, Sandino crossed into the eastern area and drove on the defenseless Pis Pis mining region near the Caribbean coast. Sandino's drive was spearheaded by the band of Manuel María Girón Ruano, a well-educated, middle-aged, grey-eyed Guatemalan, "a high type guerrilla officer; probably the most able that ever served under Sandino." [38] On

April 12 Girón seized the La Luz and the Los Angeles gold mines, properties of a company owned by Pittsburgh interests which had been operating in Nicaragua since 1901. In the next few days Sandinistas occupied the run-down Bonanza mine, also American-owned, and sacked some nearby Chinese-owned stores. Sandino arrived in the area on April 27 and made his presence felt among his turbulent followers. He summarily executed one of his officers, Antonio Galeano, for getting drunk and committing various abuses, including the violation of a local *señora*. The general, however, sanctioned the looting of American property in the area. Of three American citizens taken prisoner at the mines, two were released unharmed and one, George B. Marshall, remained a prisoner of Girón and later died of malaria in captivity.[39]

According to one of his admirers, Sandino was obsessed with the idea of ravaging these American mines, for he considered them a source of much of his country's troubles. President Díaz was once an employee of the La Luz and Los Angeles Mining Company, and the late Philander C. Knox, the author of dollar diplomacy, was thought to have been a major stockholder. On April 29, 1928, Sandino dispatched a letter to the manager of the La Luz and Los Angeles mines:

> My dear sir: I have the honor to inform you that on this date your mine has been reduced to ashes . . . to protest against the warlike invasion your government has made of our territory. . . . In the beginning I confided in the thought that the American people would not [condone] the abuses committed in Nicaragua by the Government of Calvin Coolidge, but I have been convinced that North Americans in general uphold the attitude of Coolidge; . . . for that reason . . . everything North American which falls into our hands is sure to meet its end.
>
> The losses you have had in the mine you may collect from the Government of the United States. . . .
>
> The pretext . . . Coolidge gives for his intervention . . . to protect the lives and interests of North Americans and other foreign residents . . . is a tremendous hypocrisy. We

Nicaraguans are respectable men and never in our history have there been . . . events like those now taking place, . . . the fruit harvested by the stupid policy of your Government. . . . You, the capitalists will be appreciated and respected by us as long as you treat us as equals and not . . . believing yourselves lords and masters of our lives and property.

I am your affectionate servant, Fatherland and Liberty,
A. C. SANDINO [40]

An American diplomat later conceded that the guerrilla chieftain had a point. "Sandino was indeed right when he said that we couldn't, in practice, protect American lives and property through intervention," Willard Beaulac noted. "Most foreign lives lost in Nicaragua during the period were lost after we intervened, and most of the foreign property destroyed was destroyed after we intervened." [41] In northwest Nicaragua Miguel Angel Ortez emphasized Sandino's point in a letter to an American rancher. "I wish to let you know that I have instructions from General Sandino to turn the property of all North Americans into ashes," Ortez wrote, "so that the Marines will not have the excuse of coming to Nicaragua to protect American property." [42] Instead of bringing peace to Nicaragua, American intervention was prolonging the struggle. Nicaraguans, like other nationalities, did not appreciate foreign meddling in their affairs. The government whose existence depended upon American troops found its native support dwindling, while those who resisted the foreigners gained in popular affection.

News of the seizure of the mines in the Pis Pis region came as a great surprise to American authorities in Nicaragua. The American consul at Managua criticized the Marines for driving the Sandinistas into the area. Troops and planes were rushed to the east coast late in April, and by the end of the month three Marine columns were marching on the Pis Pis region. The commander of the first column to reach the area made an "incorrect evaluation of the information received" and withdrew rapidly toward Puerto Cabezas, believing his forces were no match for the Sandinistas. By the time the other Marine columns arrived at the mines, on May 9, the guerrillas had made good their escape.[43]

Sandino and Girón had retired westward, to that portion of Jinotega department drained by the Coco and Bocay rivers. This was an area of dense jungles—where daytime visibility was usually about twenty feet—crossed by only a few known trails. Sandino set up camps and supply points on the rivers at Poteca, Wamblam, Gulke's Camp, and Garrobo. To enable him better to defend the area and to provide avenues of withdrawal, Sandino had a number of secret trails cut through the jungle, often paralleling the known trails. Across this area ran Sandino's main supply routes from Honduras.[44]

In this area, as a guerrilla deserter informed Marine intelligence, Sandino ordered his forces not to use horses, because aircraft could "spot them easily and horses could not be gotten through the brush quickly."[45] The Sandinistas traveled along the trails on foot, in single file, and closed up when the Marines were known to be far away. They crossed all open spaces on the double. When the Marines were nearby, they marched with about two paces between men. The point of a Sandinista column usually consisted of two men, followed at about a hundred yards by the chief and his staff; the main body marched a hundred yards behind the headquarters group. To move a column from one trail to another, guerrillas would leave the first trail individually at different points and make their way through the brush to some point on the second trail. Most daytime marches began at about five o'clock in the morning—never after seven. Sandinista patrols often traveled on moonlit nights, but seldom on dark nights or when it was raining. Guerrilla bands moving during the daytime usually made camp by two o'clock in the afternoon.

Sandinista camps, the deserter reported, were "temporary structures" built on hillsides. Sentries would be stationed on the hilltop above a camp, and Sandino, who "never stays more than five days in one place," would sleep in the valley below the camp "in extremely dense woods where it is never light and where it is dark by 4 P.M." The general "sleeps in houses when possible" and occasionally in caves, but always at a distance from his main body. He "seldom sees his wife" and "never has more than one woman at a time and is very kind to women and punishes with death any follower who assaults a woman." The general "dislikes dogs and does not use them for guards." He "never travels with more than fifty men. Never enters towns. Never disguises himself."

On May 9, the same day that eastern area Marines occupied the La Luz mine, a Marine patrol under Captain Robert S. Hunter left Quilali, in the northern area, with ten days' rations, to probe the area east of the town. Sandino was aware of the patrol's departure and feared that it might penetrate his "rest area"—the region around Gulke's Camp and Garrobo, where he had his main camps. To Manuel María Girón he assigned the mission of destroying or driving back this patrol. On May 14 Girón's 125-man column unexpectedly collided with Hunter's mounted column of twenty-seven Marines and nine National Guardsmen on a trail near the hamlet of La Flor. Though small, Hunter's patrol had plenty of firepower: twenty-eight rifles, three Browning automatic rifles, four Thompson submachine guns, three rifle grenade throwers, thirty rifle grenades, and twenty-four hand grenades. Besides rifles, Girón had only one Thompson submachine gun and some non-fragmentation dynamite bombs. Hunter, a veteran of World War I and the Dominican campaign, was inadvisedly marching with his point when contact was made with Girón's advance guard. After a brief exchange the Sandinista firing halted and Hunter withdrew with his point toward his main body; "thinking that when the initial bandit firing ceased that the bandits had fled," he made no attempt to reconnoiter the enemy position.[46]

"Captain Hunter's service in the Dominican Republic had probably led him to underestimate the fighting qualities of the Nicaraguan bandits," a Marine officer surmised.[47] Within five minutes Girón's men, marching on a hidden trail, had flanked Hunter's column and were engaging his main body. A Marine Thompson gunner was killed, and Captain Hunter charged forward, snatched up the dead man's weapon, and began firing at the enemy from a fully-exposed standing position. In World War I such acts of gallantry were often indispensable in leading troops out of the trenches and over the top; but in bush warfare this kind of daring was sadly inappropriate. Hunter was shot down, mortally wounded, and the patrol had to turn back to get proper medical care for the dying captain and another wounded Marine. Hunter won a posthumous Navy Cross and Girón accomplished his mission: Sandino's rest area was secure—for the time being.

The next serious threat to the area came from the east. After occupying the Pis Pis mining region early in May, eastern area patrols pushed as far west as the village of Bocay, at the junction of the Coco and Bocay rivers.[48] Soon the rainy season made overland travel practically impossible, so the Marines took to the swollen rivers in bateaux and native dugouts. On July 26 a force of forty-six Marines shoved off from Bocay to disperse a reported Sandinista concentration at Poteca, on the Coco. The Marines were commanded by Merrit A. ("Red Mike") Edson, "a short, red-haired, icy-eyed captain."[49] After two minor brushes with the enemy, Edson ordered foot patrols to hack their way along the river banks while the main body followed in boats. Meanwhile, Sandino planned to ambush Edson as his boats came around the first bend in the river above the village of Ililiquas. Girón was to execute the ambush with thirty rifles and one machine gun firing from intrenched positions on the north bank of the river; another force of thirty men under Pedro Altamirano was to be stationed on Girón's left flank to block any Marine attempt to turn that flank; a force under Sandino was to be in reserve near the south bank and available to support Girón with the fire of one Thompson, two Browning automatic rifles, and about thirty rifles. The ambush was planned for August 7, 1928, the 109th anniversary of Simón Bolívar's brilliant victory at Boyacá—the battle that assured the independence of Colombia. Girón's private secretary, a young Colombian named Rubén Ardila Gómez, looked forward eagerly to the combat.

On the morning of August 7, as Edson's patrol approached the ambush site, two Loening amphibian planes covering the patrol spotted Sandino's camp on the south bank of the Coco. They bombed and strafed the area, and Sandino, unknown to Girón, withdrew with most of his men to Wamblam—where his mistress, Teresa Villatoro, awaited him. Also unknown to Girón, Altamirano's blocking force had taken up positions on the wrong trail, too far from the river to effectively seal off Girón's left flank. Edson heard the bombing ahead of him but decided to continue cautiously poling his boats upstream. About 1:00 P.M. a party of Edson's flankers, walking along a beach below the north bank of the river, began to pass before Girón's men lying in ambush on the bank above. Girón's second-in-command, Juan Gregorio Colindres, became excited and exposed himself. The ensuing fight lasted three hours. The Marines beached their boats and overran Girón's left flank. Girón's men fought doggedly and had to be dug out of their foxholes one by one. Girón had only one man left in his command when he finally abandoned his position, leaving ten dead and three wounded behind. When Girón staggered into Wamblam late that night, he had some hot words with his chief over the mismanagement of the ambush. In the end Sandino mollified the worthy Girón by making him chief of staff.

Edson lost one Marine killed and three wounded. During the night the wounded were shipped downstream to Bocay, where Marine planes landed on a sand bar the next day and evacuated them to the American naval base at Puerto Cabezas. Like the Quilali airlift, this was a hazardous operation, both for the pilots and for the wounded, who had to be flown out in a sitting position. The difficulties encountered in evacuating wounded from the jungles of Nicaragua in 1928 spurred the Navy Department in its search for an air-

craft that had a high lift capacity and needed only a minimum of runway for take-offs and landings. Some American
naval and Marine officers believed the solution to this problem lay with rotary-winged aircraft—with the helicopter or
the autogiro. A few years later one of these revolutionary
craft would be field-tested in Nicaragua.

After his encounter with Girón, Edson pushed on upstream to Wamblam, which he found abandoned, and Poteca,
which he occupied after a brief fight on August 17. At Poteca Edson captured a large store of Sandinista clothing and
equipment, then continued on to Santa Cruz, less than fifteen
miles from Quilali. Before the month was out, another Marine patrol had ascended the Bocay River and occupied the
village of Garrobo.[50] The Marines had conquered the main
rivers, but the jungles still belonged to Sandino.

The Marines were also secure in the cities and in the
main towns, although their relations with local citizens were
not always the best. In Matagalpa feeling against the United
States ran high after a drunken Marine shot and killed a native without provocation late in 1927.[51] In Corinto Marines
added to the resentment of striking dock workers by threatening to bring in strike-breakers from the interior—a threat
that forced the workers to return to their jobs without having secured any gains. Some residents of San Rafael del Norte
became indignant about alleged mistreatment of Sandino's in-
laws when the Marines reoccupied that town in February
1928. To correct this impression, American authorities solic-
ited statements from several members of the Arauz family
denying that they had been roughly handled when the Marines searched their home.[52] General Lejeune was concerned
about the image of the occupation forces in Nicaragua, and
on March 20 he ordered General Feland to submit evidence
about the attitude of "people of better standing" toward the
Marines.[53] Throughout Nicaragua the Marines went to work
soliciting testimonials from merchants, bankers, ranchers, doctors, lawyers, politicians, priests, and prelates. Among those

warmly praising the Marine presence in Nicaragua were Canuto José, Bishop of Granada, and Anastasio Somoza, Liberal governor of the Department of León.[54]

But many Conservative politicians were not so pleased with the intervention. As early as January 23, 1928, brigade intelligence noted that "there has been a very noticeable change of late in the former friendliness shown to us by the Conservatives." [55] The ruling Conservative party generally resented Marine efforts to keep politics out of the National Guard; Conservatives also feared American control of Nicaragua's election machinery, which would assure fair elections in November that could turn them out of power. The Conservative-controlled Congress refused to ratify the Stimson-Díaz agreement establishing a non-partisan National Guard, but the Marine-led constabulary continued to operate under the presidential agreement. Conservative opposition to American-supervised elections in 1928 was a more serious matter. In March a proposed electoral law, prepared by Harold W. Dodds of Princeton University and recommended by the Department of State, was rejected by the Nicaraguan Congress. The head of the American electoral mission in Nicaragua, Army Brigadier General Frank R. McCoy, then arranged for some modifications in the bill, but Congress adjourned without acting upon it. At American insistence the compliant President Díaz on March 21 promulgated the law by decree, despite the questionable legality of such an action.[56]

The Nicaraguan political situation in the spring and summer of 1928 baffled Captain Bleasdale, the dauntless field commander who was now National Guard intelligence officer. On July 1 he wrote to Major General Lejeune:

> It is difficult to pick the truth out of the mass of lies that comes to my desk. A people, the majority of whom have spent their lives in an atmosphere of dishonesty, deception, espionage, and general crookedness, are a little difficult to cope with. . . . If, as a people, the Nicaraguans had any sense of law, order, honesty, and common ordinary decency, there

would be no occasion for the United States to lend its assistance to them to straighten out the pathetic mess they have made of their efforts to negotiate the complicated machinery of modern civilization. . . . This is a sorry country and a sorry people and the better Nicaraguan knows that when it becomes a better land, it will be because of the United States and your Marines.[57]

Brigadier General McCoy, chief of the electoral mission, thought he could contribute something toward making Nicaragua a better land. According to Carleton Beals, McCoy was "one of these iron-willed, super logical, single-track types whose stern jaw carried not an ounce of compromise." With his election law the general "had hit upon an ideal scheme for the salvation of Nicaragua—a utopian democratic perfection, which he was putting over with the faith of a Loyola, and the same inquisitorial methods." McCoy explained the election law to Beals "with fanatic zeal—as dogmatic, as undeviating as the most rabid Communist." [58] But the election law was not the Army general's only concern. "I am special representative of the President," he announced to General Feland. "If you haven't gotten Sandino in a month, I will feel that you have failed and I shall so report to the State Department." [59] In the spring of 1928 McCoy became involved in a scheme devised by the United States military attaché in Central America and Guy R. ("Machine Gun") Molony, a noted American soldier of fortune, to plant a spy in Sandino's headquarters. Implicated in the intrigue was Sandinista General Antonio Sequeira, who was later executed by Sandino for treason.[60]

Army Captain Matthew B. Ridgway, one of McCoy's assistants in Nicaragua, was also interested in matters not directly concerning the upcoming elections. "At every possible opportunity," Ridgway later recalled, "I visited the Marines in their jungle outposts and gained an abiding respect for their fighting qualities." [61] The Army captain often discussed counter-guerrilla tactics with Marine officers. Ridgway's quest for knowledge led Captain Roger W. Peard to compile

for him a "Brief Survey of Bandit Operations in the Northern Area." [62] Although Ridgway had to leave the pursuit of
"bandits" to the Marines, he did take an active part in hunting
Nicaraguan crocodiles. Carrying a 30-'06 rifle, he would
crawl on his belly through the slime at the edge of a lake,
wearing only shorts and shoes, to get a shot at a crocodile.
"I would shoot them just between those little knobs in which
their eyes are set, which is all you can see sticking up when
they are in the water." These hunts were conducted late in
the afternoon when the light was dim, and they provided "a
fine test of marksmanship." Captain Ridgway killed as many
as seven fourteen-foot crocodiles in one day. His only loss
was his West Point ring, which "slipped off my finger while
I was stalking one old bull and it's still there somewhere,
buried in the jungle muck." [63]

While Ridgway was reducing Nicaragua's crocodile population, Sandino's guerrilla forces also suffered a decline in
numbers. During the summer of 1928 some sixteen hundred
Sandinistas surrendered to the Marines and Guardsmen in the
northern area and were granted amnesty. But they brought
in few serviceable rifles and no automatic weapons. Some
Marines suspected that Sandino was encouraging these appar-
ent defections, knowing that his "part-time bandits" would
break their paroles and again flock to his standard whenever
they were needed. Early in the fall it was learned that Sandino's commanders in Nueva Segovia, Ortez and Salgado,
were organizing their reserves into a five-hundred-man "Civic
Guard." [64] Meanwhile, deep in the jungles of Jinotega, Sandino and Pedro Altamirano had made their plans to disrupt
the American-supervised elections scheduled for November
4, 1928—elections in which the "traitor," José María Moncada, would be the Liberal candidate for President, running
against the Conservatives' Adolfo Bernard. Late in September, as the period for registering voters began, Altamirano
led his band out of the wilderness and launched Sandino's
anti-election campaign.

Pedro Altamirano—better known as Pedrón, "Big Pedro"

—was well suited for the task. A laborer in his youth, he had killed a man while working on the roads; the remainder of his fifty-two years he had spent in banditry and guerrilla warfare. Still, he was able to raise a large family. His sturdy wife María accompanied him in the field and helped him make command decisions. His sons and daughters also shared their father's life of war and brigandage; Pedrón lived surrounded by his family, a most reliable bodyguard. The patriarch was slow-gaited, ponderous. Just the sight of his dark hulking form was enough to inspire terror. Pedrón's savagery was matched in its intensity only by his devotion to Sandino. There was an indissoluble bond of trust and affection between the illiterate old bandit and the articulate young revolutionist.[65]

Pedrón drifted from town to town in southern Jinotega department, warning the people not to participate in the elections. On October 2 he caught four Liberal politicians electioneering in San Marcos and killed them all. The Marines in the area were scattered, a few men at each registration place. Nevertheless, their commander, Captain Norman M. Shaw, managed to put together some strong patrols that eventually chased Pedrón back into the wilderness.[66] With Pedrón gone, election day was relatively quiet. An American officer was responsible for supervising the voting in each of Nicaragua's thirteen departments, and an enlisted man was in charge of each of the country's 432 polling places. The election was hard-fought and fair. Despite Sandino's terrorism and propaganda, 133,000 of his countrymen cast their ballots on November 4, 1928—fifty thousand more than in the last American-supervised election in 1924. The votes were quickly tabulated, revealing that General Moncada, who had received a last-minute endorsement from the exiled Dr. Sacasa, had easily defeated the Conservatives' Adolfo Bernard.[67] The blackthorn tree at Tipitapa had borne its fruit.

With their task complete, the men of the American electoral mission in Nicaragua prepared to leave for home. Counting those assigned to electoral duty, about nine hundred, the total number of American military personnel in Nicaragua reached five thousand by election day. Admiral Sellers was not sorry to see the electoral mission leave. "What a relief it is to do business," he confided to a Marine Officer, "without having General McCoy trying to throw a monkey wrench into the plans." [68]

Most of the Army officers assigned to the electoral mission returned to the United States by ship, but Captain Ridgway and Lieutenant Irving Alexander went overland. They traveled through Central America and Mexico by mule back, oxcart, canoe, bus, and train. The journey lasted three months, for they stopped off frequently along the way, enjoying the hospitality of peasant families. When he and Alexander crossed into Arizona from Nogales, Mexico, Ridgway had acquired an enduring affection for the people of Latin America.[69] Before the end of the 1920's Matthew Ridgway had demonstrated the qualities which were to win him recognition as one of the finest examples of the American professional soldier. Without pretense of "intellectuality," he was already an inveterate observer and inquirer. His curiosity would lead him to a remarkable perception of the psychological aspects of war—including revolutionary war. He could appreciate the capabilities and limitations of men—including himself. He did not suffer from the megalomania and paranoia that often afflict the minds of great soldiers. But neither could he be cast in the mediocre soldier's role of mindless "yes" man to higher authority—whether another soldier, or a civilian *fuehrer* or president. He wore his uniform proudly and, without vainglory, placed his life and his thought at the disposal of his country.

The Marines were determined to eradicate "banditry" in Nicaragua before 1928 was over, and toward this end they employed all the means at their command. One expedient, adopted during the election campaign, was a system of paid informers. A brigade memorandum to all officers outlined the system:

The practice of doling out small sums of money for reliable information should be encouraged. Larger sums should be promised and paid out for any information which results in our obtaining contact with bandits. From $25 to $100.00, depending on the results obtained, might be justifiable. One good contact is worth a lot of time and money. Payments should be made as secretly as possible so as not to jeopardize the lives of informants. . . . Try to impress upon every one that ¾ of the bandits operating in this country are foreigners and that their expulsion from this country will result in complete peace in this country.[70]

Complete peace in the country seemed close at hand after the elections of November 4. "The opinion that Sandino is 'finished' in Nicaragua," an intelligence report stated a week later, "is absolutely general amongst the natives." [71] American authorities felt the time was ripe for another attempt to reason with Sandino. At General Feland's request Don Gregorio flew to San Rafael del Norte in a Marine plane on November 16 to talk with his daughter-in-law. Don Gregorio, who as late as September 25 had warmly praised his son's cause, wanted to know Sandino's conditions for laying down his arms. Blanca suggested Don Gregorio write his son a letter which she would have delivered. In his letter Don Gregorio asked Sandino to reply directly to the American commander stating his conditions for peace.[72]

Meanwhile, the Marines had located Sandino's long-lost mother, Margarita Calderón. Margarita wrote to Blanca on November 11, saying that General Feland had personally promised her full guarantees for her son. "I suffer very much from his absence of so many years," Margarita told Blanca. She suffered even more because of her son's insurrectionary activities; "this will kill me and I beg him with my soul, this in the name of God and myself, to abandon his present rebel attitude." The letter was flown to Blanca by Marine airplane.[73] Marine aircraft also dropped thousands of leaflets over the jungle area in which Sandino had his headquarters. "The leaflets said that there were big preparations to finish us," a Sandinista physician told the press. "In small leaflets signed by Sandino's father, he [Don Gregorio] spoke of the sickness of Sandino's mother, Mrs. Margarita Calderón de Sandino, who wants him to go and see her before she dies." [74]

Late in November Admiral Sellers wrote Sandino urging him to consider laying down his arms now that the elections had been held and the impartiality and good intentions of the American forces in Nicaragua had been amply demonstrated. Sellers' letter was sent to Sandino through Blanca in San Rafael del Norte, with a covering letter from General Feland, dated December 4, that invited the guerrilla chief to a conference. Sandino replied four weeks later that he did not recognize any United States authority in Nicaragua and would not confer with American officials. He was, however, willing to deal with Moncada and give him a chance "to rectify his errors." But Sandino insisted that there would be no peace until all American troops had left Nicaragua. "Foreign lives and property will be better guaranteed by us Nicaraguans," Sandino said in closing, "than by forces of a foreign government, because every foreign intervention in our affairs only brings loss of peace and the people's ire." [75]

After replying to Sellers, Sandino wrote Moncada on New Year's Day, 1929, offering to meet with the new President. "You alone," Sandino told Moncada, "are the one with whom I want to come to an understanding for the attainment of an effective peace in Nicaragua." Sandino would not deal with "intermediaries who have no business in our internal affairs." The guerrilla chief warned Moncada that his search for an accommodation with the new administration should not be taken as a sign of weakness. "What motivates us is the desire that the Yankees not have a pretext for continuing to tread upon the soil of our Fatherland," Sandino concluded, "and [the desire] to prove to the civilized world that we Nicaraguans ourselves are capable of solving the problems of a free and sovereign nation." [76]

But Moncada spurned Sandino's overtures; he had in mind

other means for ending the rebellion of his erstwhile subordinate. Meanwhile, the war continued. On December 6 a Marine sergeant had been killed in a clash with Sandinistas near Ocotal.[77] Before the year 1928 had ended, Managua was buzzing with rumors that Sandino was planning a major offensive.[78]

7

A Stalemate and a Trip to Mexico

Lieutenant Colonel Clyde H. Metcalf, a Marine officer who
served in Nicaragua, pictured the difficulties his comrades faced in that country:

> By the beginning of 1929 it was becoming more and
> more evident that the marines in Nicaragua had been called
> upon to perform an almost impossible task. . . . They were
> expected to maintain order . . . without any control over the
> civilian population. . . . Neither the people nor their officials
> stood behind the marines in their attempt to put down law-
> lessness. . . . Notwithstanding all of their vigorous efforts,
> officers conducting the campaign were practically unanimous
> in the opinion that the military situation had reached a stale-
> mate. So long as the people would not assist the marines, the
> bandits could continue to operate in small groups and carry
> on their depredations in spite of everything the marines
> could do.[1]

It was clear from their actions and attitudes that many
Nicaraguans, perhaps a majority, regarded the Marines not
as a police force protecting them from outlaws but as an
occupying army. In the United States a new President had
been elected who was more sensitive to Latin American de-
nunciations of Yankee Imperialism. Before his inauguration in

March 1929 Herbert Hoover took a cruise to Latin America, during which he stopped off for a day at Corinto, Nicaragua. In the interests of better relations with Latin America, Hoover believed that United States forces should be promptly withdrawn from Haiti and Nicaragua. But American authorities in Nicaragua feared that chaos would result if the Marines were pulled out of the country before its government had the means to enforce its own laws. Nevertheless, Admiral Sellers thought that the withdrawal could begin early in 1929. On January 3 he recommended that the Marine brigade in Nicaragua be reduced to 3,500 officers and men. The proposed reduction in forces did not satisfy the anti-interventionists in the United States Senate, who, in February, almost succeeded in adding an amendment to the 1929 naval appropriations bill that would have cut off all funds to maintain Marines in Nicaragua, "except in cases of emergency arising hereafter." [2]

Pressure mounted steadily in Congress for the removal of the Marine brigade. As a result, attention was focused on the National Guard—the Marine-led constabulary that would have to assume responsibility for all military operations against Sandino should American combat units be withdrawn. The Marines had made considerable progress in organizing and training the National Guard since its inception in May 1927. Under Brigadier General Elias R. Beadle, a Marine lieutenant colonel who had succeeded a temporary appointee as Chief Director of the National Guard in July 1927, the organization increased to an aggregate strength of more than two thousand officers and men by the beginning of 1929. During his command as Chief Director, Beadle's policy was to take over police duties in the more peaceful parts of the country and leave the job of eliminating Sandino to the Marines. Although token forces of Guardsmen took part in some of the engagements in the eastern and northern areas, the brunt of the fighting was usually borne by the Marines. While Adolfo Díaz was President, Beadle had enjoyed the support of the Nicaraguan chief executive and of the American Minister in Managua, Charles C. Eberhardt, a middle-aged career diplomat, but not that of the commander of the Marine brigade. General Feland, a much-decorated veteran of more than thirty years of military service, resented the Chief Director's independent command: he wanted the National Guard brought under his control and sent into the field to fight guerrillas. In his dispute with Beadle, which was intensified by personal animosity, Feland found a natural ally in José María Moncada, who was inaugurated President of Nicaragua on January 1, 1929. Both were intent on destroying the independence of the Nicaraguan National Guard.[3]

"Since January 1," Minister Eberhardt informed Washington, "President Moncada has looked upon General Feland as his virtual Minister of War and adviser on military and other matters." Abetted by Feland, Moncada began to renege on the agreement he had made with Stimson at Tipitapa. The new President objected specifically to the provision that the non-partisan National Guard be "the sole military and police force of the Republic"; in addition to the Guard, Moncada wanted a "Volunteer Army" commanded by Nicaraguan officers of his own choosing. Although the President might put this new force under Feland's control at first, Eberhardt feared that in the future it could become the instrument for illegally perpetuating Moncada in power. Moncada maintained that the Tipitapa agreement was "extra-constitutional" and had been terminated on January 1, 1929, with the re-establishment of a "constitutional regime." On January 8 President Moncada began recruiting his Volunteer Army, over the strenuous objections of Eberhardt and Beadle, who favored the expansion of the non-partisan National Guard to meet the demand for native troops in the combat areas.[4]

Minister Eberhardt hoped for the enactment of a bill pending before the Moncada-controlled Congress that would clear up the ambiguous legal position of the National Guard and provide for its expansion. But the bill's prospects dimmed as serious friction developed between President Moncada and Chief Director Beadle. One source of the friction was

Beadle's refusal to give Moncada's military aide—Marine First Lieutenant Arthur D. Challacombe, a former *aide de camp* to General Feland—a major's commission in the National Guard. Eberhardt advised Washington in mid-February that the situation would be improved if both Beadle and Feland were relieved of duty in Nicaragua. Washington agreed, and the two officers were ordered to turn over their commands on March 13. The desired results were achieved and the National Guard bill was finally passed on February 19. But shortly afterward Feland was ordered to delay his departure until May 10. Eberhardt reacted indignantly to the postponement, charging Feland with "continuing a campaign of interference which has seriously damaged the prestige of the Legation, the Guardia, and the Marine Corps itself and which threatens to jeopardize our whole Nicaraguan program." [5]

By this time certain activities of General Feland were coming to light, which, in Eberhardt's words, "can only be characterized as unpatriotic." [6] After his friend Moncada was inaugurated, Feland reportedly told the representative of Pan American Airways in Managua that his "and other big American companies need not expect to get such contracts as that which they were seeking, since there is now a new deal on and 'we' are not letting the old American clique run things." The "we" included Lieutenant Challacombe, who "cabled his father-in-law to come over and get in on water and other contracts." [7] Challacombe's father-in-law, A. E. French, arrived in Nicaragua in March, and Moncada named him supervisor of the Pacific Railway, over the strenuous objections of Eberhardt and the J. G. White Company, which was managing the railroad under a contract with the Nicaraguan government.

While dissension racked the American colony in Managua, the Sandinistas intensified their operations in the countryside. On January 10, 1929, two Guardsmen were killed and four wounded in an ambush near Guanacastillo, Nueva Segovia. [8] Even less fortunate was a mounted patrol of seven Marines from the platoon of First Lieutenant Alexander Galt.

The lieutenant, who was hunting Pedrón in Jinotega department, detailed the seven men to reconnoiter the area around San Antonio. On January 19, after a ride of about six hours, the Marines, led by a private first class, arrived in the village of San Antonio, where they spent the next two nights in the home of one Ignacio Cruz. Before leaving their host on the morning of January 21, they asked him for directions to Constancia. The directions they received led them to a dead end on a coffee plantation. The disgruntled Marines turned around and retraced their steps to San Antonio, where, about three hours after their false start, they found the right trail to Constancia. Two Marines were riding and five were walking as the patrol plodded down the trail in the mid-morning heat, their weapons in their saddle boots. About two miles from San Antonio, thirty Sandinistas struck from ambush. The guerrillas killed three Marines and captured a Thompson submachine gun, four rifles, three pistols, one grenade launcher, and all the patrol's blanket rolls and saddle bags.[9]

This Marine defeat was offset two weeks later by the capture of one of Sandino's most able lieutenants. On the morning of February 3 General Manuel María Girón was riding alone along the bank of a stream near San Albino. He was tired and sick and on his way out of the country for rest and recuperation. His head was down and he was half asleep in the saddle—unaware that eight enlisted Marines were taking turns bathing in the stream ahead of him. The Marines were members of a patrol commanded by First Lieutenant Herman H. Hanneken, a veteran officer who had impressed upon his men the importance of vigilance and cunning. Four of the Marines were bathing and four were standing guard when the lone rider was spotted. The eight Marines grabbed their rifles and slipped into the bushes along the path of the approaching rider. The dozing Girón received a rude awakening as the eight riflemen pounced upon him.[10] Girón was the first, and the last, important Sandinista chief to be taken prisoner by the Marines or the National Guard.

Meanwhile, Moncada's Volunteer Army was taking shape.

On January 28 General Feland issued a statement clarifying the role of the volunteers: only a "few hundred" would be recruited, and they would not operate independently but rather would be employed as Marine headquarters in Nicaragua saw fit. The chief virtue of the volunteers, the statement continued, was that they could readily distinguish between "bandits" and the "law-abiding inhabitants" of northern Nicaragua. The volunteers would be enlisted for six months and would be considered a part of the National Guard, Feland informed General Lejeune. But most of them—two columns of one hundred men each—would be sent to the northern area and placed directly under the command of Colonel Dunlap, who was responsible to Feland and not to Guard Director Beadle. Feland would detail a force of Marines to accompany each column, and Moncada would proclaim martial law in the northern area. The Marines, however, would "take no part in applying [martial law] against anybody, but prisoners and evidence which we gather will be turned over to Nicaraguan officials for trial," Feland explained. "I believe that this application of martial law is going to have even more effect than the actual operations of the columns in the field." [11] Before the end of January a column of volunteers, nominally commanded by General Augusto Caldera, but supervised by a Marine captain, was in the field north of Ocotal.[12]

A second volunteer column took the field on February 19 to operate in the San Albino–El Chipote area. It consisted of about ninety volunteers, thirty-six Marines, and a Navy medic. The Marines manned the column's heavy weapons: five Browning automatic rifles, five Thompson submachine guns, and four grenade launchers. The three American officers rode mules, and the Marine contingent had twenty-one other mules for packing supplies and equipment. The officers of the volunteer contingent—a Mexican general and seven colonels, most of whom were Mexican or Costa Rican—were each armed with two revolvers and long, straight-edged cutaches; the general and three of the colonels were mounted. The Nicaraguan enlisted men, a motley group ranging in age from seventeen to fifty, were dressed in khaki and armed with Krag rifles. The volunteers had twenty-five pack animals —mules and oxen—to carry their rations and extra ammunition. The commander of the volunteers, General Juan Escamilla, had left his native Mexico after choosing the losing side in the de la Huerta rebellion; in Nicaragua he had served as a general in Moncada's Constitutionalist Army. He was about forty years old, slender, wiry, and sinister looking, with a big, black mustache. "I considered Escamilla an adventurer," wrote the commander of the column's Marine contingent, Lieutenant Hanneken.[13]

Accompanying Hanneken on this patrol was the lieutenant's prisoner, Manuel María Girón. After his capture the Sandinista general had been taken to Colonel Dunlap's headquarters in Ocotal. There he had been offered his freedom in return for leading the volunteers to Sandino's camp. Girón refused, but Colonel Dunlap ordered Hanneken to take him along anyway. On March 2 Hanneken turned Girón over to Escamilla, "in accordance with instructions received before clearing Ocotal." The Marines and volunteers were camped in the open, in an orange grove, on the northeast slope of El Chipote, when General Escamilla convened a general court-martial to try General Girón. The oranges were ripening and were ready to be picked.

The trial began at one o'clock in the afternoon of March 2. The military court consisted of six colonels: four judges, a prosecutor, and a defense counsel. The grey-eyed Girón rejected counsel and pleaded his own case. At the outset he charged that the court was without jurisdiction in his case, because he was a Guatemalan citizen and his country's legation in Managua had not been informed of the trial. Furthermore, since he was a member of a regular military organization—every bit as regular as the volunteers, he added—he could not be tried for carrying out the orders of a superior officer.

Girón's objections were overruled, and the charges against him were read. He was charged with acting as chief of staff for Sandino, who was in rebellion against the Nicaraguan government; commanding the rebel forces that looted the Pis Pis mines; kidnaping George Marshall, an American citizen who died in his custody; commanding rebel forces at the Bromaderos ambush, in which several Marines were killed; commanding rebel forces at La Flor that killed Captain Hunter; commanding rebel forces that ambushed Captain Edson on the Coco River. The defendant pleaded guilty to all charges, "remarking that he was only carrying out the orders of his superior officer." He was found guilty and sentenced to be shot. The trial lasted two hours. "I still have my doubts as to the legality of this trial," Hanneken wrote ten years later.

General Escamilla immediately approved the sentence and the condemned man was led away from the camp in the orange grove. A firing squad of volunteers, commanded by Colonel Isaac Solano, was designated to carry out the sentence. The only others present were Escamilla, Hanneken, and a Marine second lieutenant. At 5:30 the men of the firing squad took their positions and Colonel Solano asked Girón if he had any last words; the middle-aged Guatemalan yelled back "No, you son-of-a-bitch!" Girón "died with a sneer on his face and after the volley a designated member of the squad rushed to him and fired a coup de grâce. He was buried where he fell."

The execution of Girón left the volunteers with one prisoner: a Nicaraguan they had found caring for a mule that belonged to Sandino. This prisoner was the next victim of Escamilla's firing squad. "The bravado and calm manner displayed by the bandits that were executed made a deep impression on me," Hanneken wrote. News of these executions reached Colonel Dunlap just as he was receiving reports that General Caldera's column of volunteers had violated the Honduran border on March 17. Dunlap had a message dropped to Hanneken, telling him to make sure he stayed on his side of the border and to see that Escamilla did not exercise his court-martial authority too freely. "I was quite flabbergasted," Hanneken wrote. "At Ocotal I had been told that the power Escamilla had to convene military courts was no concern of mine. Only two men had been executed and one of them by orders of Colonel Dunlap and it was beginning to cause uneasiness at Area Headquarters."

The activities of the volunteers were also causing uneasiness in Managua and in Washington. In March 1929 Calvin Coolidge and Frank B. Kellogg were replaced as President and Secretary of State by Herbert Hoover and Henry L. Stimson. The new administration was determined to straighten out the Nicaraguan mess. General Feland was ordered out of Nicaragua before the end of March and replaced by Brigadier General Dion Williams—who had raised the first American flag on the shores of Manila Bay. Feland's principal antagonist, Minister Eberhardt, was replaced the next month by Matthew E. Hanna, "a West Point graduate who had already had a distinguished military record before joining the Diplomatic Service." He had served with Major General Leonard Wood in Cuba and helped organize the public school system there after the Spanish-American War. Hanna was "military in bearing and manner," an admiring subordinate wrote, but "a diplomat to the core." [14] Beadle's replacement as Chief Director of the National Guard was Marine Colonel Douglas C. McDougal, a former commander of the Haitian constabulary.

In Honduras Liberal President Vicente Mejía Colindres had taken office in February. The new President was inclined to cooperate with Moncada and the Marines, but this became difficult after Caldera's volunteers crossed the ill-defined Honduran border on March 17. Matters were not helped when Marine planes bombed a Sandinista band near Las Limas, a village claimed by Honduras, on March 23. On April 2 Honduran public opinion forced President Mejía Colindres to ask the United States to "retire from our territory." Four days later Marine and volunteer officers met with a Honduran general on the border and worked out plans for joint operations against the Sandinistas. But when the Hon-

Honduras

duran President declared martial law along the Nicaraguan border, his congress retaliated by reducing the size of the Honduran Army.[15]

Meanwhile, Escamilla's volunteers were carrying on in northern Nicaragua. By the end of April they had had only one inconclusive contact with Sandinista forces, but they had captured and executed three more "bandit collaborators." After a two weeks' rest, Hanneken and Escamilla moved into the Yali area late in May. The people in this region were strongly pro-Sandino, Hanneken reported; "when word was received that Escamilla's column was in the area, they ran for Yali." The refugees congregated around the Marine barracks at Yali, pleading for protection against Escamilla. According to one source, twelve hundred sought refuge there, two hundred of whom died of starvation.[16] Escamilla fed as many refugees as he could with cattle his men drove off the ranches "of known bandits." On June 3 the Hanneken-Escamilla column spied a column of Sandinistas moving on a parallel trail. The two forces opened fire simultaneously, but the guerrillas soon dispersed, leaving one dead behind. The volunteers captured one Sandinista, whom they summarily executed with their guide, who they suspected intended to lead them into ambush.

The Conservative press of Nicaragua now launched a full-scale attack against General Escamilla and his American collaborators. Escamilla was labeled a "Mexican adventurer, a mercenary soldier, a murderer and a cutthroat";[17] he was "more bloody than Pedrón."[18] *La Tribuna* of Managua taunted the United States daily with a passage that it urged everyone to memorize: "Against the insidious wiles of foreign influence—I conjure you to believe me, fellow-citizens —the jealousy of a free people ought to be constantly awake."

This use of George Washington's Farewell Address could not have pleased Henry Stimson, but the new Secretary of State realized that the Nicaraguan Conservatives had some basis for their fears that the United States was helping Moncada create a Liberal Army—a ruthless military force which could deprive the Conservatives of their political rights, their property, and their lives. Stimson instructed American authorities in Nicaragua to dissociate themselves from Escamilla's actions, and he urged Moncada to disband the volunteers without delay. The National Guard law had been enacted and Marine Colonel McDougal had been promoted to the rank of Guard major general, clearing the way for the rapid expansion of the Guard and its reorganization along military rather than police lines. With this program under way Stimson insisted that there was no longer any justification or legal basis for the Volunteer Army. In mid-June Moncada agreed to disband the volunteers, and the last members of this force were mustered out before the end of the summer, when jobs were provided for them by a government road-building project.[19]

But the concept of a Volunteer Army—a purely Nicaraguan force under native officers empowered to deal with the guerrillas as they saw fit—remained dear to the heart of President Moncada. Many American residents of Nicaragua felt the same way. H. Samuelson—a blond six-footer, "lazy, friendly, and silent," who panned gold around Somotillo and rented horses to the Marines[20]—advocated the arming of volunteers to assist the National Guard in applying a "simple remedy" for the elimination of banditry: "if the bandits were only shot as soon as captured, you could stop it in a short time." [21] J. A. Willey, a coffee grower and American consul at Matagalpa, also favored the volunteer solution and praised the work of General Escamilla. A new Volunteer Army, Willey admitted, would have to be recruited from other parts of the country, for he and his fellow coffee growers did not trust their employees enough to arm them.[22] W. G. Mosher, a rancher near Somoto, charged that Marine "higher ups," who were enjoying a good life in Managua, refused to arm volunteers because they feared this would result in the extermination of the guerrillas; "their fat jobs depend, to a great extent, upon the bandits keeping active!" [23]

Local property holders also had their differences with

Marine junior officers and enlisted men. Plantation owners sometimes told their employees that the Marines stationed on their land were there to see that they worked properly. Some Marines resented perversions of their military function. In the Pis Pis mining region Lieutenant W. W. Benson was not happy with an assignment that included preventing the natives from panning gold at the La Luz mine. And the lieutenant did not enjoy listening to the complaints of the operator of the Neptune mine, "a typical protection-begging 'Banana American.' " [24] The president of Bonanza Mines reported that the American officers he and his colleagues "had to contend with were a source of great expense, continuous trouble, inciting the workmen to their ideas, and allowing and inciting disorder at their pleasure." [25] The manager of a cinema at Puerto Cabezas complained that Marines were letting local citizens see motion pictures free at their open-air theater.[26]

Other incidents affected relations between the Marines and segments of the Nicaraguan public. On the night of June 5, 1929, the Managua cemetery was invaded by vandals who overturned crosses and statues and otherwise desecrated the graves. The Conservative newspaper *La Prensa* blamed the vandalism on drunken Marines accompanied by prostitutes. An investigation ordered by General Williams showed that no Marines had been involved in the affair, but on June 11 the entire Marine command in Managua was marched to the cemetery to place flowers on the damaged tombstones [27]— an action that must have appeared to many as an admission of guilt. Another *faux pas* was allegedly committed by Marine First Lieutenant Richard Fagan at a party given in honor of Moncada. The lieutenant questioned the "bandit" label as applied to Sandino and conceded only that the guerrilla chieftain was guilty of a "lack of judgment" in opposing the Marines. "I'm an Irishman in the service of the United States," Fagan was reported to have said, "but as an Irishman, I say that General Sandino is a patriot." [28] Much more serious were the actions of Sergeant James A. Davidson, "who deserted from the Marine Corps in Nicaragua in 1929 and went over to the bandits." [29]

The Sandinistas too had internal troubles in 1929. Early in the year General Sandino received a letter of resignation from the chief foreign representative of the Defending Army of the National Sovereignty of Nicaragua. Marine intelligence reported that Froylán Turcios "is seeking a government position in the new Honduran administration and feels that he will have less difficulty in obtaining it if he breaks with Sandino." [30] Turcios' involvement in Honduran politics had embarrassed Sandino as early as June 1928, when the poet sided with his country in a border dispute with Guatemala; "Sandino is Indo-Hispanic," the general declared to his representative, "and he has no frontiers in Latin America." [31] The final rupture between Sandino and Turcios came after the Nicaraguan elections, when the general wrote of his plan to unite the Nicaraguan Labor party and some dissident elements of the Liberal party behind a governing junta he would proclaim, headed by Pedro José Zepeda. The poet replied that he could not represent a Nicaraguan revolutionary junta and asked that he be relieved of his duties as foreign representative of Sandino's army. He suggested that the Sandinistas withdraw to Costa Rica and surrender their arms to the authorities there who would grant them amnesty. Sandino accepted the poet's resignation on January 7, 1929, and the next month pro-American President Mejía Colindres took office in Honduras and appointed Turcios Honduran consul in Paris. "When Turcios was our representative in Honduras, we were in communication with the world," Sandino recalled. "But Turcios quit and we were left isolated. . . . North American money silenced us." [32]

Deprived of the services of Turcios, Sandino decided to go abroad himself to rally foreign support for his cause. On January 6, 1929, he wrote to Mexican President Emilio Portes Gil, requesting permission to come to Mexico and discuss with the President certain "highly important projects." [33] To deliver the letter to Portes Gil, Sandino designated José de Paredes, a captain on his staff. Paredes was about twenty-one years old, a native of Guadalajara, Mexico, who had lived in Los Angeles, California, prior to joining Sandino in 1927. He was acquainted with the English language and liked to compose insulting notes to the Marines, which he left where American patrols would find them.[34]

While Captain de Paredes was away on his mission to Mexico, Sandino wrote a letter to the new President of the United States. After listing the past transgressions of the U.S. in Nicaragua, Sandino urged Hoover not to follow the course of his predecessors. Although Dr. Juan B. Sacasa, now Moncada's Ambassador to Washington, was "humiliated, prostrate on his knees" before the American government, he warned Hoover not to expect Sandino to assume a similar attitude. He would resist as long as American troops remained on Nicaraguan soil. "I am not unmindful of the material resources at the disposal of your nation," wrote Sandino, paraphrasing Rubén Darío; "you have everything, but you lack God." [35] Sandino put this letter in the hands of Rubén Ardila Gómez, the young Colombian who had been private secretary to the late General Girón. Ardila Gómez tried to deliver it to the American legation in Honduras, but when the officials there saw that it was from Sandino—and bore his official seal: a Sandinista beheading a prostrate Marine with a machete—they refused to accept it.[36]

Next, on March 20, Sandino wrote to President Hipólito Yrigoyen of Argentina. In this letter Sandino proposed that a hemispheric conference be held in Buenos Aires to which the United States would be invited. Such a conference, with Sandino representing Nicaragua, would "guarantee Indo-Hispanic sovereignty and independence and the friendship of the America of our race with the United States on a basis of equality." The conference would discuss the construction of a Nicaraguan canal—a project that would be delegated to the United States only if that country promised to respect the

sovereignty of all Hispanic America. The letter was published by *La Nación* of Buenos Aires, but the Argentine
government made no reply to it.[37]

Meanwhile, Captain de Paredes returned from Mexico
with good news for Sandino: the Mexican President would
furnish him arms and ammunition. Besides this verbal promise,
Paredes brought Honduran passports for the general and his
staff, complete with transit visas for El Salvador and Guatemala. Everything was arranged, Paredes assured his chief;
Sandino could now go to Mexico and conclude the munitions deal with President Portes Gil.[38]

But Sandino was misled. In his conversations with Portes
Gil, the young Paredes might have mistaken the Mexican
President's professed admiration for Sandino for commitments to aid his cause materially. Portes Gil later wrote that
he offered Sandino only political asylum in Mexico. The able
American Ambassador to Mexico, Dwight Morrow, assured
Portes Gil that the United States would have no objection to
Mexico's granting Sandino political asylum but would stren-
uously object to his being given a base of operations in Mexico. Morrow and Portes Gil amicably reached an agreement
whereby Sandino would be permitted to take up residence
in Mérida, on the Yucatán peninsula, but would not be allowed to come to Mexico City or to set up a "base of operations" in Mexican territory. The United States then arranged
with the governments of Honduras, El Salvador, and Guatemala for Sandino's transit across their territory.[39]

Late in May 1929 Sandino summoned his field commanders to his headquarters and then, without waiting for
them, crossed the Río Guayape into Honduras, where he and
his staff were received by troops of the Honduran Army.
Sandino's staff consisted of junior officers of various nationalities. Among those accompanying the general were Rubén
Ardila Gómez of Colombia, José de Paredes of Mexico, Gregorio Gilbert—who had been imprisoned for killing a Marine
officer in his native Dominican Republic—and Agustín Farabundo Martí, a prominent communist from El Salvador.[40]

During the first days of June the Honduran troops escorted the Sandinistas across Honduras to La Unión, El Salvador. "During the whole trip across Honduras," the American military attaché reported, Sandino "was treated strictly as a criminal." [41] Salvadoran officials were somewhat more cordial. They met Sandino with an automobile provided by the American legation and accompanied him to a railroad way station within a mile of San Salvador. Here a special train was waiting for the Sandinistas, but before it left the station the Salvadoran Minister of War and the Mexican Minister to El Salvador paid their respects to Sandino. In El Salvador, as in Honduras and Guatemala, Sandino's passage was announced only to high government officials and to the Mexican and American legations. No publicity was allowed at the time, although certain favored newsmen were permitted to interview the guerrilla chief for publication after he had safely arrived in Mexico. Only these newsmen and officials, and a few lucky bystanders who happened to be on the spot when he passed, were able to see and cheer the Indo-Hispanic hero. The humiliating circumstances of his trip did not dampen the optimism of Sandino, who told an old friend at the El Salvador–Guatemala border that he was on his way to get Mexican military aid and would return to Nicaragua in November in a Mexican government plane.

When Sandino crossed into Mexico on June 25, Mexican border troops received him with all the honors due a visiting major general. He was escorted by rail from Tapachula to Veracruz, where on June 28 he was invited to speak to the multitudes; he made a rousing speech, denouncing Yankee Imperialism. For several days Sandino waited vainly in Veracruz for permission to proceed to Mexico City. Mexican officials told him that the time was not yet ripe for him to visit the capital; he should go to Mérida, on the Yucatán Peninsula, where the government had reserved a house for him and his staff, and wait until the initial excitement of his arrival in the country had died down. On July 11 Sandino arrived in Mérida and received a tumultuous welcome from the local populace. There he began an uneasy wait for government clearance to go to Mexico City and transact his business.

In Nicaragua Sandino's forces were thrown into confusion when the general's absence became known. In June 1929 all the principal Sandinista chiefs, except Ortez, met in the mountains north of Remanzo, near the Honduran border. Sandinista General José León Díaz presented to the assembly a letter from Sandino dated May 20. In the letter the guerrilla generalissimo informed his chiefs of the Mexican trip and designated Francisco Estrada—who had headed the short-lived departmental government in "Sandino City"—commander-in-chief during his absence. But Estrada was not pleased with this new honor. Equally dissatisfied was the man Sandino named deputy commander-in-chief, Pedro Irías. Estrada and Irías favored retiring to Honduras to await further orders from Sandino. José León Díaz, the next in command, was willing to carry on the war, but he had little personal following.[42]

Only Pedrón Altamirano had the means and the will to continue the fight. Wanted for brigandage on both sides of the border, Pedrón would take his chances in Nicaragua. The assembled chiefs elected Pedrón head of the revolution during Sandino's absence and ordered their own men to turn in their arms. When this had been done, Pedrón and his hundred men selected the best of the pooled weapons—including three Thompson submachine guns, two Browning automatic rifles, and one Lewis light machine gun. The remaining weapons were hidden in the mountains, and the retiring guerrillas and their chiefs "were directed to proceed to Honduras in small groups of two and three, unarmed, for the purpose of procuring more arms and ammunition there, to return to Nicaragua when directed by Sandino."[43] By the end of July the Honduran government had interned a number of Sandinista generals, including Estrada and Irías. In Mexico Sandino admitted the possibility of a "slight demoralization in our forces" during his absence.[44] Nevertheless, two of Sandino's most able lieutenants remained in Nicaragua to carry on the struggle. Besides Pedrón, young Miguel Angel Ortez, who had not attended the Remanzo meeting, chose to stay in the field.

Just before Sandino's departure for Mexico, the new Marine commander in Nicaragua had commented on the military situation: banditry had always been present in Central America, Brigadier General Dion Williams pointed out, and the situation in Nicaragua was "not susceptible to improvement." [45] After Sandino had gone, Pedrón served notice on the Marines that he would not accept peace in the country. On the Fourth of July he laid an ambush north of Jícaro for a twenty-man National Guard patrol led by two Marines. But Pedrón's men were unfamiliar with their new automatic weapons, and they opened fire too soon. The patrol found excellent cover in a ditch, and after about an hour the attackers began to withdraw under heavy fire from the Guardsmen, taking their casualties with them. The Guardsmen had only two wounded: an American lieutenant and a Nicaraguan private. [46]

The performance of the National Guard on this and other occasions seemed to vindicate the practice of replacing Marine units with Guardsmen in the combat zones—though many of the Guardsmen received only "a short course in field training" before being sent into "bandit country." [47] During the spring and summer of 1929 the Marine brigade in Nicaragua was reduced to under fifteen hundred men, despite the protests of the American chargé, who contended that Sandino's influence in the country was greater on July 23 than when he left for Mexico. [48] Washington had discarded the policy of sending in the Marines to wipe out the Sandinistas. Henceforth, the Marines in Nicaragua would be concerned mainly with training the National Guard, which, they hoped, could at least contain the guerrillas and prevent the violent overthrow of the recognized government.

By the end of August 1929 there were three battalions of Guardsmen in the combat zone: 609 men in the northern area—Nueva Segovia and the adjoining areas of Estelí and

Jinotega departments; 414 men in the central area—Mata-galpa and southern Jinotega; and 257 men in the eastern area —roughly the entire eastern half of the country. These men, plus about nine hundred of the thirteen hundred Marines re-maining in Nicaragua, were scattered over a huge area in dozens of stations, sometimes manned by units no larger than a squad.[49] It was a vast, sparsely settled region stretching from the mangrove swamps and savannas along the Mosquito Coast, inland across the steaming rain forest, to the cool, piney-wooded mountaintops of Jinotega and Nueva Segovia.

Communications between the far-flung posts in this vast region, and with their roving patrols, was a major problem. Telegraph service between the larger towns in the northern and central areas was fair. Actually the telegraph service was remarkable under the conditions: hundreds of miles of wire stretched through Sandinista-infested jungles, nailed to trees, with beer bottles and cow horns used as insulators. Guerrillas would sometimes cut the wire in order to ambush the repairmen, so only well-armed patrols could be sent to repair breaks in the lines. After 1927 it became impossible to maintain telegraph service between the east and west coasts.[50] Except for the cities, telephone service was either non-exis-tent or completely unreliable. Fourteen medium-frequency radio sets were brought into the combat zone and netted with the Standard Fruit Company station at Puerto Cabezas, but "constant communication could not be maintained with these sets owing to their low power and the distance over which they worked." [51]

Marine aviation furnished a more reliable means of com-munication in the combat zone. Instead of joining the grad-ual Marine withdrawal from Nicaragua begun in the spring of 1929, Marine aviation remained at full strength to furnish undiminished air support for ground operations against the Sandinistas. The planes kept the scattered units in touch with each other and with Managua by relaying both written and signal-panel messages. Aviation also furnished indispensable combat support to small, isolated outposts of Marines and

Guardsmen. These stations seemed to invite Sandinista attacks, but siege was practically impossible, for the guerrillas would not try to withstand the attack of combat planes that appeared almost daily over every outpost. If a garrison could hold out for twenty-four hours, it was usually safe. Marine aviation also provided support for ground patrols and sometimes could detect an ambush on the trail ahead of a friendly force. But air cover for ground patrols was a mixed blessing, for the presence of planes alerted the enemy to the possibility that troops were in the area.[52]

Another major problem faced by Guardsmen and Marines in the combat zone was transportation. Much of the region was mountainous, with no suitable roads and only a few trails—which in the rainy season were often knee-deep in mud and impassable even for oxcarts. Marine aviation helped the situation, airlifting men and materiel to the combat zone when possible, but the need for reliable means of surface transportation remained. Pack animals or new roads were solutions to the problem, and both were applied to some extent.

By the spring of 1929 there were some one thousand Nicaraguan mules in service in the northern and central areas. But these native animals were small and most could not use quartermaster harness or pack saddles without major alterations. American mule skinners longed for full-sized U.S. Army mules, so sixty-five of these animals were shipped in and stationed at Matagalpa. The puny native animals could subsist on local corn and foliage, but the Army mules required American-style oats and hay. Enough feed to last these animals through a six-month rainy season had to be shipped to Corinto by steamer and transported by rail from there to León, where 225 oxcarts had to be assembled to haul the shipment the rest of the way to Matagalpa. After one such experience, no more American mules were shipped to the Marines in Nicaragua. Marine officers were advised to purchase native mules between four and ten years of age that stood at least twelve hands high; the maximum pack load for these animals was 135 pounds. Nicaraguan horses were less desirable: they required more feed and had less stamina.[53] This sensible switch to an appropriate, indigenous means of battlefield locomotion was a rare accomplishment for American troops engaged in twentieth-century anti-guerrilla operations. In similar situations United States forces would cling to their cherished, technically advanced means of transportation, which are geared to conventional warfare and which, combined with the improper tactics they inspire, make success against guerrillas practically impossible.

General Williams of the Marine brigade, General McDougal of the National Guard, and Mr. Hanna of the American Legation all favored a program of building all-weather roads into the mountains. The project was launched in the summer of 1929 with funds allocated by the Nicaraguan government. Marine officers of the National Guard played a major part in supervising this project. In addition to improving the transportation system, it provided gainful employment for many country people who might otherwise have been engaging in Sandinista activity. In the Yali area Captain A. T. Lewis hired 125 known ex-guerrillas to work on the roads at fifty cents a day. Also employed by this roadbuilding program were many veterans of Moncada's Volunteer Army; General Escamilla became chief of road construction in the department of León.[54]

In addition to gaining road-building experience, the National Guard received considerable on-the-job training during 1929. From April 7, when General McDougal took command, through October—roughly the rainy season—Guardsmen clashed with Sandinistas seventeen times, losing only one sergeant killed and claiming heavy enemy casualties. The busiest month was August, when the Guardsmen at Jícaro repelled a determined Sandinista attack on their barracks.[55]

This record was marred by two serious mutinies at Telpaneca in October, in which an American officer was killed. The mutineers, led by Sergeant Fernando Larios, resented their commanding officer's refusal to allow enlisted men to accompany him to a local dance. When the officer—a National Guard lieutenant who was a sergeant in the Marine Corps—returned from the dance late at night, he was machine-gunned to death by the troops. The mutineers told investigating officers that the lieutenant was killed during a bandit attack on the garrison; when it appeared that this explanation would not be accepted, the troops mutinied again on October 29. Some fled across the border into Honduras, but Sergeant Larios was captured. There was a great public outcry when it was announced that Larios would be tried by a court-martial composed entirely of Americans—since only Americans were officers in the National Guard. Many Nicaraguans objected to the pending trial of their fellow citizen by foreigners, and their protests led to the commissioning of six native officers to sit on the Larios court-martial. Larios received a three-year sentence.[56]

With the end of the rainy season guerrilla activity increased. In the fall of 1929 Sandino circulated from Mexico a "Manifesto to the People of Nicaragua," calling for a more determined effort against the "barbarians of the north." [57] Responding to his chief's call, Pedrón rode out of the jungles of Jinotega and invaded the coffee country of Matagalpa department. Marine reinforcements were rushed to the area, but on November 11 brigade intelligence reported that "the campaign has reached a near impasse, where further progress will be dearly paid for unless our status in Nicaragua is in some way modified." General Williams requested authority to convene "exceptional military courts" to try "civilians who commit offenses against our military forces." [58]

Washington denied Williams' request, and Pedrón continued to pillage coffee plantations and assault the "forces of law and order." On the morning of November 27 Pedrón and about fifty men took positions on a hillside overlooking the National Guard barracks at the village of La Colonia, in northern Matagalpa department. There were only ten Guardsmen, commanded by a Nicaraguan sergeant, in La Colonia at the time; most of the Guardsmen and Marine officers assigned to the area were stationed on coffee plantations. At 8:30 A.M. Pedrón opened fire on the barracks with automatic weapons, rifles, and rifle grenades. Two Guardsmen were killed in the first burst of fire, and their sergeant was wounded. Yelling *"Viva Sandino!"* the guerrillas maintained a heavy volume of fire. After another Guardsman was killed the defenders fled the barracks and scattered into the countryside. Twenty minutes after it started, the firing ended and Pedrón's men marched into the barracks to collect the spoils: a Lewis machine gun, a Thompson submachine gun, seven rifles, nineteen hand grenades, and about a thousand rounds of ammunition. Then the guerrillas returned toward the north.[59] In the north, along the Honduran border, the bands of Miguel Angel Ortez and several lesser chiefs were operating. On December 18, 1929, guerrillas attacked San Francisco de Cuajiniguilapa and chased away a five-man National Guard detachment, killing one Guardsman and two civilians in the raid.[60]

While his forces in Nicaragua were winning an occasional victory, Sandino was faring badly in Mexico. In his small, government-provided villa on South Sixtieth Street, on the outskirts of Mérida, the general marked the passage of weeks and months, waiting for a summons to go to Mexico City and confer with the President. He began to suspect that the Mexican government had no intention of supporting his army and that President Portes Gil and Captain de Paredes had conspired with American officials to lure him away from Nicaragua with false promises of aid and make him a virtual prisoner in Yucatán. The general felt he was under surveillance by Mexican and American agents in Mérida, and he began making plans to elude his guards and return to the fighting front. He bitterly castigated Paredes, expelled him from his staff, and advised him to be grateful that he was not shot. "Almost with tears in his eyes" the young captain begged forgiveness.[61] He had not consciously betrayed his chief, Paredes insisted, and to prove his loyalty he returned to Nicaragua where he resumed his service with the guerrillas.

In Mexico three forces fought for the mind of General Sandino. Dr. Pedro José Zepeda, Sandino's representative in Mexico City, urged adherence to a broad united front of anti-imperialists of all classes and counseled patience and moderation in dealing with the Mexican government. More radical was the position of APRA—the Peru-based "American Popular Revolutionary Alliance"—which preached vague doctrines of racism and social revolution and was represented at Sandino's villa in Mérida by the Peruvian Esteban Pavletich. The third force, the Communist International, was represented on Sandino's staff by the Salvadoran Agustín Farabundo Martí. Venezuelan communist Gustavo Machado was engaged in a smear campaign against Dr. Zepeda, who since mid-1928 had vigorously resisted Machado's efforts to oust him as Sandino's personal representative in Mexico City. Sandino, who did not want to alienate any of his supporters, realized the advantages of the broad united front advocated by the Nicaraguan physician, but the radicals on his staff in Mérida, Pavletich and Martí, were closer to the general ideologically than was Dr. Zepeda. "Neither extreme right, nor extreme left, but United Front is our motto," Sandino wrote his representative in Guatemala on September 9, 1929. "Nevertheless," the general continued, "organizations of the extreme left are the ones that can make us think—those of us who preach determined social doctrines. You must have complete confidence that this is the direction we shall take." [62]

But Sandino steadfastly refused to submit to communist dictation. Finally, in December 1929 Gustavo Machado's "Hands Off Nicaragua Committee" turned on Sandino. The communists charged the general with betraying the party—specifically, of accepting their money to carry on the fight in Nicaragua and then taking a $60,000 bribe from the United States to exile himself in Mexico. Stung by the accusation, Sandino wrote to the Secretary General of the

Mexican Communist party, Hernán Laborde, on January 2, 1930, pleading innocence. He denied accepting any money from the United States. He differed with the Communist party on some matters, but he had not betrayed it. Sandino acknowledged that communists in Mexico had raised $1,000 and given it to Gustavo Machado to deliver to him in Nicaragua; but after Machado's round-trip expenses were deducted, the guerrilla chief was left with only $250. Accepting this paltry sum, Sandino insisted, did not commit him to follow the Communist party line. Sócrates Sandino, who up to this time had been a faithful tool of the communists, declared that his brother could not have betrayed the party because he had never been a member. An investigation ordered by Laborde cleared Sandino of the bribe-taking charge, but the inference that Sandino had somehow betrayed the communist movement remained.[63]

The communist attack on Sandino made the guerrilla chief more amenable to the advice of Dr. Zepeda, who was working quietly to arrange interviews for Sandino with President Portes Gil and with former President Calles, the power behind the Mexican chief executive. When the interviews were finally arranged, late in January 1930, the Salvadoran communist Martí warned Sandino not to meet with Calles, because the Mexican strongman had plans to poison him. Sandino had finally had his fill of communist machinations, and he ordered Martí out of his sight forever. About the same time the general expelled from his staff Zepeda's principal non-communist antagonist, the Aprista Pavletich.[64] The Nicaraguan physician was now secure as Sandino's chief adviser and his personal representative in the Mexican capital.

In January 1930, after more than six months' waiting, Sandino was at last able to go to Mexico City to confer with Calles and with the President of the Republic.[65] The Nicaraguan general apparently had lost all hope of securing Mexican aid for his guerrilla forces long before he met with Portes Gil on January 29, but he knew that the meeting would add to his prestige and that of his cause. Sandino probably re-

ceived no material aid as a result of the conference, but he undoubtedly fulfilled one of the purposes for which he had
come to Mexico: to discuss with the President matters of
great importance. Now he could return to Nicaragua.

César Falcón, a sophisticated Peruvian writer who interviewed Sandino in Mexico early in 1930, described the general:

> Short in stature . . . delicate without being skinny, nerv-
> ous. . . . His face is dry, hard. . . . His eyes say nothing; one
> might say that they had never seen anything. He does not
> know how to smile, although he laughs frequently; it is then
> that his eyes acquire a certain lustre, but his face remains
> serious—only his mouth laughs; one might say that his laugh
> does not laugh; this is not tragic, but it is very uncomfort-
> able. Sandino personally is not ugly; he is not repulsive; he
> is just insipid. . . .
>
> Now we hear him speak; we see him gesticulate. . . . "I
> will not abandon my mountains while even one Gringo re-
> mains in Nicaragua; I will not abandon my struggle as long
> as my people are denied even one right. My cause is the
> cause of my people, the cause of America, the cause of all
> oppressed peoples." Although he doesn't know how to talk,
> he is expressive, vehement; he says everything he feels, some-
> times even that which he does not feel. . . . He is the Creole
> type, one hundred percent, a talker—in general, a bit
> swaggering.[66]

After his talk with Portes Gil, Sandino returned to
Mérida and soon began making automobile trips into the
nearby countryside, ostensibly looking for a farm to buy. It
was during the dry season, and Sandino's automobile could
move over the plains of northern Yucatán with considerable
freedom. American and Mexican authorities who were watch-
ing Sandino's movements had difficulty keeping track of him.
But after a few days in the country the general and his party
would return to the villa in Mérida, so no one became alarmed
—until after Sandino and three aides went for a ride late in
April 1930 and did not return. The Sandinistas had slipped
aboard a ship at Progreso and disembarked at Veracruz. From

there they traveled incognito by train and automobile across southern Mexico, Guatemala, El Salvador, and Honduras. By mid-May, when Mexican officials realized the significance of their absence, they were already in Nicaragua.[67]

Curiously, Sandino's return to the battlefront did not please the communists.

> MEXICO CITY, MAY 29. AP—General Agustino Sandino, Nicaraguan leader, was charged by Mexican Communists today with having turned traitor to the cause of world anti-imperialism and with having gone back to Nicaragua "to sell out to the highest bidder."
>
> A Communist Party statement said that Sandino, after accepting Communist money and agreeing to a world tour against imperialism, obtained funds from other sources and returned to his homeland to renew the fight with small bourgeois groups for control of the country.
>
> The statement asserted that the United States was willing to let the fight proceed "in order to hold the menace of a Sandino victory over the Moncada Government or enter into an agreement with Sandino if he gained sufficient power." [68]

Sandino and the Communist International had parted company for good. The general's erstwhile secretary, the communist Martí, explained the break shortly before he faced a firing squad in his native El Salvador. Sandino's "banner was only a banner of independence, banner of emancipation," the Salvadoran declared. Martí broke with his chief because Sandino "did not want to embrace the communist program for which I was fighting." But "two steps from his execution" in February 1932, Agustín Farabundo Martí bore no resentment for his former commanding officer: "I solemnly declare that General Sandino is the greatest patriot in the world." [69]

8

The National Guard Offensive

D uring the first half of 1930 all Marine units in Nicaragua —except some on guard duty at foreign-owned plantations or mines—were concentrated in the cities and larger towns, and all offensive operations against the guerrillas in the countryside were turned over to the National Guard.[1] In the preceding year the Guardsmen in the combat areas had met with an occasional setback, but generally they had performed their duties well. The pattern was much the same during the early months of 1930, as the Guardsmen took over the last combat posts from the Marines.

In the northern area the National Guard was challenged by Miguel Angel Ortez and his "Defending Army of Nicaraguan Autonomy." Ortez issued a proclamation on New Year's Day, calling upon all Liberals in Chinandega and the mountain departments to support his army. In this proclamation Ortez praised Sandino, who was then in Mexico, but Ortez gave no indication that he considered himself subordinate to the absent chieftain.[2] Ortez's influence was especially strong around his home town of Ocotal, headquarters of the northern area. When the area commander, Colonel Robert L. Denig, departed from Ocotal to inspect posts to the east early in January, word was passed to the guerrillas in that region. To protect the colonel on the trail to Quilali, a National Guard patrol was sent out from that town on the morning of January 12 to meet Denig's party at Buena Vista.[3]

Guard Second Lieutenant Harold A. Uhrig rode out of Quilali on a white horse early in the morning of January 12, accompanied by ten Nicaraguan Guardsmen on foot. The Nicaraguans were armed with rifles; the American lieutenant had an automatic pistol. Sometime before nine o'clock, "a man mounted and a boy walking came from a house in the brush and proceeded in front of my patrol by two hundred feet or so," Uhrig noted in his report; they "kept looking back at us every once in a while." At about nine o'clock the man and boy disappeared around a bend in the trail; a few seconds later a shout of "Viva!" came from the ridge along the right side of the trail. About twenty-five guerrillas opened fire with rifles, pistols, and dynamite bombs, all along Uhrig's right flank. The lieutenant quickly dismounted and was pinned down with the rest of the patrol. Guerrillas crossed the trail and began firing on the Guardsmen from the left side. Two Guardsmen got up and ran to the rear and Uhrig "hollered out not to run away but to hurry back to where I was." The two kept going, and when the lieutenant heard crackling noises in the brush on both sides of the trail, he knew the enemy was closing in on him and he ordered a retreat. Uhrig and his men fled through the brush on the left side of the trail and up a mountainside, while guerrillas "followed us up with heavy fire and all yelling like maniacs." The guerrillas soon gave up the chase, and late in the afternoon Uhrig found his way back to the trail where he was joined by a relief patrol from Quilali. Besides one man killed and one wounded, the lieutenant had lost his automatic pistol and his white horse. Inglorious as it was, the National Guard action effectively disrupted an ambush that was intended for Colonel Denig.

News of guerrilla success in the north reached Pedrón in the central area, and he sent his compliments to Ortez and suggested they combine forces for an attack on the town of Jinotega. In his reply dated February 4, Ortez congratulated Pedrón for his victory at La Colonia and promised to give "special attention" to the proposed attack on Jinotega. In the meantime, Ortez asked Pedrón to send him a Springfield rifle, since he had four Springfield grenade launchers and not enough rifles of this type with which to employ the "bomb throwers." Ortez also expressed his belief "that we will have in a short time our supreme chief." [4] This was good news for Pedrón, who, probably more than any of the other guerrilla leaders, longed for the return of Sandino—the *político* who had raised him from bandit to general. While he waited for his mentor, the faithful Pedrón carried on Sandino's war: on February 11 his band opened fire on a twenty-man National Guard patrol near Guapinol, killing one Guardsman and wounding four others in five minutes before melting away into the jungle.[5]

During March 1930 Guardsmen clashed with the enemy seven times, losing none of their own and claiming to have killed a number of "bandits." On the first day of April a Guardsman was killed and one wounded when guerrillas attacked the garrison at Yali.[6] A more decisive blow was struck by Ortez's men on May 7. On that day, near Bálsamo, the guerrillas ambushed a sixteen-man National Guard patrol led by Second Lieutenant Edward L. Livermore as it crossed a river bed. Four Guardsmen were killed and two wounded before the guerrillas withdrew two and a half hours after opening fire. During the fight Livermore lost all his pack animals and supplies. The Guardsmen had taken cover on a high embankment where they withstood the guerrilla attack, but when the enemy retired they were unable to pursue, because of their wounded and a shortage of ammunition. Guerrilla losses, as in most such engagements, were unknown, for the attackers took their casualties with them when they withdrew. Blood found in their line of withdrawal indicated some casualties. Equally difficult to determine was the number of guerrillas taking part in the fight; Lieutenant Livermore guessed that the force that attacked him numbered "about one hundred." [7] Both sides employed rifles and automatic weapons.

The National Guard learned that the guerrilla band that had attacked Livermore in eastern Nueva Segovia "belonged to Ortez." [8] They already knew that the young chieftain was operating as far to the west as eastern Chinandega department. H. Samuelson, the miner-rancher who tried to keep the Guard posted on guerrilla activity in this area, had to send in handwritten reports after March 22, 1930, because "Miguel Angel Ortez stole my typewriter when he raided this place" (San Francisco de Cuajiniguilapa).[9] Many residents of northern Nicaragua, however, regarded Ortez as a tropical Robin Hood and freely contributed to the support of his band. In May 1930 the National Guard acted to reduce Ortez's base of support among the civilian population of Nueva Segovia. In the departmental capital of Ocotal, Ortez's father, grandfather, and four brothers were arrested on May 16 and deported to León. The father insisted that it was not his fault that his son was a "bandit"; in fact, when he first learned that Miguel Angel was thinking of joining Sandino, in September 1927, the father said he took his son to National Guard headquarters in Ocotal and asked that he be locked up; the father's request was refused, and the wayward son fled to the hills to take up a life of banditry.[10]

The removal of Ortez's relatives to León was sanctioned by President Moncada, who also approved a National Guard program to resettle forcibly the rural inhabitants of certain pro-guerrilla areas of Nueva Segovia in towns protected by Marine or National Guard garrisons. Late in May the program was extended to other parts of the northern and central areas. Anyone caught in the restricted zones after June 1 was to be considered a bandit. The American Minister, Matthew Hanna, who had not been consulted on this move, protested to President Moncada, who agreed to suspend execution of the order until June 10. In the meantime, refugees continued to stream out of the restricted zones in what the American consul in Matagalpa termed a "distressful stampede."[11] At Hanna's insistence Moncada canceled the concentration order on June 5, except as it applied to the areas of Nueva Segovia that had already been evacuated. The President then sent his military aide, Captain Marvin Scott, and his Deputy Minister of Foreign Affairs, Anastasio Somoza, to investigate conditions in the affected areas. On their recommendation the concentration program was definitely abandoned, and most of the refugees from Nueva Segovia were allowed to return to their homes in July. Ortez's relatives were not released from confinement in León until September.

Shortly after the concentration program was announced, in mid-May, Sandino crossed into Nicaragua from Honduras, reportedly accompanied by two renegade Marines who were expert machine gunners.[12] Traveling incognito, Sandino made the trip from Mexico with three companions and a pair of dismantled submachine guns, which had been disguised as carpenter's tools to deceive Central American customs inspectors. On May 24 Sandino ordered Pedrón to meet him on El Chipote mountain, "at the same place where our headquarters were," so that they could "formulate new plans for the army."[13] Pedrón sold Sandino on his plan to attack Jinotega, and early in June the two chieftains moved into the central area where they called up their reserves and began concentrating their forces on Yucapuca mountain in preparation for the attack.

In the northern area Ortez's camp near Tamarindo was attacked by a National Guard patrol under Richard Fagan on June 6. Ortez's men fell back and then launched a furious counterattack, maintaining a "terrific fire at close range" for an hour, after which Fagan "was forced to retire due to shortage of ammunition."[14] Although he inflicted no casualties on his enemy, Ortez considered the Tamarindo engagement a great victory for his forces, and he issued a proclamation to that effect. This displeased Sandino, who ordered Ortez to stop publishing proclamations that gave him an "air of independence" and might lead people to "make fun of our

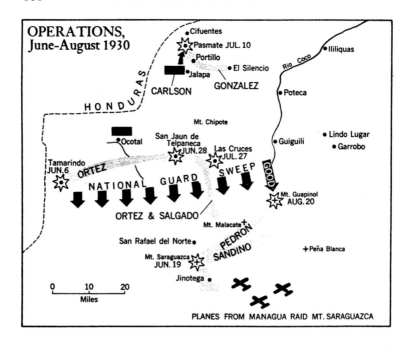

OPERATIONS,
June-August 1930

HONDURAS

• Cifuentes
✵ Pasmate JUL. 10
• Portillo
▮ • Jalapa
• El Silencio
CARLSON   GONZALEZ
Río Coco
• Ililiquas
• Poteca

Mt. Chipote
San Jaun de
Telpaneca
✵ JUN. 28
Las Cruces
✵ JUL. 27
• Guiguili
• Lindo Lugar
• Garrobo

Tamarindo
JUN. 6
✵ ORTEZ   ▮ Ocotal
NATIONAL GUARD SWEEP GOOD
✵ Mt. Guapinol
AUG. 20

ORTEZ & SALGADO
Mt. Malacate +
San Rafael del Norte •   PEDRON
SANDINO
+ Peña Blanca
Mt. Saraguazca ✵
JUN. 19 ✵
Jinotega •

0   10   20
Miles

PLANES FROM MANAGUA RAID MT. SARAGUAZCA

military institutions." [15] By the end of June Ortez acknowledged that he was operating in northern Nicaragua under
the authority of Sandino.[16] After this, Sandino's authority
over all significant guerrilla bands operating in Nicaragua
was unquestioned.

On June 18, 1930, Sandino personally led four hundred
men to El Saraguazca mountain, within striking distance of
Jinotega. The Sandinistas had ten automatic weapons and at
least two hundred good rifles. It was the most formidable
guerrilla force assembled in Nicaragua up to that time. "We
would have captured Jinotega," a Sandinista prisoner later
told his captors, "if it were not for the airplanes." [17] Two
Marine planes headed for Managua spotted the Sandinista
concentration on the morning of June 19 and immediately
attacked. After they had expended all their ammunition, the
planes dropped a warning message to the Jinotega garrison
and flew away to Managua to give the alarm there. While a
strong National Guard force was being assembled at Jinotega

and six Marine planes were being checked out at Managua for an attack on El Saraguazca, a Guard patrol that happened to be in the area made contact with the Sandinistas about noon. Two members of the patrol were wounded, and when the six planes from Managua appeared over El Saraguazca, the aviators could see stretcher-bearers carrying the casualties down the mountainside.

The Sandinistas on El Saraguazca fought off the attacking troops and planes from behind trees and boulders. The guerrillas were well protected and generally invisible to the airmen, who covered the area with bombs and machine-gun fire, hoping to keep the enemy pinned down until the Jinotega column arrived on the scene. But the Jinotega column was late, and when it arrived the planes had no more ammunition. About fifteen minutes after the aircraft flew away the Guardsmen from Jinotega began their attack; but soon, as it began to get dark, contact was broken, and during the night the Sandinistas slipped away toward the north. Casualties were light on both sides. There were two wounded Guardsmen; Sandino admitted to one killed and two wounded— including himself. The guerrilla general was hit in the leg by a piece of shrapnel, and a doctor was brought in from Honduras to treat him in his jungle hideout. Also summoned to Sandino's side from Honduras was Teresa Villatoro. With this kind of attention the general made a complete recovery. Blanca, Sandino's wife, was unable to attend to him in his hour of need because the National Guard was keeping her "relocated" in León.

The Marine airmen who raided El Saraguazca suffered no casualties, but their planes were hit several times by ground fire. Back in Managua a spent bullet was removed from the nose cowling of one of the planes and identified by Lieutenant Vernon E. Megee as a 172-grain dovetail projectile from a .30-'06 cartridge—a new American-made bullet that had not yet been issued to the Marine Corps. Sandino was being supplied—from the United States—with better ammunition than the Marines were receiving. The Marine Corps urged American munitions dealers not to sell war materiel to customers who were likely to ship it to the Sandinistas. In Mexico City Dr. Zepeda denied that Sandino was buying munitions from American firms; the Sandinistas, Zepeda claimed, were resupplied only with arms and ammunition captured on the battlefield. The guerrillas did capture some war materiel, but the amount was insignificant compared to what they purchased—in the United States, Nicaragua, and elsewhere. At least three boatloads of munitions reached Sandino from Mexico. Sandinista agents in Nicaraguan towns actively procured ammunition from members of the National Guard. Guardsmen sometimes deserted with their weapons, which they later sold or donated to the guerrillas. In March 1930 two Guardsmen deserted with a pair of Thompson submachine guns.[18]

With Sandino back in Nicaragua the guerrillas increased their operations. On June 28, 1930, Ortez ambushed a patrol from San Juan de Telpaneca, led by Captain J. P. Schwerin, killing one Guardsman and wounding two others—including the captain. Two days later, as part of a plan to strengthen the National Guard in the northern area, a captain, a lieutenant, and forty Guardsmen were sent to Jalapa to establish a garrison there.[19] Operating in this area was Sandinista General Simón González, "a Honduran day laborer and fugitive from justice," an enemy characterized him, "completely illiterate." [20] Sandino considered González "a simple man, but valiant and sincere." [21] The guerrilla chieftain awarded González the rank of general but later found it necessary to put him under the command of a colonel. The National Guard captain who challenged General González in the Jalapa district was Evans F. Carlson—a lean and intense man, the son of a New England minister.

Simón González was proceeding from El Silencio to the Honduran border on July 9 with about seventy guerrillas; all were traveling on foot except the chief and five others. They marched west from El Silencio until about sundown, then swung north just above Jalapa as they entered the

Camino Real—the main road from Ocotal to the border town of Cifuentes. The moon was full, and the band continued up the Camino Real after dark, looting as they went. One woman along the way warned the guerrillas that she would report them to the National Guard at Jalapa if they stole her clothes. General González "replied that it would do her no good as the Guardia never went out at night." [22]

At 8:30 that evening a native galloped up to Captain Carlson's headquarters with the news that guerrillas were pillaging the village of Portillo, three miles to the north. Although Carlson realized that the reported disturbances might be a ruse to lure some of his troops away from Jalapa prior to a guerrilla attack on his headquarters, the captain decided to divide his forces and himself go after the enemy at Portillo. Carlson had been a military man for eighteen years, and he was eager for his first taste of battle. He requisitioned fresh horses from the townspeople of Jalapa for himself and sixteen enlisted men and, at nine o'clock, set out for Portillo, leaving a lieutenant and eighteen men to defend the Jalapa garrison. When Carlson reached Portillo, González had gone. Acting on information received at Portillo, Carlson resumed his ride to the north in pursuit of the guerrilla column. Along the way the four Guardsmen comprising Carlson's rear guard deserted.

About two o'clock in the morning Carlson caught a glimpse of the enemy column as its rear guard crossed a river just south of Pasmate. He decided to flank the unsuspecting guerrillas, and he ordered his men to dismount and secure their animals in the woods. Then he led his twelve men across the river and through a pasture to the right of the road. "When the patrol reached the north side of the pasture," Carlson wrote in his report, "we had come to within one hundred and fifty yards of the column. . . . Rather than chance the underbrush beyond I decided to let them have it from that point and gave the order to fire." The range was too great for the captain's repeating shotgun, but his men employed their ten rifles and two submachine guns with good effect. Five Sandinistas fell in the first burst of fire; mounted guerrillas then picked up the casualties and galloped away up the trail while their comrades on foot took cover in the underbrush on both sides of the road.

Carlson led his men to the road, formed a skirmish line, and advanced toward the enemy. The guerrillas began firing back from the brush and the Guardsmen started running toward the enemy, firing wildly and shouting "*Viva la Guardia Nacional!*" With some difficulty Carlson restrained his men and ordered them into prone positions from which they began pouring an effective fire into the brush. A few minutes later the guerrilla firing ceased. It began to rain. The enemy had disappeared into the darkness, except for one who was dead and one who was wounded and crying pathetically for "*Mamita . . . Mamita.*" The Guardsmen, who suffered no casualties, searched the area after the action and recovered, among other things, two stolen horses, one white duck coat, one bolt of dress material, one lady's blouse, and one brassiere. The wounded guerrilla was interrogated and, Captain Carlson's report stated, "was later killed while trying to escape."

Elsewhere in the northern area a Guard patrol was ambushed on July 27 at Las Cruces—an action in which a lieutenant was mortally wounded and an enlisted man deserted with a Thompson submachine gun.[23] In mid-August the National Guard launched the first phase of a much discussed offensive against the guerrillas in the northern and central areas. Nine strong combat patrols were lined up from east to west in the northern area and ordered to sweep south into the central area, destroying all guerrillas before them. The most successful of these patrols was the one on the extreme left flank, led by Captain George F. Good, Jr.[24]

Captain Good and his men were hacking their way cross-country, following a compass course through the uncharted jungles of Jinotega, when, on August 20, they arrived at the base of a formidable mountain. The captain decided to hold to his course, so his patrol had to scale the precipitous northwest slope of Mount Guapinol, man-handling mules and cargo. At dusk, as the Guardsmen entered some open pine woods near the summit, they were greeted by the strains of a guitar drifting through the still clear air. "In an area known to be uninhabited by law-abiding citizens this could mean but one thing: a bandit camp." [25]

Leaving his mules behind with a suitable guard, Captain Good led about twenty men to within thirty yards of the camp, which he attempted to envelop. But before the movement could be completed the Guardsmen were discovered and fired upon. Good's men replied immediately with a barrage of rifle grenades and the fire of three automatic weapons and ten rifles. There were some fifteen people in the camp, and one, a man between twenty-five and thirty years of age, was killed immediately. "The other bandits, women, and children fled to the south" as the Guardsmen rushed the camp. After five minutes the patrol ceased firing and from the woods "a woman's voice was heard to cry 'They have killed papa.' This remark is thought to have referred to Pedrón Altamirano." [26] They had not killed Pedrón, but they had sneaked up on him and routed him out of his camp—something no other Marine or National Guard patrol was ever able to do. In the encounter Pedrón lost one man—perhaps a son—six good rifles, a large quantity of food and clothing, and the Altamirano family papers. But the chieftain and his band—the bulk of which had probably been camped nearby—made good their escape in the gathering twilight.

Captain Good's victory over Pedrón was the only important direct result of the sweep from the north, but the operation had other ramifications. The concentration of National Guard troops in Nueva Segovia before the drive into Jinotega had induced Miguel Angel Ortez to leave his native territory and strike far to the south, into the relatively unprotected Department of Matagalpa. There Ortez, Carlos Salgado, and about eighty guerrillas raided coffee plantations and villages during the first two weeks of August, collecting much booty. Then, late in the second week, the guerrillas, all mounted and armed with rifles and two submachine guns,

turned to the north and crossed into Jinotega department.
On August 16 they camped on Malacate mountain and gave
their animals a needed rest. The next day some of the guerrillas made a foray on foot in the direction of Vencedora,
and before noon they ran into a National Guard patrol under
First Lieutenant Avery Graves. The Guardsmen lost one
killed and three wounded in their contact and were unable to
pursue the Sandinistas, who returned to their camp on Malacate. Later that day Marine aircraft spotted the guerrillas'
mounts grazing in a pasture about three miles from their
camp and swooped down on the animals, killing nine of
them.[27]

Meanwhile, a thirty-man National Guard patrol from
Jinotega, led by Captain Lewis B. Puller, was closing in on
Ortez. After a week in the field Puller picked up Ortez's
trail at the Tuma river on August 16 and followed it to
Malacate mountain. Puller made a surprise attack on the
guerrilla camp late in the afternoon of August 19; twelve of
his Guardsmen struck from a flank and the rest charged
straight ahead. The guerrillas did not try to defend their
camp, "but they did make a determined effort to save their
animals which they rode from their camp on a trail leading
northwestward that was almost impassable." [28] Puller pursued
the fleeing guerrillas through a heavy rain until dark; by then
most of the Sandinistas had abandoned their animals and
other loot and dispersed into the jungle. Puller's hard-driving
Guardsmen, who suffered no casualties themselves, found
the bodies of two guerrillas they had killed and captured
fifty-two horses and mules and a large quantity of food and
supplies.

Captain Puller was "a wiry, stocky, deepchested individual of medium height [who] possessed a disarming Virginia
drawl and a reticent manner . . . [but] was hard as nails."
The captain's aptitude for bush warfare had won him command of a permanent roving patrol based at Jinotega, one
that was not liable for garrison duty. This outfit, "M" Company, consisted of Puller, thirty Nicaraguan enlisted men,

and First Lieutenant William A. Lee—"a tall lanky native
of Massachusetts," a Marine sergeant who "was a woodsman
by instinct." [29] "M" Company was armed with six automatic
weapons (Thompson submachine guns and Browning automatic rifles) and twenty-four rifles—four with grenade
launchers.

Lewis Puller thoroughly understood bush warfare. He
realized that mobility was of prime importance, but he refused to use horses: a guerrilla fighter has to stay close to the
ground—he travels fast, but he travels on foot. Horsemen
make splendid targets, and great numbers of horsemen tend
to pile up on twisting jungle trails—they cannot move as
fast as foot soldiers. But Puller did favor the use of a limited
number of sturdy little Nicaraguan mules for packing ammunition and supplies. These pack mules could sustain themselves on the leaves of trees chopped down for them, but
horses required grass—something not always available in the
jungle. Puller had high praise for the Thompson submachine
gun, but he always stressed the importance of accurate fire.
Carelessly aimed automatic fire can sometimes invoke terror
in a poorly trained or unseasoned enemy, but it inflicts few
casualties. Puller's men were constantly alert for signs of ambushes, but they were always eager for combat and on occasion charged into some difficult situations. "M" Company's
training and discipline, together with poor enemy marksmanship, explained the unit's remarkably low casualty figures.
Puller, Lee, and their Nicaraguan sharpshooters accounted
for many more Sandinista casualties. Puller was "hardboiled
and aggressive, but he was unfailing in his devotion to . . . his
men," who worshiped him and dubbed him "The Tiger of
the Mountains." [30]

Not all relations between Nicaraguan Guardsmen and
their American officers were as good as those between Puller
and his men. National Guardsmen mutinied ten times during
the war against Sandino and killed five American officers.[31]
Marines found the Nicaraguans to be a good-natured, warm-
hearted, and sturdy people; native soldiers were capable of

enduring great physical hardship and pain, but they seemed excessively sensitive to criticism, sometimes preferring death to embarrassment. The officer who insulted or humiliated a Guardsman was courting violent death; the attack did not always come immediately, but it usually came suddenly— after a brooding resentment had been transformed into a murderous compulsion. Parris Island training methods were not appropriate in Nicaragua; threats of courts-martial could not move a balky patrol on a lonely jungle trail or subdue a mutinous garrison in an isolated village. The National Guard officer could draw little strength from military institutions; the effectiveness of his leadership—and his life—depended upon the force of his own personality. The successful Guard officer had the qualities of "fearlessness, common sense, a knowledge of human nature, an enduring patience and good humor, and a working fluency in the Spanish tongue." [32] Officers who possessed these qualities won the fierce loyalty of their men and inspired them to extraordinary acts of heroism.

Americans serving with the Nicaraguan National Guard, many of whom were veterans of World War I, had to get away from "the large war idea." They learned that a successful operation was one in which the enemy suffered casualties and they had none. Just one wounded Guardsman could become an incapacitating liability for a combat patrol: if he could not be carried along until the mission was completed, the entire patrol would have to suspend operations and convey the casualty to the nearest garrison. Under Nicaraguan conditions many of the doctrines of warfare were useless. Guardsmen found it impossible to maintain contact with an enemy who would disperse into the jungle after a few minutes of firing and reassemble at a prearranged place hours later. American officers tried to combat the enemy with some of his own techniques—principally the ambush—but they were not always successful. "We were too nervous," a National Guard officer admitted. "One of those fellows could lie in ambush for a week where you couldn't do it for two hours. You'd get to worrying why nobody came along." [33]

American officers shared with Nicaraguan enlisted men the hardships and dangers of life on the trail and, more often than not, formed bonds of comradeship with the native soldiers. Together they trudged through sweltering valleys, endured torrential downpours, forded swirling rivers, inched their way up precipitous mountainsides, and shivered through the nights in rain- or sweat-soaked clothing—lying in hammocks rocked by tropical breezes that could seem as cold as an arctic blast. They ate the same food: rice and black beans, supplemented by whatever fruit and meat they could procure en route. Officers and men shared the same jokes, were bitten alike by mosquitoes, ticks, and fleas. Americans as well as Nicaraguans could succumb to Sandinista bullets, drowning, or malaria; in the jungle the prick of a thorn or the bite of an insect could lead to a crippling infection. Accidents took their toll: Guard Second Lieutenant Donald L. Truesdale lost a hand trying to toss away an activated rifle grenade that had fallen from a grenadier's belt. Truesdale's heroism saved several Nicaraguan lives and won him the Congressional Medal of Honor.[34]

The selfless devotion to duty displayed by the officers and men of the National Guard in the field was not shared by the government in Managua. Almost as soon as he took office, President Moncada began harassing American authorities in Nicaragua with efforts to extend his political control over the "non-partisan" Guard. As long as all the Guard officers were American Marines, some semblance of non-partisanship was maintained. But when the first Nicaraguan officers were commissioned, in 1930, the picture began to change. Candidates for the Marine-administered Military Academy at Managua were chosen by President Moncada each year from a list of names compiled from the recommendations of Guard officers and "influential citizens." In selecting from this list Moncada naturally paid "particular attention to family connections and political affiliations." [35] Candidates thus selected were admitted to the academy as cadets if they passed a

written examination. They were commissioned second lieutenants in the Guard upon completion of nine months of
school and one month of field training. This was a slow
process, and by July 1932 still more than two-thirds of the
Guard officers were Marines. These American officers received their regular Marine Corps pay plus a stipend from
the Nicaraguan government.[36]

The conduct of military operations against the guerrillas
was not the only responsibility of the American officers of
the Nicaraguan National Guard. They also had police duties
and, in the towns and villages of the combat zones, sometimes
had judicial functions as well. In Jalapa Captain Carlson held
court several nights a week, "acting as judge, jury, and
prosecutor" in cases involving local citizens. "Constantly referring to his big English-Spanish dictionary," Carlson
"played Solomon and Dorothy Dix in disputes that ranged
from murder to obstreperous fathers-in-law." The captain
"never punished a man unless he admitted his guilt." [37] In the
cities and larger towns, where civilian courts were available,
Guard officers on police duty encountered many frustrations.
Close cooperation between police and judiciary for the maintenance of law and order was frequently hampered because
of the reluctance of native judges to sentence offenders or
even to arraign suspects brought before them by Guard officers. Captain Carlson, who became chief of police in Managua
after his tour of duty in Jalapa, suspected that "in many
cases this reluctance is due to personal opposition to American intervention, and the determination to impede American
supervision of the Guardia." Some matters not involving
criminal offenses could be handled by American officers without reference to native judges. Captain Carlson discovered
that Nicaraguans

> take all their troubles to the police. The Chief of Police is
> regarded as the arbiter in all controversies, as well as a father-
> confessor. It is not unusual, for example, for a wife whose
> husband forgets his marriage vows and compromises himself
> with other women, to request the Chief of Police to call the

husband before him and to point out the error of his ways. And, curiously enough, the husband usually admits his fault and departs promising to mend his ways, and thanks the Chief of Police for his "mucho consideracion." Patience, a knowledge of psychology and a comprehensive knowledge of the Spanish language are indispensable attributes of a successful police officer in Nicaragua. In probably fifty percent of the complaints which come before police officials it is only necessary to have the patience to hear the case out and to give a word of sympathy in order that the person may depart feeling that the police have rendered him an invaluable service. In common with the rest of humanity the Nicaraguans are human. When they have troubles they yearn for a willing ear in which to pour them—and they find the police. A measure of confidence has been established, and little by little the regard for justice and the authority of the police is strengthened.[38]

Besides providing this counseling service, American officers supervised the registration and treatment of prostitutes and the building of pit-type latrines for townspeople without sanitary facilities, and conducted drives against stray dogs, pigs, and cattle.[39]

The President of Nicaragua was alert to opportunities for exercising his prerogatives as commander-in-chief of the National Guard. In the autumn of 1929, alleging a Sandinista plot, he ordered wholesale arrests of his political opponents. After American officers had supervised the deportation of eight Nicaraguans, including two newspaper editors, the U.S. Department of State warned Moncada against adopting a "general policy of imprisoning those whose political activities seem aimed against his administration." Washington was especially concerned because such a policy "would involve the Guardia Nacional and consequently the American Marine officers who are detailed to duty with that organization."[40] Little more than a year later the State Department had occasion to protest Moncada's use of the Guard in the "arrest and deportation, apparently for political reasons, of members of the Conservative Party." [41] In these instances Moncada could only bow to the will of Washington; he realized that it would be useless for him to order American Guard officers to carry out policies contrary to those of their government. This led him to renew his agitation for the creation of an armed force independent of the National Guard. Moncada was dependent on the Marine-led Guard for protection against Sandino, but he needed a more willing instrument to cow the less violent enemies of his regime.

Washington consistently vetoed Moncada's proposals for a national army, but the United States did approve the enlistment of a force of "auxiliaries" late in 1930. These auxiliaries, however, came under the control of the National Guard. They included short-term enlistees, unpaid civilian militia who were to report to local guard garrisons in time of emergency, and municipal police in cities and towns that agreed to support such a force. The enlistment of auxiliaries was one of the effects of the world depression that began to be felt in Nicaragua in 1930. The regular National Guard had reached a total strength of 2,256 by October 1930, but financial difficulties forced a reduction to 160 officers and 1,650 enlisted men by the end of the year. The auxiliaries partly compensated for this reduction in force. In another economy move, the pay scale for the National Guard was adjusted downward in 1930, but most officers were promoted before the cut went into effect and their salaries remained much the same. [42]

As the Nicaraguan economy deteriorated in 1930, guerrilla activity continued unabated. Matthew Hanna, the American Minister in Managua, warned the Department of State in October that "banditry cannot be eliminated and order restored by present means and methods." [43] He urged that the United States financially support an expanded road-building program in Nicaragua. The project would not only aid military operations against the guerrillas but would also help check the growing unemployment that was providing fertile ground for Sandinista agitation. Secretary of State Stimson admitted that the guerrilla situation had not improved since his visit to Nicaragua three years before and agreed that the country could not be pacified by military action alone. He liked the road-building program but realized that his government had enough economic problems to solve at home and would not appropriate money for the Nicaraguan project. Without American aid the Nicaraguan government was able to sustain a modest road-building program during the next year, although it had to close all public schools in the republic.[44]

Offensive operations against the guerrillas were curtailed during the autumn of 1930 so that enough Guardsmen would be available for election duty. Captain Alfred W. Johnson of the U.S. Navy was appointed by President Hoover to head the American electoral mission to Nicaragua that year. The United States reluctantly agreed to supervise these congressional elections after the Nicaraguan Conservative party announced it would make no nominations for Congress otherwise. In addition to the National Guard, Captain Johnson had help from about six hundred American military personnel who were assigned to his electoral mission. Voters were registered late in September, and the balloting was held on November 2. The total vote cast was about 72 percent of that cast in the presidential election of 1928. The Liberals gained seats in both houses of Congress.[45]

After the elections the National Guard launched a major offensive along the Honduran border. In this operation the Guard had the support of the Church hierarchy, which urged the Sandinistas to abandon "the useless armed struggle" in the mountains and "return to the life of home and of labor, and to the fulfillment of their religious duties, in order that the peace of Christ may cause Christian customs to flourish in our north."[46] The offensive was designed to clear the Sandinistas out of the area adjoining the Honduran border and cut the enemy's main supply routes into Honduras. The

Honduran towns of Choluteca and Danlí were important collection points for Sandinista munitions and supplies, and the
local citizens did a profitable business exchanging war materiel for the cattle, gold, and other "confiscated" goods
brought in by the Sandinistas. Shipments of munitions into
these towns came up the several rivers and trails on the Honduran side of the border from the Gulf of Fonseca on the
Pacific. Other war materiel was disembarked on the Caribbean coast and shipped up Honduran rivers to be distributed
to the Sandinistas at points as far west as Bocay. Although
the government of Honduras cooperated with the United
States in some matters—such as arresting Marine deserters in
Honduras and turning them over to American authorities—
Marine officers in Nicaragua felt that Honduran authorities
were both unable and unwilling to halt the arms traffic.[47]

The National Guard operations along the border were
doomed to failure. By early 1931 it was evident that the closing of a few main trails did not cut off Sandino's supplies.
This could be done only by a continuous occupation of the
whole five-hundred-mile border—impossible for the National
Guard, even after its strength was raised to 2,350 officers and
men in January 1931. Neither could the massed forces of the
Guard win any important victory over Sandinista troops in
the north, because

> due to the character of the terrain a large force could not
> live in the bandit country without carrying supplies and
> hence was limited to the main trails and was out of commu-
> nication with its base. The bandits could not be compelled
> to fight for any terrain feature or other objective. . . . Large
> bodies of troops had not the mobility necessary to overtake
> bandit groups and force them to decisive action.[48]

While his colleagues eluded the National Guard in the
north, Pedrón was active in the south. He combined his band
with that of Ismael Peralta and marched into western Matagalpa department early in November. With a force of more
than a hundred men, the guerrillas fell upon the ten-man Na-

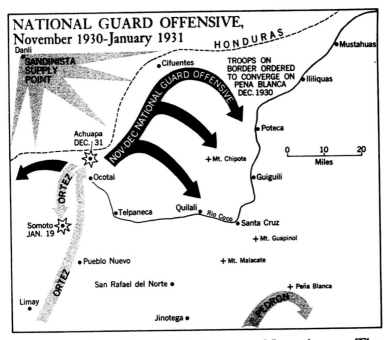

NATIONAL GUARD OFFENSIVE,
November 1930-January 1931

tional Guard garrison at Matiguas on November 5. The Nicaraguan sergeant in charge of the Guardsmen ordered a retreat after an hour and a half of fighting, and the town was abandoned to the guerrillas. The Sandinistas robbed all the stores in Matiguas and burned the National Guard barracks to the ground before withdrawing to the north. The town was reoccupied by Guardsmen from Matagalpa City on November 6, and the next day a patrol of two officers and fifteen men departed Matiguas in pursuit of the guerrillas. The patrol spotted the guerrillas near Apante, on the Tuma River. In a remarkably inept maneuver, the Guardsmen got themselves pinned down for three hours in an exchange of fire with the guerrillas across the river. The Guard commander was mortally wounded, and under cover of darkness his patrol broke contact and withdrew to the south while Pedrón and Peralta resumed their march to the north.[49]

The National Guard guessed Pedrón was heading for the mountains of central Jinotega. In December 1930 Guard forces operating along the Honduran border were ordered to converge on the area around Peña Blanca, where Pedrón was believed to be hiding out. But Pedrón eluded the dragnet, and while the Guardsmen struggled through the jungles of Jinotega he began raiding the coffee plantations around Matagalpa City. The Guard offensive also tended to drive guerrillas to the south in western Nicaragua. On November 19 Sandinistas struck as far south as Telica, in the Department of León, killing one Guardsman and wounding another.[50] This could have been the work of Miguel Angel Ortez, who was known to have been in northwestern Estelí a few days before.

In mid-November 1930 Juan Midence, a butcher from Pueblo Nuevo, was on a cattle-buying trip in the mountains between his town and San Juan de Limay. Late one afternoon, as he approached the house of one Señor Acevedo, the butcher was taken prisoner ·by guerrillas. His captors relieved Midence of his cigarettes and $5 and then took him to their leader, who was visiting Señor Acevedo. "He was taken to the house and within was Miguel Angel himself." The young general was "perfumed and powdered and rather well groomed"; he "was dressed in puttees, black trousers, khaki shirt and broad brimmed hat rolled at the sides." [51] The general questioned the butcher about his family and about the garrison in Pueblo Nuevo. Ortez seemed satisfied with Midence's answers, and he invited him to have supper with him and stay overnight as his guest in Acevedo's house. The butcher accepted, and about this time a man walked in whom Ortez addressed as "colonel" and told "to make the usual disposition for the night."

After supper Ortez took from his pocket some papers that he said were reports from Generals Carlos Salgado, José León Díaz, and two colonels, and "then discoursed at some length on the situation." The outlook was "very good," Ortez declared; soon all Nicaragua would rise up in arms and expel the Yankees from the country and Moncada from the presidency. Sandino was at that moment in Mexico and would soon return with fifty machine guns, five thousand rifles, and twenty cannons. The Mexican government was already giving the guerrillas $5,000 a month, Ortez claimed, and they were getting funds from other sources which the general did not specify. Ortez flourished his automatic pistol before his guest and "said that he took it from a Yankee in some battle." When the time came to retire, the general "took off his pistol, laid it on the table and went to sleep on a bench." Ortez got up early the next morning and forced Señor Acevedo, the owner of the house, to furnish him a horse and act as his guide. Ortez formed his troops—forty men and a thirteen-year-old boy, none of whom were mounted—and they marched away at six o'clock with the fair-haired chieftain riding in the center of the column. Juan Midence watched them depart, noting that all the men seemed to carry rifles and that the boy was armed with a revolver. He did not notice any machine guns.

On New Year's Eve, 1930, Ortez struck a blow that had far-reaching consequences. While National Guard troops stormed through the countryside on their ill-conceived offensive, Marine units manned garrisons in the cities and larger towns and performed other supporting functions—one of which was the maintenance of telephone lines. On December 31 a heavily armed mounted patrol of ten Marines left Ocotal to repair the telephone line to San Fernando. Ortez ambushed the Marines that day near Achuapa, killing all but two who managed to escape with their lives, although both were wounded. In this engagement the guerrillas captured two Browning automatic rifles, one Thompson submachine gun, three Springfield rifles, and eight fully equipped mules. Ortez then swung to the west and on January 19, 1931, bottled up the Guardsmen at Somoto in their barracks and looted the town.[52]

The deaths of the eight Marines at Achuapa caused consternation in Washington. The chairman of the Senate Foreign Relations Committee, William E. Borah—who had straddled the intervention issue for four years—on January 2 came out strongly for the speedy withdrawal of all American

forces from Nicaragua. From Mexico José Constantino González, who had represented Sandino at the Frankfurt Anti-
Imperialist Congress, wired Borah promising that the guerrilla chieftain would lay down his arms as soon as all Marines
had left Nicaragua—thus attempting to fix the blame for any
further bloodshed upon the United States.[53] Henry L. Stimson would not be intimidated, but the Secretary of State realized that something had to be done. Minister Hanna, Brigadier General Williams of the Marine brigade, and Major
General McDougal of the National Guard were all summoned to Washington from Nicaragua to confer with Stimson early in February 1931.

During the week of February 5, 1931, Hanna, Williams,
and McDougal met several times with Stimson and Brigadier
General McCoy. The five men agreed to the withdrawal
from Nicaragua by June 1, 1931, of all Marine units except
"an instruction battalion in the city of Managua and the
aviation force"; all Marines serving with the National Guard
would leave after the 1932 Nicaraguan elections.[54] While this
decision was being made, the Marine Corps Commandant,
Major General Ben H. Fuller, testified before the House Appropriations Committee against such a withdrawal:

> It would not do to take all the Marines away, leaving
> American officers in charge of those Indians, because they
> would be very likely to mutiny and chase the American offi-
> cers out. Also, it takes a good while to make a good soldier
> out of anybody, and it takes much longer to make one out
> of a Nicaraguan.[55]

Secretary Stimson surprised General Fuller and the Navy
Department on February 13 by announcing a plan for the
immediate withdrawal of one thousand of the fifteen hundred
Marines in Nicaragua, with the rest to be recalled after the
1932 elections. A few days before the announcement, Major
Douglas C. McDougal was relieved of the command of the
Nicaraguan National Guard.[56]

President Hoover and Secretary Stimson were determined

to extricate the United States from the Nicaraguan mess as soon as possible without permitting the collapse of the Managua government. They realized that an American military victory in Nicaragua was impossible without a large-scale commitment of American forces. Such a victory would hardly be worth its price in American lives, in damage to the already shaken American economy, in further perturbation of the tumultuous domestic political scene, and in detriment to the American image abroad—waging a full-sized war against bands of Nicaraguan guerrillas would seem unworthy of a great power and a great democracy. Hoover and Stimson were firmly opposed to escalation of the Nicaraguan conflict, and they refused to be panicked by the massacre of the Marines at Achuapa. The Hoover administration hoped to cool off the Nicaraguan crisis by de-escalation—by a staged withdrawal of the American forces whose presence in Nicaragua had inflamed the passions of the natives. This policy was to be put to some severe tests in the coming months.

9

Guerrilla Offensives

☞

Henry L. Stimson's announcement that the number of Marines in Nicaragua would be drastically reduced early in 1931 did not satisfy Sandino's demand for the immediate withdrawal of all American forces from his homeland. At his headquarters, somewhere in the Segovia mountains, the guerrilla generalissimo began making plans for a large-scale assault on American property in Nicaragua. His attention had been attracted to the Mosquito Coast, where export industries were being hard hit by the world depression and there was much unrest. Around Bluefields an association of banana planters was withholding produce from market in an attempt to raise prices and was using force against small farmers who tried to sell their bananas to American shippers. Late in January hungry crowds had sacked a Chinese store and two United Fruit Company commissaries in the area. Further up the coast, around Puerto Cabezas, the Standard Fruit Company was considering closing down its banana plantations because of low prices and a plant disease. The Standard-owned Bragman's Bluff Lumber Company in the same area did close in March, throwing several hundred natives out of work. Further inland, in the Pis Pis region, the American-owned gold mines were "almost at a standstill." [1] Before the end of March Sandino had ordered attacks on American property around Puerto Cabezas and in the mining district.[2]

The inhabitants of the region from the mines to the coast

were of varied racial and cultural stock. Chinese, Syrians, and European Jews engaged in retail trade in the mining camps and along the rivers, while other foreigners—principally Americans and Canadians—held supervisory positions with the mining and fruit companies. A minority of Spanish-speaking *ladinos*—of mixed Spanish-Indian blood, mostly recent immigrants from western Nicaragua—held most government positions in the coastal towns and were employed as foremen at the mines, lumber camps, and banana plantations. Much of the manual labor on the banana plantations was done by English- and French-speaking Negroes imported from the West Indies for this work since the turn of the century. Much earlier, in the eighteenth century, Negroes had been brought to the Mosquito Coast as slaves by English settlers. In later years these Negroes mixed with the native Mosquito Indians. If a descendant of Indians and Negroes was black and spoke English, he was called a Creole; if he was brown and preferred the indigenous tongue, he was an Indian. Most of the Indians—few of whom were pure blood—also spoke some English and felt a keen nostalgia for the days of the Mosquito Kingdom when they ruled the coast under the protection of the British Empire. The Indians got along well with their Creole kinsmen but lived "in a state of strained mutual tolerance" with the Spanish-speaking *ladinos*.[3]

An anthropologist who studied the Mosquito Coast in 1931 characterized the typical Indian as "very frank and outspoken, silent, phlegmatic, honest, and reliable, but also somewhat revengeful and ungrateful and inclined to drunkenness." He also discovered that "all these Indians are somewhat inclined to laziness and are fond of passing whole days in their hammocks."[4] What work they did consisted mainly of collecting and selling crocodile skins and the sap from wild rubber trees. Otherwise, they sustained themselves on the abundant game of the great rain forest that extended westward from the savanna country bordering the seashore. One enlightening influence in the lives of these people was provided by the Moravian Church, which had been sending

English, German, and Swiss missionaries to the Mosquito Coast for a hundred years. The Moravians brought to remote Indian communities the "glimmerings of hygiene, nutrition sense and practical agriculture, effective medical care and training in home economics, carpentry and rural ethics." Although most of the Indians of eastern Nicaragua were intensely loyal to the Moravian Church, they seldom adhered to the standards of Christian living preached by the missionaries. Each year—for about a month, beginning in early April—the Indians held erotic dances around certain big trees, to the accompaniment of drums and guitars. These affairs were called "Maypole" by the Anglophile Indians, and the way they sustained the birth rate would have gratified the pagan originators of the Maypole festival in ancient Britain. During the rest of the year the Mosquito Indians liked to congregate after dark in front of their community stores to drink native rum "and sing Moravian hymns and raise a terrific uproar." [5]

General Sandino had two able collaborators who were well acquainted with the Mosquito Indians. One was Abraham Rivera, a chubby, middle-aged mulatto who spoke both English and Spanish. During the early years of Sandino's revolt, Rivera, a Bluefields tradesman, had been jailed on suspicion of revolutionary activity; upon his release he had gone to the mountains and become a close friend and confidant of the guerrilla leader and a colonel in his army. Early in 1931 Sandino sent Rivera down the Coco River to Bocay, the gateway to the Mosquito territory. By the end of February the National Guard was receiving reports on Rivera's activities around Bocay. On March 2 Marine intelligence concluded that Rivera's efforts to win the support of the indigenous population had "met with considerable success." Exactly what the mulatto colonel had done "to gain the confidence of the Bocay Indians is not known, but their feelings and sympathy have been clearly brought over to the side of the bandits." [6]

Further down the Coco River, around Sacklin, another Sandinista officer exerted a powerful influence over the na-

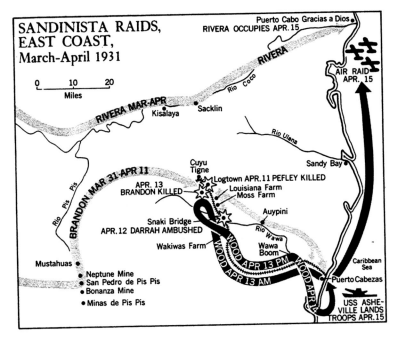

SANDINISTA RAIDS,
EAST COAST,
March–April 1931

0   10   20
Miles

Puerto Cabo Gracias a Dios
RIVERA OCCUPIES APR. 15

RIVERA

AIR RAID
APR. 15

Rio Coco

RIVERA MAR–APR
Kisalaya   Sacklin

Rio Ulana

Cuyu Tigne   Sandy Bay

BRANDON MAR 31–APR 11
APR. 13 BRANDON KILLED
Logtown APR. 11 PEFLEY KILLED
Louisiana Farm
Moss Farm

Rio Pis Pis

Auypini

Snaki Bridge
APR. 12 DARRAH AMBUSHED
Rio Wawa

Wakiwas Farm
Wawa Boom

WOOD APR 13 PM

WOOD APR 13 AM

WOOD APR 1

Caribbean Sea

Mustahuas
Neptune Mine
San Pedro de Pis Pis
Bonanza Mine
Minas de Pis Pis

Puerto Cabezas

USS ASHE-
VILLE LANDS
TROOPS APR. 15

tives. Unknown to the Marines and Guardsmen in early 1931, Adolfo Cockburn, a landowner and Liberal member of the Nicaraguan Congress, had been secretly commissioned a Sandinista general during the previous year. Cockburn had been born on Grand Cayman Island, the son of an English father and a Mosquito Indian mother. His wife was also a Mosquito woman, and he was fluent in the Indian language as well as in English and Spanish. A man of great stature, weighing some 240 pounds, Cockburn was in effect the chief of the Indians of the lower Coco River valley. They all greeted him with *"Naxan madam"*—"Good day, our father."[7] In the spring of 1931 Cockburn figured in Colonel Rivera's plans to seize Cabo Gracias a Dios, at the mouth of the Coco River. But the main Sandinista effort on the Mosquito Coast was to be made further to the south, against the Standard Fruit Company holdings west of Puerto Cabezas. This drive was to be led by General Pedro Blandón.

Pedro Blandón had worked in the mahogany lumber

camps in the lower Coco River valley before becoming a
Sandinista general in the Segovia mountains. He was a
squarely built white man in his early thirties, whose wide
dark mustache made him appear older. Handsome and rather
distinguished looking, this guerrilla chief was blind in one
eye and usually wore dark glasses.[8] On his way to the coast
from the mountains of Jinotega, Blandón fell upon San Pedro
de Pis Pis late in March and blew up the machinery of the
American-owned Neptune mine. He left San Pedro on March
30 and proceeded down the Pis Pis River, arriving at Musahuas the next day. At Musahuas the guerrillas encountered
the Reverend Otto Brezenger, a Moravian missionary and
German citizen. Blandón mistook the German for an American and charged him with being a Yankee spy and a "miserable deceiver" and oppressor of the Indians. Blandón's henchmen carried out his order that the missionary's "head be separated from his body." [9] The day Blandón left the Pis Pis district on his bloody march to the sea, Sandino ordered Pedrón
to follow in his wake.[10] The next day a natural holocaust
struck the city of Managua.

Willard Beaulac was in charge of the American legation
in Managua while Minister Hanna and his wife spent the
1931 Easter holidays in Guatemala. On March 31 the earth
moved laterally a few inches in a series of convulsions lasting eight seconds. Beaulac was standing on the legation porch
when the tremors started, and he watched the walls of the
building buckle outward as masonry, cement balustrades,
columns, portions of the roof, and the entire west wing of
the structure crashed to the ground. The scene on the street
in front of the legation was one of "desolation and terror." In
both directions the road was littered with the debris of fallen
buildings. Nothing seemed to be intact. "People in the street
were screaming or appeared to be numbed by shock," Beaulac noted. "A horse ran by, stiff-legged with terror." [11] Fire
broke out, and only a few minutes after the earthquake flames
were mounting to the sky.

The earthquake and fire destroyed more than thirty

blocks in Managua and left only about a dozen buildings intact. In the rest of the country the tremors were hardly felt. Many of the 35,000 residents of Managua had gone to the mountains or the seashore for the Holy Week and thus escaped personal injury. Of those who remained, 1,450 Nicaraguans and four Americans lost their lives in the destruction. Most Nicaraguan government officials were absent from the city, but Anastasio Somoza, the Deputy Minister of Foreign Affairs, was on hand and won the praise of Chargé Beaulac for his conduct during the disaster. Nicaraguan civilians led by Somoza joined National Guardsmen and American military personnel in fighting the fire, clearing the wreckage, policing the ruins, providing food and shelter for the homeless, burying and cremating the dead, and treating the wounded. Medical supplies flown in from American naval bases in Cuba and the Canal Zone began arriving in Managua the day after the earthquake, in time to prevent serious epidemics of smallpox and typhoid. Other valuable services were rendered by Major Dan I. Sultan and a company of U.S. Army Engineers who had been surveying the proposed Nicaraguan canal near Granada when the quake struck. Sultan arrived in Managua only hours later with a trainload of demolitions and other needed materials and took command of the fire-fighting effort. One of Sultan's subordinates, Lieutenant Leslie R. Groves, stopped the landslides at the Managua reservoir and put the city water pumps back into operation "after several days of arduous and dangerous work."[12]

The devastation of Managua, Sandino announced to his guerrillas in April, "clearly demonstrates to the doubters that divine gestures are guiding our actions in Nicaragua." The general told his troops not to "tremble before these things of divine origin, precisely for the reason that our army itself has sprung from this same invisible impulse."[13] While Sandino pondered the meaning of the Managua earthquake, his troops were busy spreading death and destruction on the Mosquito Coast.

Early in April Pedro Blandón and some one hundred guerrillas descended upon the Bragman's Bluff Lumber Company compound at Logtown. They looted the company store and then burned it to the ground with all other buildings there except the homes of some workers. Part of the stolen merchandise was distributed among the natives, many of whom were destitute, having been laid off their jobs the preceding month. From Logtown Blandón's forces—augmented by local recruits—raided the banana country along the Standard Fruit Company railroad to Puerto Cabezas.[14] Eight American employees of the company were captured and beheaded, as were two British subjects mistaken for Yankees. At Louisiana Farm the guerrillas captured the overseer, a Canadian named Austin Murphy who had once worked with Blandón in the mahogany camps. The guerrilla general ordered his old friend released immediately and provided him with a safe conduct pass. Blandón was proud of his sword and he showed it to Murphy; it had rodeo and hunting scenes engraved on the blade.

Meanwhile, word of the trouble at Logtown reached Puerto Cabezas, sixty miles away by rail. Underestimating the strength of the guerrillas, National Guard Captain Harlan Pefley left Puerto Cabezas early on the morning of April 11 with a squad of Guardsmen and an American civilian traveling on a railroad motor car. The patrol dismounted just short of Logtown and was ambushed as it approached the town on foot. The two Americans were wounded, and the Nicaraguan Guardsmen loaded them onto the motor car and beat a hasty retreat to Puerto Cabezas; Captain Pefley died on the return trip. With the captain dead, Lieutenant Clyde Darrah took command of the Puerto Cabezas garrison and radioed Managua for help. The American *chargé d'affaires*, Willard Beaulac, seized the initiative and radioed the Canal Zone, ordering an American warship to Puerto Cabezas. The admiral commanding the Special Service Squadron questioned the propriety of the order, but he complied. Major General Calvin B. Matthews, the new Chief Director of the National Guard, protested that he and not Beaulac was responsible for the protection of lives and property in Nicaragua and that any action to meet this responsibility should be taken by him. The chargé replied that he was the representative of the United States government in Nicaragua and could not delegate the protection of American interests to anyone. "If the Guard was not able to protect them," Beaulac informed Matthews, "then I had to find other means of doing so." [15]

The closest National Guard garrison to Puerto Cabezas was at Bluefields, where there were few troops to spare. On the afternoon of April 11 Lieutenant Darrah was promised two Loening amphibian aircraft from Managua the next day and was told that the *USS Asheville* would arrive with a naval landing force from the Canal Zone within twenty hours. Rather than allow the guerrillas to continue their destruction of American lives and property in the meantime, Darrah decided to strike before the reinforcements arrived. He left nine Guardsmen and thirty armed civilian auxiliaries in charge of the garrison, loaded thirty Guardsmen, a Canadian guide, and two other armed civilians aboard a special train, and rolled out of Puerto Cabezas late in the afternoon. The men arrived at Logtown before dark and found nothing but destruction. They continued on to the end of the line, near Cuyu Tigni, where they spent the night.

The next morning, April 12, Lieutenant Darrah and his men boarded the train and started back toward Puerto Cabezas. Just north of the Snaki bridge, a 480-foot steel structure spanning the Wawa River, Darrah's train was ambushed. The engineer was killed and the boiler punctured; the track on the bridge had been torn up, and the guerrillas held a commanding position on a hill overlooking the bridge. The promised planes from Managua appeared shortly after the train was halted and attacked the guerrillas intrenched on the hill but did not dislodge them. The Guardsmen were cut off from Puerto Cabezas, fifty-five miles down the railroad, leaving the town practically defenseless. While Sandinistas held the Guardsmen at Snaki bridge, other guerrillas from

Blandón's band were marching toward Puerto Cabezas on the Auypini trail. When the planes landed at Puerto Cabezas with news of Lieutenant Darrah's predicament, terror gripped the port town, and local residents frantically sought refuge on the boats in the harbor.

Late in the afternoon Lieutenant Darrah forced a crossing of the Snaki bridge, during which one of his men was seriously wounded. The damaged locomotive was left north of the bridge and the Guardsmen proceeded on foot to Wakiwas Farm, where they established telephone communications with Puerto Cabezas. By this time Captain John C. Wood, a Guard lieutenant, two medical officers, and four enlisted men had arrived at Puerto Cabezas from Bluefields on a chartered schooner. After restoring a semblance of order in the frightened town, the captain, the four enlisted men, and a medical officer set out for Wakiwas Farm where Darrah was spending the night.

At three o'clock on the morning of April 13 a locomotive pulling a tender, a flatcar, and a banana car rolled out of Puerto Cabezas, preceded at three hundred yards by a railroad motor car. The flatcar was fortified with a row of sandbags around the platform. The two officers aboard the train were armed with pistols and the four enlisted men with rifles. The engineer was ordered to run the locomotive at top speed and not to blow the whistle or ring the bell. The operator of the motor car was to signal the locomotive upon sighting guerrillas, torn up rails, or any other obstruction in the track ahead. After making two water stops the train reached Wakiwas Farm shortly after six o'clock, and Captain Wood took command of the Guardsmen there. From Wakiwas, Wood telephoned Puerto Cabezas for air support; then he and his forty-two men climbed aboard the train and headed toward Logtown in search of the enemy. The train stopped at Snaki bridge about ten o'clock, and Captain Wood's patrol crossed it on foot without drawing enemy fire. A section of track was missing from the steel bridge, and a few hundred yards ahead smoke could be seen rising from a burning wooden trestle. The patrol continued up the track on foot and forded the stream below the burning trestle as two Marine airplanes reconnoitered the area ahead. At 12:35 the patrol entered Logtown.

Guerrillas opened fire from the nearby woods and from the stilted workers' shacks at Logtown. Captain Wood quickly deployed his two machine guns to riddle the huts from below, formed his riflemen into a skirmish line, and advanced into the elevated shanty town. The Guardsmen were eager for combat, and Wood had difficulty keeping them from overrunning the firing line. Until this time Puerto Cabezas Guardsmen had not reacted aggressively under fire, and the guerrillas had little reason to expect such a spirited attack. Blandón's men fell back in disorder as the patrol swept through the town. Ralph Beardsley, Lieutenant Darrah's Canadian guide, spotted a well-dressed guerrilla making for cover under a shack and shot him at close range with his rifle. "The bandit staggered a few steps, was hit again, and fell to his hands and knees when a dozen Guardia saw him and opened fire." [16] It was Pedro Blandón; he died about an hour later. In the meantime, the surviving Sandinistas fled into the woods where they were bombed and strafed by the planes and pursued by Wood's patrol until they had completely dispersed. After the battle the bodies of eighteen guerrillas were counted in and around Logtown; one Guardsman was slightly wounded.

Although they had killed the top guerrilla leader in the area, Wood's men had not ended the threat to Puerto Cabezas. The force defeated at Logtown had numbered no more than seventy men, armed only with about forty-five pistols and rifles—some of which were muzzle-loaders. Upon returning to Wakiwas Farm, about sundown, Captain Wood was informed by telephone that a larger and better-armed guerrilla force was on the outskirts of Puerto Cabezas; he was urged to hurry back to town. Wood loaded his troops on the train and continued down the track until the operator of a motor car coming from the direction of Puerto Cabezas informed him that a strong force of guerrillas was blockading the track eight miles out of town. Rather than risk an ambush in the dark, Wood decided to camp for the night at Wawa Boom, some fifteen miles by rail from the port. The guerrillas had not cut the telephone line, and Wood was able to communicate with Puerto Cabezas from Wawa Boom. Wood—and any English-speaking guerrillas who might have been listening—learned that the USS Asheville had steamed into Puerto Cabezas, but, astonishingly, the ship's captain refused to land troops. The rumor spread through town that there were so many Sandinistas in the area that the Marines aboard the Asheville were afraid to go ashore. Once again panic-stricken residents of Puerto Cabezas crowded onto the boats in the harbor.

On the morning of April 14 a Marine plane dropped a message at Wawa Boom, informing Captain Wood that Puerto Cabezas was surrounded by guerrillas and that a trestle about a mile down the track from the guard position was on fire. Wood decided to relieve the town by sea. At nine o'clock he loaded his troops aboard an old electric-powered banana launch that Ralph Beardsley made operational with telephone batteries and shoved off from Wawa Boom down the Wawa River toward the sea. They crossed the Wawa bar with difficulty and headed north along the coast, arriving at Puerto Cabezas a few minutes after noon. The next morning, April 15, a naval force was finally landed from the USS Asheville, and Captain Wood led a National Guard combat patrol out of Puerto Cabezas in search of the enemy. But the guerrillas who had terrorized the port for four days had left the area. Later in the day Marine planes reported that Sandinistas were occupying Cabo Gracias a Dios, seventy miles up the coast.

The guerrilla drive against Cabo Gracias a Dios was led by Abraham Rivera. The mulatto colonel and some forty guerrillas, armed with about ten old rifles and a few pistols, came down the Coco River from Bocay in small boats paddled by some forty-five Indians. The National Guard post at Kisalaya, manned by a handful of Mosquito Indians, offered no resistance. The guerrillas took the garrison's typewriter, and Rivera presented it to Adolfo Cockburn at his hacienda near Sacklin. From Sacklin, Rivera's fleet paddled downstream to Cabo Gracias a Dios, arriving before dawn on April 15. The coastal town was completely without defenses, a temporary garrison of one officer and ten Guardsmen having been withdrawn some weeks before.[17]

Rivera occupied Cabo Gracias a Dios at about five o'clock in the morning without firing a shot. His men seized the customs warehouse and hauled away everything of value—principally $500 worth of shoes and $50 worth of medicine. The customs collector—Lisandro Salazar, an old acquaintance of Colonel Rivera—explained that bad economic conditions were responsible for a drop in imports; there were only a few dollars in the customs safe. After the mulatto colonel left the customs office, a *ladino* officer entered, "armed with every weapon invented up to date," and asked the customs collector if he would "voluntarily" write a kind thought about General Sandino in the officer's notebook. Salazar later recalled that he wrote "about fifty expressions," to which he affixed the official stamp of the Nicaraguan Customs Service.[18]

All the stores in Cabo Gracias a Dios were ransacked for food, medicine, clothing, and American dollars. Nicaraguan money was refused by the guerrillas, who said they wanted only hard currency to buy arms and ammunition abroad. No one was killed, despite the fact that some American citizens resided in the town. The American manager of Standard Fruit's Tropical Radio Station at Cabo Gracias was spending the night aboard his yacht in the harbor when the guerrillas seized the town; he was able to slip away without injury. Another well-known American in town was Albert Fagot, a merchant, whose "head was not cut off because Mr. Rivera . . . was employed by Mr. Fagot for about twenty-five or thirty years and was the recipient of many favors from him." [19] Fagot and other storekeepers were robbed of some

$12,000 in cash and merchandise, and $1,000 damage was done to the Tropical Radio Station.

The looting ended at about 3:30 in the afternoon of April 15, when the guerrillas heard the sound of airplanes approaching Cabo Gracias a Dios. The Sandinistas ripped their black and red insignias from their shirts and hats and ran into and under the houses. Without warning the American planes dropped fourteen bombs on the town—but did serious damage to only one store. "The bombardment would have taken serious proportions with great losses," the customs collector reported, "if it had not been for the fearlessness of Mr. Hugo Fagot in raising the American flag on his father's house." [20] When it was dark and the planes had gone, Colonel Rivera and his men boarded their vessels and paddled up the Coco River toward Sacklin.

The Standard Fruit Company bore the brunt of the Sandinista raids. From April 11 to 15 its radio station was put out of commission; its lumber camp was burned to the ground; commissaries and other buildings on its banana plantations were looted and burned; its railroad track was torn up, its trestles burned, and its locomotives damaged; and more than a dozen Standard employees were killed, including eight American citizens. For four days the National Guard had been powerless to halt the guerrilla rampage. Standard begged Washington for more protection, but Secretary of State Stimson was not receptive; he considered American businessmen on the Mosquito Coast "a pampered lot of people" who thought they had "a right to call for troops whenever any danger apprehends." [21] Nevertheless, the day Stimson wrote these words in his diary, April 15, he authorized the landing of troops from the USS Asheville at Puerto Cabezas. With naval forces holding the port, Stimson hoped the National Guard would be able to overtake and destroy the guerrillas on the outskirts of the town. The next day, April 16, when he learned that the Sandinistas had escaped, Stimson thought he had rather strong evidence that the Marine work with the National Guard had been a failure. [22] The same day he wired the American legation in Nicaragua that the United States government

> cannot undertake general protection of Americans throughout that country with American forces. To do so would lead to difficulties and commitments which this Government does not propose to undertake. Therefore, the Department recommends to all Americans who do not feel secure under the protection afforded them by the Nicaraguan Government . . . to withdraw from the country, or at least to the coast towns whence they can be protected or evacuated in case of necessity.[23]

This was a radical departure from the traditional American policy of protecting the lives and property of citizens abroad. Announcement of the policy change was delayed, probably to allow the administration to prepare for the reaction of the American people—some of whom were already loudly demanding massive military operations against the bandits who dared to molest American citizens. The State Department condemned the outrages but on April 17 implied that American armed forces would have a difficult time combating irregulars who rejected "open warfare" and employed "the stealthy and ruthless tactics which characterized the savages who fell upon American settlers in our country 150 years ago." [24] That same day the naval landing force was withdrawn from Puerto Cabezas, and the next day Stimson's warning to American citizens in Nicaragua was made public. Washington refused to send more Marines to Nicaragua, and a landing force that had gone ashore at Bluefields was reembarked on April 29. That day, as a courtesy to his former chief, and perhaps in an effort to head off opposition from the man who had launched the intervention in Nicaragua, Stimson explained his policy to former President Coolidge:

> I feel that it would be unnecessary, as well as very regrettable, if we should be led by the pressure of unfounded criticism into sending new forces of the Marines back again into

the bandit provinces. The Marines, brave and efficient as they are for their proper work, are not adapted to such service.[25]

Many Americans cheered the abandonment of the policy of using the Marines to protect American property abroad. In the depression years of the early 1930's big business—the kind responsible for most foreign investment—was becoming increasingly unpopular in the United States. These businesses paid few, if any, taxes on their foreign operations, yet demanded that American tax money and American lives be expended for their protection. Even when businessmen were conceded the right to call for troops to protect their foreign investments, their wisdom in exercising this right was sometimes questioned. American property in Nicaragua was generally respected by all native factions and was relatively secure, even in the midst of revolution, until the Marines occupied the country in 1927 and Sandino began waging total war against the invading nation. As long as the Marines remained in Nicaragua, some observers suspected, American lives and property would not be safe in any part of the republic.[26]

Despite its great losses the Standard Fruit Company received scant sympathy from the American left wing. Equally unsympathetic was a growing band of American nationalists who were coming to the conclusion that American capitalism, as it then existed, was doomed; these people admired Huey Long of Louisiana and Benito Mussolini of Italy and demanded that the American economy be reorganized and freed from the clutches of international bankers. Some of these nationalists suspected that corporations like Standard Fruit, which demanded increased American intervention in Latin America, were paving the way for the importation of harmful foreign influences with their bananas. The fascistic Lawrence Dennis, erstwhile American *chargé d'affaires* in Managua, warned that "indefinitely prolonged interventions" in Latin America would result in the United States "assimilating the Mediterranean, Indian, and Negro races and cultures found in the republics immediately to the south of us." [27]

But such considerations were hardly responsible for Henry Stimson's determination to liquidate the Nicaraguan adventure as rapidly as possible. Over the protests of American investors in Nicaragua, Stimson reaffirmed in April 1931 the decision announced in February—to withdraw all Marines from Nicaragua by the end of 1932. In September 1931 Japan occupied Manchuria and gave the Secretary of State more reason for ending the Nicaraguan intervention. When Stimson lectured the Japanese on the evils of aggression, they protested that they were acting only to protect the lives and property of their citizens in Manchuria, just as the United States had long been doing in Nicaragua. "The State Department's hand could be strengthened considerably in its policy toward Japan if it had no Manchuria of its own." [28]

In Nicaragua General Sandino announced the advent of another world war in which two-thirds of mankind would perish. In the meantime, the guerrilla oracle declared on May 10, 1931, that catastrophes like the Managua earthquake would occur in other places "where injustice reigns." The Sandinistas had an important place in this scheme of things: "we have been chosen by Divine Justice to exercise Her rights." [29] Sandino's guerrillas continued to exercise these destructive rights after their attacks on Puerto Cabezas and Cabo Gracias a Dios. Before the east coast raids had subsided, Pedrón withdrew from Matagalpa department; he swung back through his Jinotega jungle heartland and surprised the National Guard by raiding the Pis Pis mining district early in May. American officers who served with the Guard conceded that Pedrón had the "arts of ambush, subsisting on the country, subterfuge, surprise, rapidity, and secrecy of movement down to a fine point and his use of interior lines was masterly." [30] While Pedrón raided the mines, Ortez was active in Nueva Segovia.

In May 1931 General Miguel Angel Ortez was commanding a first-class guerrilla outfit of more than a hundred men, many of whom were professional revolutionaries from Honduras. Hondurans were highly respected throughout Central America for their fighting qualities, and Ortez's Honduran second-in-command, Colonel Juan Pablo Umanzor, lived up to this reputation. Umanzor was several years younger than the thirty-six-year-old Ortez. In appearance they differed strikingly: Ortez was fair, trim, and fine-featured, while Umanzor was dark, sloppy, and Negroid. In military talent Umanzor would prove himself Ortez's equal, if not his superior. On the night of May 14–15 Ortez and Umanzor attacked the National Guard barracks at Palacaguina.[31]

The Guardsmen at Palacaguina were housed in a long, rectangular building facing an open plaza; it was directly across from the church, one hundred yards away. Reinforced firing positions had been prepared in the walls of the adobe barracks, and there was a machine gun tower at the north end of the building. The garrison consisted of two officers—First Lieutenant J. Ogden Brauer, commander, and Second Lieutenant Harry E. Kipp, second-in-command—and twenty-four enlisted men; they were armed with eighteen Krag rifles, two grenade launchers, two machine guns, and a Browning automatic rifle. The night of May 14 was drizzly and dark, though gas lights around the barracks provided some illumination. Sentries were stationed outside the barracks, but after midnight the guard in front of the building fell asleep at his post.

Ortez's guerrillas infiltrated Palacaguina early in the morning of May 15. Juana Martínez, night attendant at one of the local stores, heard marauders approaching, and she ran from the store and hid in an outhouse. At 1:50 A.M. a new sentry came on post in front of the barracks and noticed men moving about the church. He challenged a mounted man who answered him with pistol fire. A Sandinista blew a bugle call and firing began on all sides of the barracks; the heaviest fire came from the front, from the direction of the church. The Guardsmen quickly manned their battle stations to face a determined guerrilla effort to take the barracks from three directions. "Their attack was well directed," Lieutenant Brauer wrote in his report, "and they took every advantage of the surrounding terrain. The attackers were far more tenacious than ordinarily." Besides rifles and dynamite bombs, the guerrillas employed two submachine guns, a machine gun, and two grenade launchers. The machine gun was emplaced near the church and effectively supported the three-pronged assault by raking the front of the barracks. The Sandinista rifle grenadiers fired from positions closer to the barracks, which should have been within range of the building, but their grenades fell short.

National Guard rifle grenades proved more effective— although only about one in three exploded. Since the grenades had to be launched through the windows of the barracks, high-angle fire was impossible and the weapons had to be fired from the shoulder. Private José López spotted a Sandinista officer in the open near a gas light and he fired a rifle grenade at him. The grenade exploded in the officer's stomach and he crumpled to the ground. Guerrillas rushed to the officer's side and found him still conscious but bleeding profusely. They pulled him out of the line of fire and unbuckled his sword belt and cast it aside. From the outhouse Juana Martínez watched the guerrillas carry General Miguel Angel Ortez into her store. They laid him on a bed, and Ortez ordered them to leave him there and retire from the town. Ortez did not fear capture—he knew he was going to die— but his troops would not abandon him. He summoned his officers to his side and said, "The chief is now General Juan Pablo Umanzor," and then he died.[32] At 4:15 a Sandinista bugler sounded retreat and the guerrillas withdrew from Palacaguina, taking with them the body of the dead general. They buried Miguel Angel Ortez near the base of El Cuje hill, about four miles from Palacaguina.

Ortez won posthumous laurels from his enemies, who eulogized him as one of Sandino's most "active and successful" chiefs, "one of the few . . . who continued to fight after the first burst of fire . . . and made valiant attacks on garrisons." [33] Ortez's attack on Palacaguina was valiant, but it was not good guerrilla practice. Guerrillas seldom can overrun fortifications manned by disciplined soldiers—no matter what the numerical odds. Furthermore, the leaders of a peasant army are scarce natural commodities and must be conserved. Military academies and Marine Corps schools in the United States could turn out a limitless supply of officers for the Nicaraguan National Guard, but Sandino had no such machinery for replacing leaders like Girón and Ortez. No doubt Ortez's valor accounted for much of his strength as a leader, but in the final analysis he was not as effective a guerrilla commander as the illiterate Pedrón, who seldom exposed himself to fire.

By early June 1931 Pedrón had returned from the Pis Pis district to the area around Peña Blanca. Mounted on a fine big mule, wearing tall, handsome boots, with a forty-five caliber revolver and a German automatic strapped to his hips, and with gold rings and chains glistening in the sun, the formidable Pedrón led 150 well-armed Sandinistas westward in search of the enemy. About 2:00 P.M. on June 15 Pedrón's advance guard crossed a rise near Embocaderos and spotted its quarry: a seventeen-man National Guard patrol making its way to a house in the valley below. The Guardsmen stopped for lunch at the flimsy pine-board house, and Pedrón's men silently formed a horseshoe around the building at a distance varying from fifty to 150 yards. The Sandinistas opened fire at three o'clock and had soon killed the commander of the Guardsmen, Captain Lester E. Power, and his second-in-command, Lieutenant William H. McGhee. With their officers gone, the Guardsmen fled, running the gantlet through the open end of Pedrón's horseshoe. Besides the officers, one enlisted Guardsman was killed and four wounded in this encounter near Embocaderos.[34]

During the summer of 1931 Sandinista bands raided every Nicaraguan department north of Managua. The guerrillas were almost constantly on the move, searching for new op-

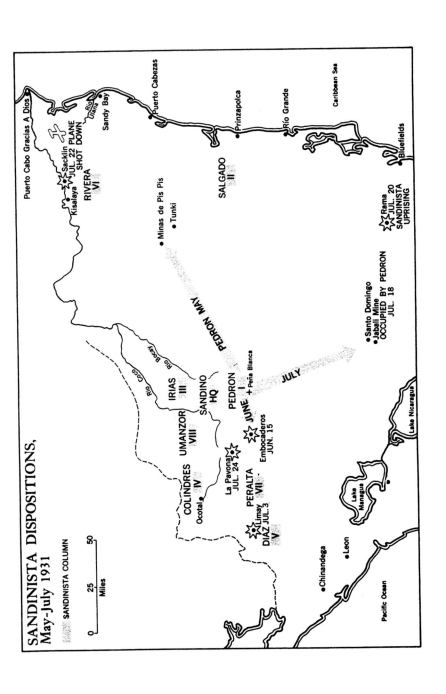

SANDINISTA DISPOSITIONS,
May-July 1931

▨▨ SANDINISTA COLUMN

0   25   50
        Miles

Puerto Cabo Gracias A Dios

Sacklin
Kisalaya ☆~☆ JUL. 22 PLANE
                SHOT DOWN
RIVERA
VI

Río Uana
Sandy Bay

Puerto Cabezas

Prinzapolca

Río Grande

Caribbean Sea

Bluefields

Minas de Pis Pis
Tunki

SALGADO
II

☆ Rama
JUL. 20
SANDINISTA
UPRISING

PEDRON MAY

Santo Domingo
Jabalí Mine
OCCUPIED BY PEDRON
JUL. 18

Peña Blanca

Río Bocay
Río Coco

IRIAS
III

SANDINO
HQ

PEDRON
I

JUNE

JULY

UMANZOR
VIII

COLINDRES
IV

Embocaderos
JUN. 15

La Pavona
JUL. 24 ☆

Ocotal
PERALTA
VII

Limay
DIAZ JUL. 3
V

Lake
Managua

Lake Nicaragua

León

Chinandega

Pacific Ocean

portunities to plunder private property or to strike at under-
manned National Guard detachments. The Defending Army
of the National Sovereignty of Nicaragua was organized into
eight "columns" of from seventy-five to 150 men. The First
Column was Pedrón's, based in southern Jinotega and raiding
the departments of Matagalpa and Chontales and across cen-
tral Jinotega to within sixty miles of the east coast. North of
Pedrón, in Jinotega department, the Third Column operated
under the command of General Pedro Antonio Irías. In the
Mosquito Coast departments were the Second Column under
General Carlos Salgado and the Sixth Column under General
Abraham Rivera. The late General Ortez's command in
Nueva Segovia was divided into the Eighth Column under
General Juan Pablo Umanzor and the Fourth Column under
General Juan Gregorio Colindres. South and west of Nueva
Segovia—in Estelí and the adjoining areas of León and Chin-
andega departments—roamed General Ismael Peralta's Sev-
enth Column and General José León Díaz's Fifth Column.
After Marine planes wounded Sandino in their attack on El
Saraguazca in June 1930, the guerrilla generalissimo took
pains to conceal his own whereabouts. A Sandino communiqué dated July 28, 1931, stated that his general headquarters
were located in the center of the eight departments he
claimed to control, at a place he called "El Chipotón," and
that his columns were "mobilized with mathematical precision, equally to the right and the left of our general headquarters." [35]

Early in July 1931 José León Díaz failed in an attempt to
hold the Guardsmen at Limay in their barracks and loot the
town. More successful were the combined forces of Umanzor and Colindres, who drove off a twenty-three man Guard
patrol near La Pavona on July 24, killing one Guardsman.[36]
One of the most spectacular Sandinista operations during the
month of July was Pedrón's raid into Chontales, a department heretofore free of guerrilla activity. On the afternoon
of July 18 Pedrón's troops occupied the ungarrisoned town

of Santo Domingo and the Jabali gold mine. At the mine a group of guerrillas captured W. Pfaeffle and his son, Otto. They tied the prisoners' hands with hemp rope and dragged the "Yankees" around for several hours, exhibiting them to their comrades. Herr Pfaeffle protested that they were Germans and was finally recognized by two guerrillas who had worked with him at another mine. Pfaeffle and son were then escorted to Santo Domingo to see Pedrón, who apologized for the treatment the Germans had received. It was a "simple mistake," Pedrón explained; they "were making war against North Americans and in no case against foreigners of other nationalities." Pedrón announced that they had come to win friends for their cause and ordered two proclamations from Sandino read to the people of Santo Domingo. The cause, however, was not helped by arbitrary looting on the part of some of the guerrillas, "something their chiefs could not prevent, although they wanted to." [37] After the Santo Domingo raid Pedrón eluded a heavily armed patrol of forty-five National Guardsmen and returned to Jinotega department.[38]

While Pedrón was raiding in Chontales, Sandinistas in southern Bluefields department briefly occupied the National Guard barracks at Rama—another area previously untouched by guerrilla activity. A sentry and the sergeant of the guard at Rama were standing outside the barracks when seven or eight natives approached them and asked for a light. As the sentry reached for a match, one of the natives shouted "Sandino!" and drew two pistols and killed the sentry. The other natives drew knives and wounded the sergeant and two or three unarmed Guardsmen who were sitting on the porch of the two-story barracks. Eighteen more Sandinistas suddenly appeared from two directions, and the wounded Guardsmen and two others who were inside abandoned the building to the attackers. Lieutenant Fred Riewe, the garrison commander, saw the encounter from his quarters across the square. He went into the street, rallied his men, and organized a counterattack that drove the Sandinistas out of the barracks about thirty minutes after they had seized it. Some of the Sandinistas were strangers to Rama, but at least half of them were local residents. They escaped with two rifles.[39]

North of Rama, in the lower Coco River valley, guerrilla activity resumed after a brief lull following the April raids. In mid-July two-plane air patrols began flying a daily triangular pattern from Puerto Cabezas to Sacklin to Cabo Gracias a Dios and back to Puerto Cabezas. Sacklin, a Coco River town in the bailiwick of Congressman Adolfo Cockburn, appeared deserted to the airmen on the first four days of the patrol. On the morning of the fifth day, July 22, they noticed a horse tied to the corner of a house. The planes swooped down to investigate and were greeted by gunfire. "By being fired upon," one of the pilots explained, "we were justified in bombing the town, which we proceeded to do." The Loening amphibians dropped nineteen bombs, scoring hits on several boats and thatched huts. Since the Loenings did not mount machine guns, the observers used Thompson submachine guns against the personnel driven from the houses by the bombs. Both planes were hit several times by ground fire, and one was forced to land in a "sea of mud and mire" three miles east of Sacklin, at about ten o'clock in the morning. The crew was uninjured, but the plane was beyond repair. Lieutenant Herbert P. Becker, the patrol leader and pilot of the surviving aircraft, signaled the pilot of the downed plane, Staff Sergeant Gordon B. Heritage, to burn his craft. Lieutenant Becker then flew away to Puerto Cabezas and notified the garrison of the crash. Becker intended to return to the scene to help Heritage and his observer, Corporal Orville B. Simmons, find their way back to Puerto Cabezas, but it rained so hard that afternoon that the lieutenant was unable to get his plane off the ground.[40]

After burning their aircraft, Sergeant Heritage and Corporal Simmons set out for the coast. With great difficulty they crossed four swirling rivers on July 22, loaded down with a machete, pistol, submachine gun, ammunition, and some of their plane's instruments. They lost their compass but considered themselves lucky in not losing their lives crossing the fourth river. Already fatigued from fighting the river, they pushed on through torrents of rain and spent three hours hacking their way through about three hundred yards of jungle. At intervals one of the men would climb a tree to take bearings. Just about dusk they stumbled out of the jungle onto a path and followed it to a deserted hut where they settled down for the night. "We were stiff from the cold of the jungle night," Heritage later recalled; "our bodies became numb and turned blue from the drenching downpour." Their clothes were tattered and the exposed parts of their bodies "were bleeding from the slashes of slithering, razor-edged jungle grasses." Their "shoes had fallen apart, the tops alone remained." The airmen discovered that the containers of their emergency rations had deteriorated, but they decided to eat some hardtack anyway and they became sick to their stomachs.

After a miserable night Heritage and Simmons caught a glimpse of the rising sun in a break in the clouds and resumed their journey to the east. It began to rain again, and soon the airmen came to the largest river they had yet encountered. They crossed it, losing their submachine gun in the process, and entered a large swamp on the other side. They started across the swamp at about 8:30 in the morning and "fought our way through the morass until 3:30 in the afternoon," Heritage wrote; "at times we waded up to our necks in muck, mire, and rushes." Then they met a friendly Indian from Sandy Bay who was hunting alligators. The Indian helped the airmen aboard his dugout and poled them down the Ulana River to Sandy Bay. They arrived at the coastal village about dusk and ate a good meal with the Indians, after which they "found a Chinaman who lent us trousers and shirts." The next day an Indian took them down the coast to Puerto Cabezas in a twenty-five foot dugout rigged with jury sails.

Sandy Bay was part of Adolfo Cockburn's constituency, but the congressman's influence was less there than among the Indians along the lower Coco River. In the latter area Abraham Rivera roamed at will, collecting tribute for Sandino from local merchants. Since the Indian National Guardsmen at Kisalaya did little to remedy this situation, an American officer and some *ladino* enlisted men were brought in to strengthen the garrison. In September 1931 the National Guard came across a guerrilla "Headquarters Bulletin" which referred to Adolfo Cockburn as a Sandinista general. Early the next month Second Lieutenant Edward J. Suprenant, the new Guard commander at Kisalaya, set out with a private and a *ladino* sergeant for the congressman's hacienda near Sacklin, ostensibly to pay him a courtesy call. In his pocket the lieutenant had the serial number of a typewriter stolen from the Kisalaya garrison and reported to be in Cockburn's possession.[41]

The Guardsmen were received graciously by Adolfo Cockburn on October 3, 1931. Lieutenant Suprenant complimented him on his beautiful place, and the congressman offered to take the Guardsmen on a tour of the house. The private was left outside while the lieutenant and the sergeant, who carried a submachine gun, were escorted through Cockburn's home. The last room they visited was the office, where a portrait of President Moncada was prominent on the wall and a typewriter stood on the desk. Suprenant asked and received permission to try out the typewriter, and after he had written a few lines he announced that it was the machine stolen from the Kisalaya garrison. Cockburn turned pale and denied that this was so. Suprenant then took from his wallet the paper with the stolen typewriter's serial number and approached Cockburn to show him that it was the same as the number on his machine. The congressman bolted and grabbed an automatic pistol from a desk drawer, whereupon Sergeant Francisco Avendaño leveled his Thompson submachine gun at Cockburn and mowed him down. In the dead congressman's desk the Guardsmen found documents which proved conclusively that he had been a Sandinista collaborator. The Mosquito Indians of Sacklin and Kisalaya mourned the loss of their chief and waited patiently for the opportunity to avenge his death.

It was soon clear that Sandinista activity along the upper Mosquito Coast would not end with the death of Adolfo Cockburn. Before the end of October guerrillas were again raiding Standard Fruit Company plantations along the Cuyu Tigne–Puerto Cabezas railroad. A band of Sandinistas looted the Louisiana Farm commissary near Logtown on October 27 and withdrew to Cuyu Tigne where they were joined by other guerrillas who had been raiding in the area. A National Guard patrol, led by a Nicaraguan lieutenant, pursued the guerrillas from Louisiana Farm to Cuyu Tigne; there the Guardsmen met with stiff resistance and were driven back toward Puerto Cabezas with one dead.[42]

The troops of Augusto C. Sandino raided farms and plantations, defenseless villages and garrisoned towns, confiscating property and forcing contributions to their war effort. Although they did not always succeed, most of Sandino's officers tried to prevent indiscriminate pillaging and made a practice of giving receipts for the property they took. A measure of restraint was essential if Sandino was to retain the sympathy of the people of northern Nicaragua. He decreed the destruction of all American-owned property but tried to protect the capital of others—so that they could continue to produce revenue for his cause. Although he levied heavy "taxes" upon the rich, he tried to avoid the appearance of social radicalism, explaining that

> there is no need for the class struggle in Nicaragua, because here the worker lives well; he struggles only against the American intervention, the rich as well as the poor should back the struggle, some with their money and others with their services. . . . If our soldiers take shoes and clothing from their owners, it is because our soldier brothers need them more, and because it is not just that the men who are establishing the liberty of Nicaragua should walk in sandals.[43]

Not long after he returned from Mexico in 1930, Sandino threatened to burn all the cities in Nicaragua if the Yankees did not get out of the country—a declaration that caused concern among some of his supporters, especially Dr. Zepeda in Mexico. That year Sandino also authorized the firing squad for any merchant who refused to give up salt or medicine for free distribution among his neighbors; furthermore, any civilian who rejected his share of the distribution was to be shot as a future traitor. Sandino achieved that balance of reasonableness and terror necessary to maintain the cooperation of the inhabitants of a guerrilla zone. Peasants, merchants, and large landowners could all send protests to Sandino, and sometimes those who felt they had been treated unfairly by his troops got a hearing from the general. Occasionally Sandino would scale down the contribution demanded of a property owner when it was shown to be excessive.[44] Sandino tried not to drive his "taxpayers" out of the zones in which his guerrillas operated. But for those who refused to cooperate—and especially those who assisted the National Guard—Sandino's retribution was often terrible.

Sandinista justice was administered by several *cortes*—a Spanish word that can mean either "courts" or "cuts." The most famous of these was the *corte de chaleco*, the "vest cut": the offender's head was lopped off with a machete, after which his arms were severed at the shoulders and a design was etched on his chest with machete slashes. Pedrón invented the "vest cut" and applied it often until he tired of it in 1930 and ordered that all "traitors" receive the *corte de cumbo* instead. This *corte*, the "gourd cut," was applied by an expert machete man who sliced off a portion of the victim's skull, exposing his brain and causing him to lose his equilibrium and suffer hours of agony and convulsions before death. Less sophisticated was the *corte de bloomers*, by which the victim's legs were chopped off at the knees, eventually producing death through bleeding. "Liberty is not conquered with flowers," Sandino declared in 1931; "for this reason we must resort to the *cortes* of vest, gourd, and bloomers."[45]

These three *cortes* were the most popular among the guerrillas, but there were at least two others that were sometimes applied to the bodies of dead enemies: the "tie cut," by which the subject's throat was cut and his tongue pulled through the slit, and the "cigar cut," by which his penis was amputated and placed in his mouth. In cases not warranting the death penalty, offenders' houses were burned or their windows and doors removed and destroyed.

Men of many nationalities helped maintain the Sandinista terror in Nicaragua. Besides Latin Americans, British subjects, Germans, and Americans served in Sandino's army at one time or another, although none of them achieved prominence as leaders. All the top commanders were Central Americans. The number of Hondurans in Sandino's army, which had always been substantial, was increased after a partly communist-inspired revolt by unemployed fruit company workers was crushed on Honduras' Caribbean coast in June 1931; many of the Honduran rebels, who had risen in arms shortly after the spectacular Sandinista raids against Standard Fruit's Nicaraguan holdings, joined the guerrillas in Nicaragua when the revolt in their own country failed.[46]

The discipline of Sandino's guerrillas had been described as excellent, but "not like the army where the mechanical idea predominates over the moral idea." [47] Whether by moral idea or the force of his own personality, Sandino did dominate his officers, but they in turn were sometimes unable to control their own subordinates. Sandino executed a number of his officers, including at least two generals, for such crimes as treason, unauthorized looting, and violating women. The guerrilla generalissimo had a keen, though superstitious, sense of justice: once he exonerated a condemned man when the executioner's gun misfired, considering this a sign of the man's innocence. Sandino believed strongly in his own intuition and in fate; he was sure that he would "not come out of the struggle alive." [48]

After Sandino was wounded in the air raid on Mount Saraguazca, on June 19, 1930, he apparently took no part in

combat and devoted most of his time to organizational matters and to the search for a philosophical basis for his movement. During the summer of 1930 he decreed that all officers
and men of his army be greeted with the title "Brother." [49]
On February 15, 1931, Sandino issued a proclamation to be
read to his largely illiterate troops setting forth his version of
the creation of the universe and explaining that "when the
majority of humanity recognizes and lives by the Spirit, Injustice will cease forever and there will reign only Divine
Justice: the only daughter of Love." [50] Simple peasant soldiers
stood in awe of their philosopher-general and even claimed
to have seen the end of a rainbow rest on his head.[51]

Sócrates Sandino returned from Mexico late in 1930 and
soon joined his brother in the Nicaraguan mountains. Early
the next year Sandino decided to break with Teresa Villatoro
and summon his wife to his headquarters deep in the jungles
of the central Coco River valley. "For the good of our
cause," Sandino wrote Abraham Rivera in February,[52] "it is
quite possible that I will soon be reunited with my wife
Blanca." The only kind of marriage recognized by divine
law, Sandino explained, "is that of pure and free love," but
for the present "we cannot escape from the laws of men and
will have to accept them." Sandino said he was telling Rivera
this so that "I will not be considered injust in any act of my
life." In any case, he continued, "the one who enjoys my un-
limited affection is Blanca. Teresa is highly esteemed by me
and I will aid her all my life, but our characters are as different as the heavens and the earth." When Sandino wrote this,
Teresa had already departed for her native El Salvador.[53]

Blanca de Sandino arrived at her husband's headquarters
in March 1931, accompanied by her brothers Luís Rubén and
Pedro Antonio Arauz. Sandino employed the young men as
his secretaries, but a conflict soon developed between the
general and his brothers-in-law. In August it was reported
that Sandino was about ready to shoot Luís Rubén and Pedro
Antonio. Both fled the general's camp and returned to San
Rafael del Norte, where they hid from both guerrillas and

Guardsmen until Luís Rubén turned himself in to the National Guard on August 28; Pedro Antonio surrendered a few days later. Blanca remained devoted to Sandino, but most of the general's in-laws had turned against him by mid-1931. About this time Sandino apparently authorized his troops to steal his in-law's cattle. Blanca's father, Pablo Arauz, had been dead for several years, and one of her aunts concluded that Sandino was a communist because he did not believe in the Church and used masonic symbols.[54]

"My little Blanca," Sandino wrote Abraham Rivera in 1931, "has her .32 Special pistol and her .44 Winchester rifle and I cannot stop her from shooting up much ammunition daily"; she "is manly, like Mary, the wife of Joseph, was, and all I can do is permit her to do everything she likes." [55] One day some Mosquito Indians arrived at Sandino's camp with an old Jamaican Negro whom they had captured after he had abandoned a village school-teaching position assigned to him by Abraham Rivera. Blanca was on hand, and she decided that the Jamaican, Ruben Brown, had done nothing to warrant punishment. She gave him a job as camp cook. According to Brown,

> Doña Blanca awarded me affection for the great care I took in preparing her meals, and soon she would not let anyone else fix them for her. One day Sandino had demons in his head and called in a loud voice for four armed men so that they could shoot me. I became very sad and said goodbye to life, having informed Doña Blanca that they were going to kill me so that she could look for another cook. She told me that she would not permit this even for one moment, and thus it was that when they came to take me out and put me to death, she intervened and the men went away. . . .
>
> So it is, then, that I owe my life to my cooking spoon and to Doña Blanca.[56]

During the autumn of 1931 the Sandinistas displayed surprising strength. On November 2 the combined forces of José León Díaz and Carlos Salgado routed a fifteen-man National Guard patrol under Second Lieutenant D. H. Hutch-

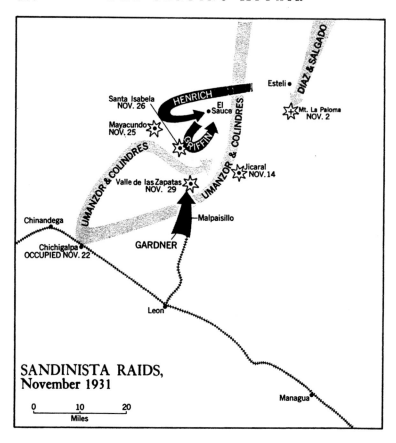

SANDINISTA RAIDS,
November 1931

croft at La Paloma mountain, in Estelí department, killing three Guardsmen, wounding one, and capturing a Thompson submachine gun and three rifles. Then the forces of Juan Pablo Umanzor and Juan Gregorio Colindres drove deep into León department and overran the small National Guard garrison at Jicaral on November 14. They continued on to Chichigalpa, on the Managua-Corinto railway, which they occupied on November 22. Managua was thrown into a panic, and Moncada issued a call for volunteers to deal with the worsening situation. As the United States was still opposed to an independent Moncadista army, the three hundred volunteers who responded to the President's call were incorporated into the National Guard as auxiliaries. But even the expanded National Guard was not considered adequate to handle the situation, and Secretary of State Stimson authorized Marines to operate outside Managua for the first time since the preceding spring, to serve as guards on Nicaraguan passenger trains.[57]

Umanzor and Colindres gave up the railroad town of Chichigalpa on the night of November 22 and withdrew northward. Three days later a patrol of six Nicaraguan Military Academy cadets and ten auxiliaries under Second Lieutenant Charles Henrich intercepted the guerrillas near Mayacundo. The Sandinistas deployed, launched a determined attack on Henrich's patrol, and drove it back to El Sauce. A larger patrol, fifty-one Guardsmen commanded by Captain R. G. Griffin, Jr., marched south from El Sauce and occupied Santa Isabela on November 26. Late that afternoon Umanzor and Colindres attacked Captain Griffin at Santa Isabela and drove him out of town, to a "better defensive position" where he spent the night; at dawn the next morning Griffin retired to El Sauce "for ammunition and supplies."[58] A still larger patrol, ten Guardsmen and fifty-three auxiliaries under Second Lieutenant George E. Gardner, marched north from the railroad at Malpaisillo and overtook the Sandinistas near Valle de las Zapatas on November 29. After a brief exchange of fire with Gardner's patrol, the guerrillas dispersed and escaped to the north and to the west.

The guerrilla operations in November "showed considerable organization and indications of more or less efficient leadership," National Guard intelligence noted. The Sandinistas displayed "marked aggressiveness on quite a few occasions" and appeared "to be quite adept at spreading misinformation to cover their movements." The area they chose for their operations surprised the National Guard; "it was not thought they possessed enough strength in money, arms, ammunition, and equipment to dare to operate so close to this thickly populated area and the railroad."[59] American *Chargé d'Affaires* Willard Beaulac, who had served in Managua since the spring of 1929, reported on November 25 that "the bandit situation appears as grave as, or graver than, at any time since I have been in Nicaragua." [60] Nevertheless, two weeks later President Herbert Hoover reaffirmed U.S. intention to withdraw the last of the Marines after the 1932 Nicaraguan elections.[61]

President Hoover and Secretary Stimson were well aware of the limitations of American power in a foreign guerrilla war. They wanted peace in Nicaragua but doubted that it could be achieved by American military force. They would not jeopardize United States prestige by seeking victory in an impossible war. By making it unmistakably clear that the remaining Marines would be withdrawn after the 1932 elections, Washington was paving the way for negotiations between the Sandinistas and those political elements from which the next Nicaraguan administration would be drawn. There would be no repetition of the situation following the 1928 elections, when the Marines remained in Nicaragua and encouraged incoming President Moncada to reject Sandino's peace overtures and try to exterminate the guerrillas. The next Nicaraguan administration would either have to come to terms with the Sandinistas or carry on the war without U.S. military support.

10

The End of a Banana War

The Sandinista threat to west central Nicaragua subsided during the winter of 1931–1932, and the centers of guerrilla activity shifted back to the north and the east. On December 22, 1931, guerrillas occupied San Isidro, in western Matagalpa department, and besieged the local garrison. After an unsuccessful attempt to ambush a National Guard relief patrol from La Trinidad, the Sandinistas abandoned San Isidro and withdrew to the north.[1] In the jungles near El Chipote a patrol led by Captain Granville K. Frisbie and Lieutenant Donald L. Truesdale discovered a secret trail and followed it to a guerrilla camp on December 26. The Guardsmen were detected as they approached the camp, and they opened fire, killing two Sandinistas and probably mortally wounding another. "One of the two killed outright proved to be a woman, dressed with clothing trimmed at the neck and sleeves with red and black." Another woman, the wife of Sandinista Major Rafael Altamirano, was captured, but others in the camp escaped. During the next two days Señora Altamirano led the patrol to several unoccupied guerrilla camps, each stocked with ammunition and a hundred bushels of corn. Some "were of fairly good construction, being of split cedar shingle roofs. All had fields nearby of corn and sugar cane." There was a field of tobacco near one camp, which the Guardsmen destroyed with all the other guerrilla facilities.[2]

Early in 1932 Pedrón swung to the east and on January 28 sacked the store at Tunki in the Pis Pis district. A week later he was forced to abandon most of his loot when his band was overtaken and five of his men killed by an aggressive National Guard patrol under Second Lieutenant Earl T. Gray. While Pedrón was in the east, some lesser chiefs were active in southern Jinotega. Daniel Hernández and Perfecto Gutiérrez killed two Guardsmen and wounded two others in a series of engagements in the Peña Blanca area from February 1 to 4. Another Guardsman was killed near San Antonio on February 14. In Nueva Segovia, Second Lieutenant C. H. Clark lost one man killed and four wounded near Posa Honda on February 24 but achieved some significant results: he routed Umanzor's band and captured a large quantity of Sandinista equipment and supplies.[3]

While the Guardsmen chased guerrillas in the north and the east, politicians were maneuvering in Managua. Elections were to be held in November 1932 to choose a successor to President José María Moncada, who was constitutionally ineligible to succeed himself. Late in 1931 the Nicaraguan chief executive suggested that the McCoy Election Law, the National Guard Law, and the Bryan-Chamorro Treaty were all unconstitutional and advocated the election of a constitutional convention to clarify these matters. Nicaraguan Conservatives feared that if such an assembly were convened, Moncada would push through a constitutional amendment prolonging his own term. The U.S. State Department admitted that Nicaraguan constitutional reform was none of its business but announced that the United States would not supervise the regular 1932 elections if a constitutional convention were elected that year. Without American supervision the Conservatives would have little chance in the elections and a Liberal dictatorship could result—especially if the Conservatives boycotted the elections as they were threatening to do.

It mattered little to Washington which party ruled Nicaragua—neither was likely to jeopardize American interests.

What mattered was that the appearances of representative democracy be maintained in the occupied republic. American acquiescence in the establishment of a Nicaraguan dictatorship or American supervision of boycotted elections would not sit well with U.S. or world public opinion. And the intervention certainly would be harshly judged if, upon the withdrawal of the Marines, the republic lapsed into a state of revolution and anarchy. Some means had to be devised for ending the mutual distrust of Liberals and Conservatives and inducing both parties to participate in the democratic process. The task fell to American Minister Matthew Hanna, who was instructed to bring the two parties together in an agreement that would permit meaningful American-supervised elections in November 1932. "All the loss of American lives and treasure," Willard Beaulac noted, "would avail nothing in bringing peace to Nicaragua so long as this senseless enmity between the two parties continued." [4]

After some hesitation President Moncada agreed to attend a dinner given by Minister Hanna, to which the Conservative former Presidents Adolfo Díaz and Emiliano Chamorro were also invited. The enmity between Moncada and Chamorro, the strongman of the Conservative party, was especially deep and long-standing. The dinner was scheduled for January 12, 1932, at the American legation, and the guest of honor was Rear Admiral Clark K. Woodward, the man President Hoover had appointed to head the American electoral mission to Nicaragua before Moncada announced his plans for constitutional reform. The legation's first secretary, Willard Beaulac, described the evening.

> The two ex-presidents and most of the other guests arrived early. President Moncada arrived a few minutes after the appointed time, accompanied by his aides and by a squad of guards armed with rifles and submachine guns. The guards proceeded to station themselves at strategic locations inside and outside the legation. I met the president downstairs and escorted him to the living room on the second floor where the other guests were assembled. As we approached the liv-

ing room, a hum of conversation greeted us. When we reached the door all conversation ceased, and the well known pin, if it had been dropped, would have sounded like a sledge hammer. Mrs. Hanna quickly came to the door, greeted the president cordially, and took him over to where Emiliano Chamorro was standing. The two old opponents shook hands. People started to breathe again . . . Conversation was resumed, subdued at first, but gathering in momentum as the minutes passed. By the time we went downstairs to the dining room, it might almost be said that we were gay. There was, of course, a shade of hysteria beneath the surface.

The sight of armed guards within the legation had a so-bering effect on the party, and it was a solemn assembly that seated itself at the table. . . . The Hannas, nevertheless, exuded good cheer and merriment, and Matt's deep voice and laughter reverberated around the room. The company gradually relaxed. However, the evening had one more thrill for us. Champagne was served, and the minister toasted the president. All others in turn raised their glasses and drank. The president, raising his glass, looked across the table at Emiliano Chamorro, who still had his glass raised. Catching Chamorro's eye, the president asked, "Por qué le tiembla la mano, General?" (Why is your hand trembling, General?) All conversation ceased, all eyes were on Chamorro. He was equal to the occasion. "De emoción, Señor Presidente" (From emotion, Mr. President), he replied. We drank with the president and the ex-president, and the guards doubtless lowered their Tommy guns.[5]

Moncada and Chamorro conversed amicably after dinner. Before long a thaw in relations between the Conservative and Liberal parties was evident. Moncada dropped his proposals for constitutional reform, and the Hoover administration went ahead with plans to supervise the Nicaraguan elections. But this undertaking was hardly popular with the American public, and congressional opposition to any further involvement in Nicaragua intensified during the spring of 1932 as the Marine-led National Guard suffered a series of shocking reverses.

In March Juan Pablo Umanzor, Juan Gregorio Colindres, and Sócrates Sandino swept south into León department and again threatened Jicaral and Valle de las Zapatas. As the. Guardsmen chased these guerrillas back into the northern departments, a Sandinista force crossed into the department of Rivas from Costa Rica. This band, which numbered no more than twenty, was routed by a National Guard patrol on April 5 and driven back across the border. But while the National Guard dealt successfully with the threats to León and Rivas, its principal garrison on the lower Coco River at Kisalaya rose in mutiny and killed an American officer.[6]

Sergeant Sebastián Jiménez, a Sandinista sympathizer in the National Guard at Kisalaya, played upon the desires of the garrison's Mosquito Indians to avenge the death of Adolfo Cockburn—the congressman they had revered almost as a king. The persons they held responsible for the killing— Lieutenant Suprenant and Sergeant Avendaño—had been replaced at Kisalaya, but the mutinous Sergeant Jiménez managed to transfer the Indians' hostility to the new commanding officer, Lieutenant Charles J. Levonski, and his second-in-command, Nicaraguan Second Lieutenant Carlos Reyes. Sergeant Jiménez called in the Mosquito Guardsmen and auxiliaries on April 4, issued them arms, and led them in revolt against their officers. They killed Levonski and wounded Reyes, then withdrew to the mountains where they delivered twenty-one rifles, a machine gun, a Browning automatic rifle, a submachine gun, and twenty-one grenades to the Sandinistas. A few of the mutineers, including Sebastián Jiménez, joined the guerrilla army, but most of them, considering the death of their chief avenged, returned to more peaceful pursuits in the great rain forest they knew so well.

Exactly a week after the Kisalaya mutiny, a sergeant and two other Guardsmen from the Quilali garrison deserted to the guerrillas with three automatic weapons. The next day, April 12, Umanzor sacked Valle de las Zapatas in León department.[7] On April 21, on a trail in Nueva Segovia, Salgado and Colindres handed the National Guard one of its worst defeats. Second Lieutenant Laurin T. Covington was leading his patrol from Apalí to Jalapa when it was ambushed while crossing a stream near Las Puertas. Four Guardsmen were killed before Covington could break contact and link up with a relief column under First Lieutenants C. W. Johnson and Laurence C. Brunton. Using a secret trail, Salgado and Colindres moved their men rapidly to Los Leones, a point further down the main trail, and set up an ambush there for the combined Guard patrols. In the fight that ensued the Guardsmen were routed and six more of them were killed, including Lieutenants Covington, Brunton, and Finis L. Whitehead, a medical officer. The guerrillas captured a Browning automatic rifle, five rifles, and three automatic pistols.[8]

The victors in this encounter, Salgado and Colindres, had held important commands in Sandino's army for five years, and both had taken part in the first battle with the Americans at Ocotal. Both were natives of Nueva Segovia, but there the similarity ended. General Carlos Salgado had been a day laborer before becoming a guerrilla; he was middle aged, short and slight—a harmless looking little Indian whose profile resembled the one on the American five-cent piece. General Juan Gregorio Colindres, on the other hand, was from a well-to-do gold-mining family and was regarded even by his American enemies as "intelligent and courteous."[9] Colindres was about thirty-eight, of medium height, gaunt but rather handsome; he had light hair, a full mustache, and the look of a man of considerable character. Colindres was undoubtedly a Nicaraguan patriot, and he committed his family's wealth and prestige to Sandino's cause. Combinations like that of Salgado and Colindres were not uncommon in Sandino's army; semi-savage Indian generals were often paired with officers of more civilized demeanor who were better equipped for political agitation. In the summer of 1932 the illiterate Simón González was operating on the Mosquito Coast with Francisco Estrada, a mechanic by profession who fancied himself a poet. About thirty years old in 1932, Estrada had headed the short-lived government at Sandino City five years before; he was white, tall, well built, and of good appearance.

During the spring and summer of 1932 there was fierce fighting in almost every department of Nicaragua. Between April and September the National Guard clashed with guerrilla forces 104 times. The Sandinistas became increasingly aggressive; they made numerous attacks on Guard patrols and garrisons and, sometimes, stood their ground when attacked, fighting pitched battles for as long as three hours. On April 21 Sandinistas attacked the new National Guard garrison at Kisalaya and were repelled, losing several men killed, including the mutinous ex-Sergeant Sebastián Jiménez. In May Pedrón was again raiding the Pis Pis mining district, and in June a Nicaraguan officer of the National Guard garrison at San Isidro led a mutiny and killed his commanding officer, Second Lieutenant Edward H. Schmierer. In July Simón González and Francisco Estrada pillaged and burned Standard Fruit Company property near Puerto Cabezas.[10]

Economic distress in the banana country was exploited by both communists and Sandinistas. While they raided Standard Fruit plantations in Nicaragua, Estrada and González helped stir up trouble in Honduras by charging that the Yankees were dispatching troops to the neighboring republic to protect the property of the United Fruit Company there.[11] The communists, who had long been active in Honduras, organized cells in Nicaragua during the winter of 1931–1932. The Managua police, headed by Captain Evans F. Carlson, first learned of a communist movement in that city early in January 1932. On the night of February 19 Carlson's policemen raided "the houses of ten persons suspected of being instrumental in the organization of communism in Nicaragua" and arrested twenty-one "for having in their possession subversive literature, or for suspicion of being connected with the Communist movement."[12] In June 1932 J. Edgar Hoover, Director of the Federal Bureau of Investigation, warned that "an energetic campaign is planned by the Communist Party of the United States on behalf of the movement in Nicaragua." The American communists planned "to issue propaganda against the policy of the United States in keeping armed forces in Nicaragua, to secure financial and moral support for Nicaraguan sympathizers of the Liberation Movement, to organize demonstrations in the United States, and to conduct a propaganda campaign among the American armed forces in Nicaragua." [13]

Sandino and the Communist International were battling the same enemy, but there was little cooperation between the two. Sandino rejected orthodox communist ideology and liked to boast of how he frustrated the efforts of Gustavo Machado and Agustín Farabundo Martí to take over the Sandinista movement for the Comintern. "This movement is national and anti-imperialist," Sandino insisted; "we fly the banner of liberty for Nicaragua and for all Hispanic America." But there was more to Sandinismo than just Hispanic American nationalism. "This is a people's movement," the general declared, "and we take an advanced position in regard to social aspirations." [14] But Sandino said his army would wait for the "approaching world conflagration" before undertaking its "humanitarian program . . . in favor of the world proletariat." [15] In the autograph book of a Spanish visitor the general wrote that "Spain and America will communize the earth." [16] Another visitor to Sandino's headquarters explained that the general used the word "communize" as a synonym for "fraternize." [17] Despite this nebulosity—or perhaps because of it—Sandinismo proved more attractive to Nicaraguan workingmen and university students than orthodox communism. In 1932 the National Guard was well aware of Sandinista subversion in Nicaraguan cities and ports; particular attention was paid to the University of León, a virtual hotbed of Sandinismo. [18]

While Captain Carlson's police force hunted subversives in Managua, Marine airmen were amusing the residents of the capital city with a new machine. "At 9:00 yesterday an autogiro flew under our skies for the first time," La Prensa reported on June 28, 1932.

The people of the city saw it in flight and groups of curious ones gathered on the plazas and open places to watch with interest the maneuvers of the bird. It has a kind of windmill of four blades on its upper side, these blades drooping slightly when the machine is on the ground. The machine now in Nicaragua arrived practically "knocked down" on the naval transport *Vega* two weeks ago, was brought from Corinto by rail and was put together at Zacharias Field.[19]

The prototype of the Marine autogiro—invented by Juan de la Cierva, a Spanish engineer—had been successfully flown for the first time in 1923. The autogiro was the world's first practicable rotary-wing aircraft. In addition to the rotor, the craft had stubby fixed wings and a forward propeller. Unlike the true helicopter, which was still in the experimental stage in 1932, the autogiro's rotor was geared to the engine only while the craft was on the ground, just before take-off. Once the rotor was properly spinning, the pilot threw a clutch and transferred power to the propeller for forward motion. Vertical ascent was thus impossible, but the autogiro could take off on much less runway than required by conventional aircraft. It depended on "autorotation"—the free whirling of the rotor during forward motion—for the necessary lift to keep the craft airborne. When forward motion ceased, the autogiro would settle; with a stiff wind activating the rotor, the craft could make a nearly vertical landing. *La Prensa* reported that Marine pilots on the ground at Managua saluted the autogiro "with a chorus of laughter when they saw it land the first time with the exact precision of a game bird." Throughout the summer the autogiro continued to delight the residents of Managua, who gave it affectionate nicknames. "The United States autogiro," *Diario Moderno* reported on August 13, "spent part of yesterday morning going through aerial acrobatics. The 'turkey hen' was admired for a long time by the curiosity seekers."

The autogiro's performance in its Nicaraguan field tests

was disappointing to the Marines. With a crew of two, the aircraft's take-off distance averaged less than one hundred yards, but the Marines found that it could carry only fifty pounds of cargo efficiently. An evaluation board of three Marine pilots recommended against using it for airlifting supplies but found the craft suited for inspecting small landing fields prior to their use by conventional planes, evacuating medical sitting cases from landing areas unsuited for other aircraft, and "to ferry important personnel to the same kind of landing areas."

In addition to amusing the people of Managua with the autogiro, Marine aviators dusted the city's lake front with conventional aircraft "at regular intervals to kill mosquitoes and . . . materially decreased the number of cases of malaria." The Marines also continued their patrol flights over the combat zones, but with "strict orders to take all care of the security and safety of the civilian population and . . . bomb only when they feel perfectly sure certain groups are really bandits—if they are carrying guns, if they are in the vicinity of a recent hold-up, or give themselves away by running to cover." [20] These restrictions did not preclude all abuses and left Marine aviators open to enemy charges that they made inhuman attacks against peaceful citizens.

The airmen were not the only Marines charged with atrocities by the Sandinistas. American officers serving with the National Guard were accused of a wide variety of crimes, many of which must have been purely imaginary. A widely circulated story about a Marine officer tossing a Nicaraguan baby into the air and catching it on the point of his bayonet was reminiscent of Allied propaganda against the Germans in World War I. Other tales had American officers burning old women alive, tearing babies apart with their hands, and eating human hearts.[21] Other stories—concerning the shooting and rough handling of prisoners,[22] using the water treatment,[23] and mutilating the bodies of dead guerrillas—are not so easily dismissed. Lieutenant O. E. Pennington of the Matagalpa National Guard detachment posed for a photograph holding

the severed head of a guerrilla. The picture fell into Sandinista hands and was widely published in Latin America in
1932. Pennington admitted that the photograph was genuine
but denied personally beheading the guerrilla.[24]

"M" Company, the roving patrol based in Jinotega, was
frequently mentioned in anti-American atrocity propaganda.
A photograph of six members of the company holding three
severed heads fell into Sandinista hands and was circulated
with the Pennington photograph.[25] The company commander, Captain Lewis B. Puller, was sometimes mentioned in
this propaganda. Lieutenant William A. Lee, second-in-command and acting company commander while Puller was on
assignment in the United States during much of 1931 and
1932, was probably the subject of more atrocity stories than
any other American officer in Nicaragua. In guerrilla warfare "only the aggressive and ruthless may expect to survive,"
Marine General Vernon E. Megee wrote; "Puller and Lee
were eminently qualified on both counts." [26] The officers of
"M" Company were worthy opponents of a savage foe, but
they could not have been guilty of all the Sandinista accusa-
tions against them—many of which were patently absurd.[27]
The guerrillas certainly feared "M" Company. A Nicaraguan
who had been held prisoner by Pedrón's band reported that
the Sandinistas were most afraid of "Lt. Lee and a one-armed
officer who fought like Lee, named Gutiérrez" [28] The one-
armed officer was Nicaraguan Lieutenant Policarpo Gutiérrez, who had lost his left arm in the 1927–1928 campaign
against El Chipote.

All Nicaraguan officers did not fight like Policarpo Gutiérrez, and American military men had misgivings about how
the National Guard would fare when the Marine officers left
its service. Nevertheless, Washington's policy of withdrawing
all Marines from Nicaragua after the elections of 1932 was
irreversible. The date set for the departure of the last of
the Marines was January 2, 1933, and all command and
staff positions in the Guard had to be turned over to
Nicaraguan officers before that date. There were not enough

Nicaraguan officers, so the length of the course at the Nicaraguan Military Academy was cut and the classes were expanded. By mid-1932, as plans were being made to turn over the higher ranks of the Guard to Nicaraguans, American officers came to realize that these ranks "without question, will be for deserving politicians, and eventually will all be of the party in power." It was clear that "politics control the appointments in what was hoped to be a non-partisan military force." [29] The idea of the National Guard as a disinterested stabilizing force for Nicaraguan democracy had been questioned by Lawrence Duggan of the Department of State as early as November 1931.[30]

Despite the disappointments of the intervention, Secretary of State Stimson was determined to fulfill a commitment made to the two Nicaraguan parties in 1928 for American supervision of the 1932 elections. But in June 1932 Congress refused to appropriate funds to send five hundred more American servicemen to Nicaragua for election duty. As a result, the National Guard had to provide most of the personnel for supervising the election, although some American servicemen from the Canal Zone and the Special Service Squadron were assigned to temporary duty in Nicaragua with the electoral mission.[31]

Nicaraguan *políticos* realized that the withdrawal of the Marines after the November balloting would leave the frightening problem of dealing with Sandino in the hands of the victorious party. The leaders of both parties considered the pacification of Sandino to be the gravest problem facing the country; the Sandinista threat drove the Liberals and Conservatives together. In the summer of 1932 delegates from the two parties began negotiating a series of agreements whereby the victor in the November elections would share with the vanquished the spoils and burdens of government. The first of the agreements—signed on October 3 by the authorized representatives of both parties but not made public until after the elections—called for a united front in dealing with Sandino.[32] Since there was little hope of the National

Guard winning a military victory over the guerrillas, the agreement stated that "peaceful and conciliatory methods are to be preferred and an effort will be made to treat with Sandino along these lines immediately." In arriving at this agreement the Liberals and Conservatives were assisted by the "Patriotic Group," an organization affiliated with neither traditional party, which also offered to serve as an intermediary in transactions between the Sandinistas and the old-line politicians. The United States voiced no objections to the activities of the Patriotic Group—even though its leader, Sofonías Salvatierra, was an avowed anti-interventionist—and did not oppose offering Sandino concessions to induce him to lay down his arms.

General Sandino announced his terms for peace early in the summer. He insisted that the Marines be withdrawn *before* the elections, and he called upon all parties and political groups in Nicaragua to join in nominating a candidate of national unity for the presidency. As it became clear that the politicians had little enthusiasm for Sandino's proposals, the guerrilla chieftain announced his own presidential candidate and vowed to install him in office by force of arms if necessary. Sandino's choice was Horacio Portocarrero, an old Liberal general who had been living for many years in exile in El Salvador. General Portocarrero was a "symbol of past struggles," a "perfect gentleman" who "carried his more than seventy years with the bearing of an ancient conqueror." [33] But the politicians were of no mind to endorse Sandino's choice and went on to nominate their own presidential candidates: Adolfo Díaz by the Conservatives and Doctor Juan B. Sacasa by the Liberals. Shortly after his nomination, Sacasa sent an emissary to Washington to ask that the Marines be retained in Nicaragua for some time after the new President took office. But Secretary of State Stimson refused the request and "averred that it was essential to adhere to the plan of withdrawing the Marines as scheduled." [34]

As the political campaign got under way, Sandinista propaganda urged the Nicaraguan people to take no part in

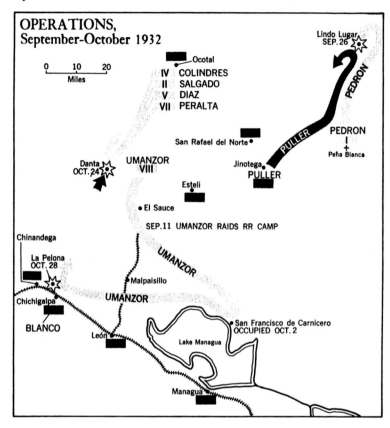

OPERATIONS,
September-October 1932

0   10   20
Miles

IV   COLINDRES
II   SALGADO
V   DIAZ
VII PERALTA

Ocotal

Lindo Lugar
SEP. 26

PEDRON

PEDRON
I
+
Peña Blanca

San Rafael del Norte

PULLER

Danta
OCT. 24

UMANZOR
VIII

Jinotega
PULLER

Esteli

El Sauce

SEP. 11 UMANZOR RAIDS RR CAMP

Chinandega

La Pelona
OCT. 28

UMANZOR

Chichigalpa

UMANZOR

Malpaisillo

BLANCO

León

San Francisco de Carnicero
OCCUPIED OCT. 2

Lake Managua

Managua

the election. In a show of guerrilla strength, Umanzor once again drove south and on September 11 raided a construction camp on the railroad being built between León and El Sauce.[35] Further to the east, in Jinotega department, the National Guard took the offensive. On September 20 Captain Puller's "M" Company plunged into the jungles around Peña Blanca with thirty days' rations and the intent to destroy the permanent Sandinista camps believed to be in that area. On September 26 Puller was ambushed by Pedrón at Lindo Lugar. With 150 men and at least seven automatic weapons, with hand and rifle grenades as well as dynamite bombs, Pedrón opened fire from a natural "V" position—hoping to do to Puller what he had done to Captain Power at Embocaderos the year before. But Puller and his men struck back vigorously, and within thirty minutes they had driven Pedrón's men out of their ambush positions. "M" Company, however, lost two men killed and several wounded, including Lieutenant Lee. Because of the wounded, Puller was forced to turn back to Jinotega. The company was ambushed twice along its line of withdrawal but suffered no further casualties.[36]

Meanwhile, Umanzor continued his march to the south and on October 2 seized the town of San Francisco del Carnicero on the shores of Lake Managua. While Umanzor was in the south, the combined forces of Colindres, Salgado, José León Díaz, and Ismael Peralta marched westward from Nueva Segovia and Estelí into Chinandega department. This force, estimated by the National Guard at three hundred, was attacked near Danta by twenty-four Nicaraguan Guardsmen, led by two American officers, who forced the guerrillas to withdraw to the east.[37] While Colindres and his associates abandoned northern Chinandega, Umanzor moved into the southern part of the department and camped at La Pelona hacienda near Chichigalpa. Information that Umanzor was at La Pelona reached Chichigalpa on the afternoon of October 27, and that night a force of eleven regular Guardsmen, twenty-five auxiliaries, and two Nicaraguan officers prepared to attack the guerrillas the next morning.[38]

Second Lieutenant Federico Davidson Blanco's thirty-eight-man patrol—armed with rifles, four automatic weapons, and two grenade launchers—was attacked by guerrillas at 6:45 on the morning of October 28 as it approached Umanzor's camp at La Pelona. Many of the auxiliaries broke ranks and ran after the first shots, and the regular Guardsmen soon found themselves surrounded by Sandinistas. Lieutenant Blanco's regulars fought fiercely to break out of the encirclement and finally succeeded at about 11:15. During the rest of the day the survivors of the patrol straggled into Chichigalpa and Chinandega, leaving Umanzor in command of the battlefield at La Pelona. Eleven Guardsmen were killed, five wounded, and two captured. The patrol also lost thirteen rifles, two Browning automatic rifles, and two grenade launchers. Lieutenant Blanco claimed in his report that the Sandinistas suffered much heavier losses, and he praised the performance of his regular Guardsmen while admitting that "the majority of the auxiliaries were a real bunch of cowards."

An encounter five days later in Nueva Segovia revealed the cowardice of a regular National Guard officer. On the night of November 2 a guerrilla force led by ex-Sergeant José García, a deserter from the Quilali garrison, attacked the National Guard barracks at Jícaro. The Guard commander, Second Lieutenant Jacob G. Keller, directed the Guardsmen in resisting the enemy, but his second-in-command, Nicaraguan Second Lieutenant Jorge Bernheim, retired to his room after the first few shots, one of which had wounded him "very slightly . . . on the outer edge of the skin between the thumb and forefinger of the right hand." Bernheim told Lieutenant Keller that he could not leave his room to take his battle station because "he was wounded too badly." The injured lieutenant "did fire 36 rounds from a 16 gauge shotgun through the screen door of his room from a sitting position on the floor." This fire could not have done much damage to the attackers—who never came closer to the barracks than fifteen yards—since there was a breast-high adobe wall immediately in front of Bernheim's door. The enlisted Guardsmen " 'razzed' Bernheim just as much as they did the bandits during the attack." [39]

Umanzor's raids and the poor showing of some native National Guardsmen caused consternation in Managua. Leaders of both political parties were frantic and pleaded for the retention of the Marines in their country. American Minister Hanna tried to console the native *políticos* by pointing out that "the possibility of conciliating Sandino will be greater if no Marines remain in Nicaragua." Hanna recognized that American occupation of Nicaragua was "the principal excuse for [Sandino's] belligerency" [40] and in effect admitted that the intervention was actually fomenting the bloodshed it was supposed to prevent.

United States forces in Nicaragua had already been reduced to such an extent that by election day, November 6, there were only enough American servicemen to supervise 182 of the country's 429 polling places. No Americans were assigned to the polls in "districts where their nationality would expose them to attack by the Sandinistas." [41] By November 7 enough returns had been produced to show that Sacasa and the incumbent Liberal party had carried the elections by a substantial majority. Soon after the results were announced, a split developed in General Sandino's forces. Juan Gregorio Colindres, whose band was operating in northern Chinandega at the time of the elections, proclaimed himself Provisional President of Nicaragua in the name of Sandino's army, but without the generalissimo's approval. On November 9, from his headquarters in eastern Nueva Segovia, Sandino ordered Ismael Peralta, Colindres' second-in-command, to arrest Colindres and assume command of his column and bring it to the generalissimo's headquarters. Peralta and Colindres arrived at Sandino's camp about the first of December, where the arrested officer begged forgiveness and Sandino relented. Sandino believed Colindres was the victim of the bad advice of Doctor Arturo Vega, a physician from León and sometime Liberal politician. [42]

In diplomatic and political affairs General Sandino was listening to the advice of Horacio Portocarrero in El Salvador and Pedro José Zepeda in Mexico. Before the elections Sandino had considered proclaiming a provisional government in northern Nicaragua, but he dropped the idea when it became clear that no Latin American nation would recognize his government. In mid-November the general was thinking of coming to an "honorable understanding" with the new Nicaraguan administration, whereby his army would be given military control of the republic and his followers would occupy the Ministries of War, Treasury, and Foreign Relations in Sacasa's government. If these concessions were not granted,

Sandino believed that Zepeda and Portocarrero could secure enough military equipment abroad to enable his forces to wage open warfare against the Nicaraguan government after the first of the year.[43] While Sandino was formulating his demands, he learned who would command Sacasa's armed forces.

On November 15 it was announced that the first Nicaraguan Chief Director of the National Guard was to be Moncada's Foreign Minister, Anastasio Somoza—the erstwhile Liberal general who, in 1927, had rushed to pay his respects to Henry L. Stimson even before Moncada had seen the American envoy. Somoza was to assume his command on January 1, 1933, and, in the meantime, was to gain experience as the assistant to General Matthews, the outgoing commander. The new fifty highest-ranking officers of the Guard, with the exception of the Chief Director and his chief of staff, were all recommended by President-elect Sacasa and automatically appointed by President Moncada in accordance with a pre-election agreement: during the campaign each of the two presidential candidates had submitted a list of fifty men, equally divided between Liberals and Conservatives, so that the successful candidate's choices would be appointed understudies to the departing American officers in time to gain several weeks' experience before assuming their commands. But the selection of the Chief Director and the chief of staff—Brigadier General Gustavo Abaunza, a Liberal newspaper publisher—were not left entirely to Sacasa. Somoza was commissioned major general and designated Chief Director of the National Guard by President Moncada, apparently with the concurrence of Sacasa and General Matthews, and certainly with the warm approval of the American Minister in Nicaragua.[44]

Anastasio "Tacho" Somoza was born in 1896 at San Marcos, only a few miles from Sandino's birthplace at Niquinohomo. As youths Sandino and Somoza attended the same high school in Granada, but not at the same time. Although Somoza's father was a farmer of only modest means, a succession of good coffee crops enabled him to send his son to the United States for further education. In Philadelphia young Somoza took a business course at the Pearce School and met Salvadora Debayle, a student at a local girl's school and a member of an aristocratic Nicaraguan family. Returning to their homeland, the couple were married in 1919 despite the objections of Salvadora's family. After the wedding the Debayles tried to make the best of the situation and set up their son-in-law in business as proprietor of an automobile agency. But the business soon failed, and Somoza had to take such odd jobs as boxing referee, baseball umpire, electrical meter reader, and privy inspector for a Rockefeller Foundation sanitation mission to Nicaragua. In this last job Somoza won the nickname "The Marshal," because the long flashlight he used in his work resembled a marshal's baton. Somoza was a big man—huge for a Nicaraguan—tall, well built, and athletic, but with a tendency to paunchiness. Almost always jovial and convivial, he radiated a Falstaffian charm. When the Constitutionalist Revolution broke out in 1926 Somoza took the side of his wife's uncle, Juan B. Sacasa, and his own distant relative, General Moncada. Although he did little to distinguish himself militarily, Somoza soon became one of Moncada's favorites. While Moncada was President, Somoza was successively Nicaraguan Consul in Costa Rica, Deputy Minister of Foreign Affairs, Minister of Foreign Affairs, and, finally, Chief Director Designate of the National Guard. The last appointment was partly due to the patronage of the American Minister in Nicaragua, Matthew C. Hanna. The Minister and his wife were impressed by Somoza's absolute mastery of the American language and were captivated by his effervescent personality. Mrs. Hanna thought Tacho Somoza a smooth tango and rumba dancer.

About a week after it was announced that Somoza would head the National Guard, Sofonías Salvatierra of the Patriotic Group wrote to Sandino in behalf of President-elect Sacasa, proposing a peace conference.[45] While Sandino studied these post-election developments, guerrilla activity decreased. Na-

tional Guard intelligence suspected that "the bandits are
carrying on their waiting policy until the Marines withdraw
from the country. . . . From the bandit standpoint there is
nothing for them to gain by launching an offensive movement at this time" (December 1).[46] As days and weeks passed
and Sandino made no reply to Salvatierra's letter, President-
elect Sacasa's fears of a prolonged war increased. Finally, on
December 24 Sandino wrote to Salvatierra, agreeing to the
peace conference, but delivery of the letter was delayed until
after the Marines had left the country.[47] The Sandinistas were
willing to negotiate with the incoming Sacasa administration,
but they could not resist striking one last blow against President Moncada, the man who had spurned Sandino's peace
overtures four years before.

One of President Moncada's last official acts was to be the
dedication of the new León–El Sauce railroad line on December 28. On Christmas Day rumors were circulating in Managua that Sandino was planning to crash the dedication
ceremony at El Sauce and tear up the railroad. The next
morning General Matthews dispatched Captain Puller and
seven of his best American officers with sixty-four hand-
picked enlisted Guardsmen to El Sauce to make the area secure for the formalities. At 4:30 P.M., as the locomotive pulling the three cars containing the seventy-two Guardsmen
chugged up the last grade south of the final construction
camp near El Sauce, Juan Pablo Umanzor and a force of
more than a hundred Sandinistas were looting the camp's
commissary.[48]

Umanzor heard the train and, believing it to be only
lightly guarded and carrying ammunition for the El Sauce
garrison, sent about half of his men to capture it. As the train
approached some ancient Indian ruins, Sandinista machine
guns opened up on it from both sides of the track. The
Guardsmen piled out of the cars, half following Puller to the
right side and half with Lieutenant Lee to the left. Realizing
now the true strength of his enemy, Umanzor committed

the rest of his troops. Lee's men took up defensive positions in a ditch while Puller tried to turn Umanzor's left flank. Puller's encircling party under Lieutenant Bennie M. Bunn ran head on into a Sandinista group attempting the same maneuver. Bunn grabbed a Browning automatic rifle from an enlisted Guardsman and advanced without cover toward the oncoming Sandinistas, firing short bursts from the hip. Lieutenant Bunn's heroism forced the enemy back and saved the day for the National Guard. After an hour and ten minutes of battle, Umanzor withdrew, leaving thirty-one of his dead behind. The Guard lost only three killed and three wounded. Two days later, as scheduled, Moncada presided over the dedication ceremony at El Sauce without incident.

On January 1, 1933, Juan Bautista Sacasa was sworn in as President of Nicaragua, and Anastasio Somoza took command of the National Guard. The next day the last of the Marines embarked at Corinto. One hundred thirty-six Marines had lost their lives during the intervention. Thirty-two were killed in action and fifteen died of wounds; eleven were murdered, five by mutinous National Guardsmen; forty-one died in accidents, fourteen of them in airplane crashes; twelve committed suicide; one was shot while resisting arrest; and twenty-four died of disease. The total number of Marine combat fatalities during the entire intervention was probably less than the Sandinista losses in the single battle of Ocotal. When the number of Marines killed by guerrillas is added to the number of native National Guardsmen killed—seventy-five, according to official Marine figures—a grand total of 122 combat deaths results. This is a remarkably low figure for nearly six years of no-quarter guerrilla warfare; the total number of Sandinistas killed at Ocotal and the El Sauce railroad—their first and last battles with the Marines and Guardsmen—was probably greater than the Marine–National Guard figure for the entire intervention. National Guard units alone claimed to have killed a total of 1,115 "bandits," [49] but this figure, and the official contention that only seventy-five native Guardsmen lost their lives fighting the guerrillas, may be reasonably questioned. The figure of forty-seven Marine combat fatalities is undoubtedly accurate.

"The Marines had come to save lives in the civil war," Henry L. Stimson noted a dozen years after the intervention; "they had remained to disarm the contenders, chase bandits, and hold an election, and they left behind in the end a country peaceful and independent. It was a job well done." [50] McGeorge Bundy, who uncritically recorded these reminiscences of the aged statesman, would later, in Vietnam and Santo Domingo, have to face the realities of American military intervention in foreign revolutions. One of Secretary Stimson's subordinates during the Nicaraguan intervention, Willard Beaulac, implied that the greatest contribution the Marines made to peace in Nicaragua was to withdraw from the country, for Sandino ended his destructive guerrilla warfare immediately after the Americans left—something he had steadfastly refused to do as long as the Marines were "maintaining law and order" in Nicaragua.[51] If the intervention was not quite the success Stimson publicly proclaimed it to be, this was due primarily to the stubborn resistance of one man. After it was all over, Dana G. Munro of the State Department admitted that Sandino was something more than a simple bandit. "It is difficult to suppose," Munro wrote in 1933, "that Sandino could have kept up the struggle, against great odds and in the face of severe hardship, if he had not been inspired by a fanatical hostility to foreign intervention." [52] Seventeen years later Munro noted that the Marine-Sandinista conflict "did more to create Latin American ill-will than any other episode in our foreign policy since the 'taking' of Panama." [53]

Militarily, the United States benefited from the intervention. "There is no doubt," one Marine officer wrote, "that the hard campaigning, the perpetual stretching of insufficient means, and the tenacity of the enemy did much to maintain the professional temper of the Corps between the two world wars." [54] The United States was fortunate to have a group of combat-hardened young Marine colonels—the lieutenants and captains of Nicaragua—when the time came to stop the march of the Japanese Empire across the Pacific. In the jungles of Guadalcanal, Edson, Hanneken, Carlson, and Puller made indispensable contributions to the success of the first American offensive of World War II. These and other veterans of the Nicaraguan campaign "brought to the geometrically expanded Marine Corps the required skills and judgments necessary for the training and indoctrination of the 'New Breed' of Marines." [55]

The fact that they were unable to put down Sandino's rebellion does not discredit the Marines. They were given an impossible task: to win a war that had no military solution. "Sandino was in every respect a wholly new phenomenon for the Marine Corps and the United States," a Marine historian has noted. He was a "modern-style guerrilla demagogue." Augusto C. Sandino, "in his articulacy, his talent for agitation, his international connections, his exploitation of the press, his deft intrigue, his cynical disregard of political commitments, his vanishing powers across 'neutral' frontiers . . . is far more readily recognizable in the 1960's than in the 1920's." [56] "Sending in the Marines" is not enough to vanquish this kind of enemy.

II

The Death of Caesar

Shortly before New Year's Day, 1933, General Sandino sent his wife from his jungle headquarters to San Rafael del Norte to make arrangements for the peace conference proposed by President Sacasa. Blanca de Sandino, now four months pregnant, was arrested by National Guard Captain Policarpo Gutiérrez when she arrived at San Rafael del Norte. The general's wife protested the arrest, informing the captain that she was Sandino's agent in charge of peace conference arrangements and as such had been guaranteed freedom of movement by President Sacasa. "I have nothing to do with the orders of the President," Gutiérrez told Blanca; "he rules in Managua and the National Guard rules here." [1] Nevertheless, on January 6 Blanca was allowed to inform Managua of Sandino's willingness to negotiate with the government. By this time the guerrilla chieftain had announced his terms for peace. He would settle for political and military control of a new department drawn up to include most of the wild Coco Valley between El Chipote and the Caribbean coast, plus the withdrawal of all records from government archives referring to the Sandinistas as bandits and the government's promise to work for an inter-American conference to discuss the proposed Nicaraguan canal. [2]

Sacasa's will to resist Sandino's demands deteriorated as his military arm—the National Guard—was wracked by internal feuding. Officers who had graduated from the Marine-run Nicaraguan Military Academy, many of whom were also veterans of anti-guerrilla combat, resented the commissioning of civilians to fill the higher ranks of the National Guard. By January 7 General Somoza was aware of a plot by a group of academy graduates to seize control of the Guard. There was little the Chief Director could do but try to reason with the mutinous officers and meet some of their demands for higher rank. In the meantime, Sandino took advantage of the situation and personally led three hundred men out of the jungles to the summit of strategic Yucapuca mountain, between San Rafael del Norte and Jinotega. Sandino camped on Mount Yucapuca on January 10, while another important peak in the area, El Saraguazca, was being occupied by the troops of Juan Pablo Umanzor.[3]

Sofonías Salvatierra, who was now Sacasa's Minister of Agriculture and Labor, urged the President to act quickly to pacify Sandino. Sacasa named Salvatierra head of a four-man delegation to go north and negotiate with Sandino. The delegation—which included Don Gregorio Sandino, ex-Constitutionalist General Alberto Reyes, and Sofonías Salvatierra's brother Alejandro—arrived in San Rafael del Norte on January 13. Blanca de Sandino, who by this time had been released from National Guard custody, was overjoyed by Salvatierra's explanation of President Sacasa's position. "I believe, my love," she wrote her husband, "that according to your ideas and those of Sacasa, you two will reach an understanding." Referring to their unborn child, Blanca wrote that "your little boy wants to see you and he is happy that his *papito* will soon be with his *mamita* making her pains easier."[4] That same night, January 13, six truck loads of National Guard "auxiliaries," commanded by ex-volunteer General Juan Escamilla, roared out of Managua for Matagalpa and points north.[5]

Sandino's wife and Sacasa's Minister of Agriculture and Labor worked vigorously to avoid a major clash between the Sandinistas and government forces. On January 19 Blanca escorted Salvatierra and his peace delegation to Sandino's

camp in the Yucapuca-Saraguazca area. The general stated
his conditions for peace, which were essentially the same as
those he had announced earlier in the month, and he and
Salvatierra agreed that these terms could serve as a basis for
further negotiations; Sandino said he was willing to go to
Managua in person to make peace. On January 21 Blanca and
the peace delegation returned to San Rafael del Norte and
Salvatierra telegraphed Sacasa, informing him of Sandino's
position. The President conferred with representatives of the
two political parties on January 23, and it was agreed that
Sacasa would proclaim a truce to facilitate further negotiations. The cease-fire was to take effect immediately, and
official notice of the truce was telegraphed to Blanca on January 24. Blanca promptly dispatched a runner to Sandino's
camp with a copy of the telegram—but that same day fighting broke out around El Saraguazca. The general's wife was
distressed:

> I beg you in the name of little Augusto, let's do every-
> thing possible to make him and ourselves happy. I am so
> concerned, because this very moment information is arriving
> that many bombs have been heard exploding on Saraguazca.
> . . . Now you know, my love, that I will be the first victim
> if all this comes to nothing. . . .
> Your little boy kisses you; you should see what a kicker
> he is now. Come and see your child; don't think of aban-
> doning him, because he will be your happiness. Right now
> a most beautiful rainbow is appearing in the west, a very
> good omen.
> Come *papasito*, don't make me cry so.[6]

The fighting around El Saraguazca stopped before the end
of the month, as Sandinistas and National Guardsmen be-
latedly began observing the truce. In the meantime, Doctor
Pedro José Zepeda arrived in Managua from Mexico aboard
an airplane he had chartered for the Nicaraguan government.
Sofonías Salvatierra met Zepeda in Managua and on January
29 flew with him to Jinotega. There they mounted mules
provided by the National Guard and rode overland to San

Rafael del Norte. After conferring with Blanca and holding a tree planting ceremony in San Rafael del Norte, Salvatierra and Zepeda proceeded to Sandino's camp in the Yucapuca-Saragauzca area, arriving on January 31. The next morning Sandino announced to the Minister of Agriculture and Labor: "I woke up today feeling romantic and tragic; I think we have to make peace in the next five days or I'm dead, and the way to do it is for me to go to Managua and deal directly with Doctor Sacasa." [7] Salvatierra lost no time in wiring Sacasa to send the airplane for Sandino immediately. Early in the morning of February 2, 1933, Julio Zincer, the plane's Mexican pilot, took off from the airfield at Managua to go to Jinotega and pick up Sandino.

General Augusto C. Sandino stepped off the plane at Managua airfield about noon on February 2, 1933. Although the government had tried to keep his arrival a secret, word of Sandino's impending visit had spread through Managua and a sizable crowd was on hand at the airfield when he landed. The general appeared in his field uniform, with a revolver on his right hip and a book in his left hand. A National Guard lieutenant saluted and stretched out his hand to the guerrilla general. "No," Sandino said to the lieutenant, "an embrace; we are brothers and I bring you peace." [8] President Sacasa's automobile was there at the airfield, waiting to carry Sandino to the presidential palace. But shortly after the plane landed Major General Anastasio Somoza, Chief Director of the National Guard, drove up in his car and invited Sandino and Doctor Zepeda to ride with him. Sandino and Somoza embraced and drove away together toward the presidential palace. The people of Managua lined the streets and cheered wildly as the guerrilla leader passed in Somoza's car. At the presidential palace Sandino was embraced by Juan B. Sacasa, and the general and his advisers were shown to a room in the west wing of the building. There Sandino declared to the press that he had come to make peace and was laying down no conditions. His advisers—General Portocarrero, Zepeda, and Salvador Calderón Ramírez, a Nicaraguan Liberal who had been associated with Zepeda in exile in Mexico, "a highly cultured gentleman" [9]—met immediately with representatives of the Conservative and Liberal parties and drew up a protocol of peace. The document was signed by President Sacasa and General Sandino at ten minutes before midnight on February 2, 1933.

By the terms of the peace agreement [10] Sandino declared his crusade for Nicaraguan liberty ended, and the Liberal and Conservative parties rendered "homage to the noble and patriotic attitude of . . . General Sandino." The guerrilla chief formally submitted to the authority of the government in Managua and agreed to the "gradual abandonment of his arms." Sandino and his followers were promised amnesty for any political or criminal offenses committed since May 4, 1927, and Sandinistas were to be given employment preference on all public works projects in the northern departments. In addition, they were to be granted a tract of government land of "sufficient amplitude" in the wilderness of the Coco Valley for an agricultural colony. To protect the colony—which had to be at least thirty-five miles from the nearest incorporated town—Sandino was allowed to retain an armed force of one hundred men, to be known as "Emergency Auxiliaries" of the Nicaraguan government. Sandino could select these men from among the members of his army; one year after the promulgation of the amnesty decree, the government could authorize the retention of his force, or reduce it in number, or place new officers in charge of it. The remainder of Sandino's troops were to turn in their arms by February 23, 1933. To supervise the disarmament and handle other matters relating to the Sandinistas, Agriculture and Labor Minister Sofonías Salvatierra was named presidential delegate to the northern departments. The Sandinistas were to surrender their arms to Salvatierra at San Rafael del Norte, and Sandino was granted military and political control of the town for the period of the disarmament.

The morning after he signed the pact with Sacasa, Sandino flew back to the north to carry out its provisions. San-

dino's peacemaking was applauded by almost everyone—
except the communists, who regarded it as confirmation of
their earlier charges of treason against the general. Sandino
had displayed no bitterness in Managua, not even toward the
United States. "I have nothing against North Americans personally," he declared. "So let them come here to work. However, I will not accept them coming as bosses again. . . . I
send my greetings to the American people." [11] Later he sent
a letter to the *New York Herald Tribune* offering condo-
lences to the families of the Americans killed in Nicaragua. A
large segment of the American press responded by hailing
Sandino as a true patriot in the tradition of Washington and
Bolívar.

Sandino's army was officially disarmed at San Rafael del
Norte on February 22, 1933. On that day Sandino, Salvatierra, and Colonel Rigoberto Reyes of the National Guard
took an official inventory of what Sandino claimed were all
his weapons, except for a few old rifles which were deposited
in the mountains and would be collected later. At San Rafael
del Norte there were 2 Lewis machine guns, 10 Browning
automatic rifles, and 6 Thompson submachine guns. There
were 337 rifles, of which 199 were Krags (the official rifle of
the National Guard), 55 were *Concones* (American Enfields
purchased by Mexico after World War I and supplied to
Sacasa's forces during the Constitutionalist revolution), and
14 were Springfields (the official rifle of the U.S. Marine
Corps). There were 6 shotguns and 3,129 cartridges for all
the weapons collected. All this ammunition and all the automatic weapons—except for one Browning automatic rifle—
were returned to Sandino after the inventory for his armed
guard of 100 men. In addition to the automatic weapons,
Sandino reclaimed for his guard 11 Springfield rifles and 71
Krags. Although only 361 weapons were accounted for,
about 1,800 Sandinista soldiers were demobilized at San
Rafael del Norte—which caused doubt "in certain quarters as to whether Sandino has turned in all his arms." [12]
Nevertheless, President Sacasa officially accepted the disarma-

ment and, on Sandino's recommendation, appointed Francisco Estrada commander of the 100 Emergency Auxiliaries.

In the spring of 1933 Sandino published a "Manifesto to the Peoples of the Earth and in Particular to the People of Nicaragua." [13] In this pamphlet the general stated his intention "to morally support Doctor Sacasa during his administration" but declared that he was "independent of the government." While Sacasa was in office Sandino said he would remain in the Segovia mountains, and, he wrote, "I will use this time to organize agricultural cooperatives in these beautiful regions that for centuries have been ignored by the statesmen." This area, centered around Guiguili on the Coco River, extended over 36,800 square kilometers, Sandino claimed, and would one day become the "Federal District of Central America."

The colonization project at Guiguili was dear to Sandino's heart. He had long embarrassed his bourgeois admirers by calling himself a "rational communist" and chiding them for not understanding that his communism was "the communism of the commune." [14] Significantly, Sandino did not advocate agrarian reform—that is, the confiscation or expropriation of private land and its redistribution among the peasantry. This, the general maintained, was not necessary in Nicaragua where there was plenty of unused public land. He saw the key to Nicaragua's advancement in the colonization of the republic's vast wilderness areas. Such an undertaking, Sandino believed, required great cooperative efforts, and for this he favored the communal organization of his Indian ancestors; at Guiguili he could set the example.

Sandino spent part of the spring of 1933 in San Rafael del Norte awaiting the birth of his child. He lived in the Arauz home with his wife, his mother-in-law, and Blanca's niece, Angelita González Arauz, of whom Sandino was very fond. On the morning of June 2, 1933, Blanca Arauz de Sandino died in childbirth. To Sandino's grief at the loss of his wife was added disappointment: "the adored 'Chico,'" the boy both parents had hoped for, "turned out to be a little girl."

The general named his daughter "Blanca Segovia," left her in the care of Blanca's mother, and retreated to the cooperative at Guiguili. There Sandino consoled himself with Blanca's niece, whom he brought to the jungle settlement as his concubine.[15]

The ex-guerrilla leader nevertheless maintained his enthusiasm for the agricultural project on the Coco River. In July he told a reporter from Managua that his colony could produce many of the goods being imported on the Caribbean coast, including cereals, lard, and meat. For export the colony could produce various tropical products, such as cacao. Planting, Sandino announced, would begin as soon as his men had finished making the Coco River navigable by deepening the channel where necessary. At first President Sacasa was apprehensive about Sandino's opening of the Coco and proposed to strengthen the National Guard detachments near the river's mouth.[16] Eventually, however, Sacasa came to realize that the greatest threat to his government came not from the Sandinistas but from the National Guard. On November 1, 1933, Sacasa's Vice-President reported to the American legation that General Somoza was conspiring to overthrow the President.[17]

Twice during 1933 Sandino bowed to Sacasa's wishes and postponed his plans to form a new political party; on at least three occasions he expressed strong support for the administration. In the meantime, relations between the Sandinistas and the National Guard deteriorated, especially after a Guard patrol opened fire on a group of Sandinistas driving livestock near Yali on August 20. Five Sandinistas were killed and one Guardsman was wounded in this fight—which was officially declared a mistake. On November 20 Sandino arrived in Managua to discuss with Sacasa the "difficulties which have arisen between Sandino's men and the Guardia Nacional in the Northern Area." [18] While he was in Managua, Sandino also conferred with Somoza, and the two generals issued "pacific and conciliatory" declarations which were published in the Managua press on December 5. Sandino committed his

Emergency Auxiliaries to "respect the institutions and authorities of the Republic," and Somoza ordered the National Guard to cooperate with the Sandinistas in maintaining order and peace in the Coco Valley. But this atmosphere of accord was shattered later in the month when Francisco Estrada, commander of Sandino's Emergency Auxiliaries, appeared in Managua and requested additional arms for his men.[19]

Somoza adamantly opposed issuing Sandino more weapons and, furthermore, demanded that Sacasa order the total disarmament of the Sandinistas in February under the terms of the peace agreement of 1933. Somoza's demand increased the tension between the National Guard commander and the President, both of whom sought help from the new American Minister to Nicaragua, Arthur Bliss Lane. Sacasa told Lane that he feared the consequences if he ordered Sandino to surrender his arms; Sacasa thought Somoza would try to overthrow his government no matter what the President did about Sandino. Somoza complained to the American Minister that Sacasa had not permitted the National Guard "to 'finish' Sandino," that the Guardsmen's pay was in arrears, and that "despite the non-payment of the troops" Sacasa had spent $20,000 of National Guard funds "for the construction of a fort just outside of León, thus showing his lack of confidence in the Guardia and his desire to fortify the region of the country most loyal to the President." Sandino's representative in Managua, Pedro José Zepeda, also called on Lane and suggested that Sacasa would need Sandino's Emergency Auxiliaries to protect him against Somoza.[20]

On January 26 Sandino wrote Sacasa pledging loyalty to the President against the "unconstitutional" National Guard. But the general declared that he would not give up his arms and hoped the government would live up to the peace agreement and not ask him to do so. The threatening tone of the letter angered Sacasa, who then "definitely refused Sandino's request for additional ammunition through Estrada" and summoned the ex-guerrilla to Managua for a "frank discussion." [21] General Somoza told Minister Lane "that he will take no action to embarrass the President and that the Guardia will be loyal" during Sandino's visit to Managua; "even if the Guardia officers should be loyal to the government," Lane reported to Washington, "I have grave doubts as to the efficiency and discipline of the organization as a whole and as to whether Somoza really controls his men." [22]

General Sandino arrived in Managua on February 16, 1934, and was lodged at the residence of Agriculture and Labor Minister Sofonías Salvatierra. Other guests in the Salvatierra home included the general's brother, Sócrates Sandino, Juan Pablo Umanzor, and Francisco Estrada. Sandino's chief adviser, Pedro José Zepeda, was in the United States on a business trip, but Horacio Portocarrero and Salvador Calderón Ramírez were on hand in Managua. American Minister Lane had great confidence in Calderón Ramírez—who had been summoned to Managua from his post as Nicaraguan *chargé d'affaires* in Mexico—and expected him to exert a moderating influence on Sandino in his dealings with Sacasa and Somoza. But Sandino antagonized Somoza the day after he arrived by declaring to the Managua press that he would never surrender his arms to the "unconstitutional" National Guard.[23]

Somoza, however, displayed no hostility toward Sandino when he met with him and Sacasa at the presidential palace on the night of February 18. The disarmament question was not settled at this meeting, but Somoza gave Sandino a safe conduct pass, and the ex-guerrilla consented to remain in Managua until an agreement could be reached. During the next two days Sandino conferred with various government officials. Salvador Calderón Ramírez attended these meetings as Sandino's adviser and "apparently exerted his influence on the side of reasonable conciliation." The "highly cultured" Calderón soon appeared "somewhat disillusioned" with the ex-guerrilla and, in conversations with Minister Lane, "referred in disparaging terms to Sandino's intellectual capacity for expressing his ideas." Sacasa's Minister of Foreign Affairs told Lane that he had listened carefully to Sandino talk for half an hour, but afterward he had no idea of what the general had been trying to say. High government officials "manifested an impatience" because so much time was "being spent in long negotiations with such a person." In an interview published in *La Prensa*, Sandino declared that the United States wanted to get him out of the Coco Valley so that the area "might fall into American hands and serve as a source of food supply in the event of war." [24]

Sandino also reiterated his charge that the National Guard was unconstitutional in a note he sent to Sacasa on February 19. The President replied the following day, stating his belief that he and Sandino could settle their differences—"particularly those concerning the National Guard." [25] The next morning, February 21, General Somoza arrived at the American legation—he "appeared unusually excited"—and informed Minister Lane that Sacasa "had exchanged letters with Sandino implying that the Guardia should be reorganized within six months" and had appointed General Horacio Portocarrero, Sandino's adviser, presidential delegate to the northern departments. Somoza declared that Portocarrero's appointment was an insult to the National Guard and would put the Guardsmen in the northern departments under the control of Sandino. The National Guard commander said he wanted to "proceed immediately against Sandino" and would "lock him up" if Lane would "merely wink [his] eye." The American Minister advised Somoza to calm down and "suggested to him the possible consequences of any violent action, such as civil war." Lane told Somoza that he would see Calderón Ramírez and try to find out exactly what was going on between Sacasa and Sandino. [26]

On the afternoon of February 21 Lane conferred with Calderón, who told him that Portocarrero, "although once a Sandino enthusiast, was now very loyal to the government and was . . . the best selection for the position of delegate." At six o'clock Lane arrived at Somoza's house and repeated to the Guard commander what Calderón had said about Portocarrero. Somoza told the American minister

> that he would not "start anything" without prior consultation with me. Somoza appeared even more nervous than in the morning and was conferring with three Guardia officers . . . when I entered his home. He said that while he accepted Calderón's estimation of Portocarrero, the Guardia would be furious at the "insult" and that things had reached a point where he could no longer control the Guardia. As I left him he again said that nothing would be done without consulting first with me.[27]

After speaking with Lane, Somoza and the three officers —one of whom was Captain Policarpo Gutiérrez—departed the Chief Director's house and went to a building in the Campo de Marte military compound where twelve other officers were already assembled. Somoza announced to the group—which included Brigadier General Gustavo Abaunza, National Guard chief of staff—that he had just come from a conference with American Minister Lane "who has assured me that the government in Washington supports and recommends the elimination of Augusto César Sandino, because they consider him a disturber of the peace of the country."[28] After a brief deliberation the officers voted unanimously to kill Sandino that night. To insure that all would share responsibility for the act, the officers signed a resolution called "The Death of Caesar." Then they made plans to eliminate the ex-guerrilla chieftain and all members of his armed guard who were in Managua that night. The officers knew that Sandino and some of his aides were then visiting Sacasa and would probably stay for dinner. Major Lisandro Delgadillo and fifteen Guardsmen were detailed to arrest Sandino and his companions as they left the presidential palace grounds. Once Sandino was in custody, Captain Policarpo Gutiérrez and fifteen other Guardsmen were to raid Sofonías Salvatierra's house and arrest the Sandinistas there. All the important prisoners were to be taken immediately to the Managua airfield and executed. When all this had been decided, Generals Somoza and Abaunza proceeded to the National Guard theater where Chilean poetess Zoila Rosa Cárdenas was giving a recital.

Dining with Sacasa and Sandino on the night of February 21, 1934, were the President's brothers, Federico and Antioco Sacasa, Sandinista Generals Juan Pablo Umanzor and Francisco Estrada, Don Gregorio Sandino, Salvador Calderón Ramírez, General Horacio Portocarrero, and Agriculture and Labor Minister Sofonías Salvatierra. Sandino was in good humor and entertained the company for awhile with war stories. Then the diners discussed the exploitation of gold mines in the Guiguili area by a company that Sacasa and Sandino had agreed to form, in which the President's wife would be the principal stockholder. The Sacasa family was impressed by the samples of gold that Sandino had brought from the mountains. The party broke up at about ten o'clock; Calderón and Portocarrero remained to discuss the duties of the new presidential delegate, while Sandino, his father, Umanzor, Estrada, and Salvatierra said good night to the President and drove away in the Agriculture and Labor Minister's car.

Salvatierra's automobile was halted at the sentry box at the exit to the palace grounds. Major Lisandro Delgadillo's heavily armed Guardsmen emerged from the shadows, and their leader ordered the Sandinistas out of their car. They obeyed, but not without protest. "Why are you doing this?" Sandino demanded of Major Delgadillo. "We are all brothers. . . . Call General Somoza and ask him to come here." [29] Sandino, Delgadillo, and Somoza were, in fact, brother Masons, and the ex-guerrilla persuaded the major to telephone Somoza at the recital. Somoza told Delgadillo that he could do nothing and refused to speak to Sandino. Don Gregorio Sandino and Sofonías Salvatierra were locked up in Hormiguero jail, and Major Delgadillo loaded Generals Sandino, Estrada, and Umanzor onto a truck with his fifteen Guardsmen and drove away toward the airfield. About twenty minutes after the truck departed Hormiguero jail, Salvatierra and Don Gregorio could hear the sound of distant gunfire. "They are killing them now," General Sandino's father remarked. "Thus it will always be: he who makes himself a redeemer dies crucified." [30]

What Don Gregorio heard was an attack on Salvatierra's residence by the men of Captain Policarpo Gutiérrez. Most of the Agriculture and Labor Minister's family was out of town, but his son-in-law was at the house and was killed in the attack. One of Salvatierra's Sandinista guests, Colonel Juan Ferretti, escaped, but Sócrates Sandino, the general's brother, was captured by Captain Gutiérrez. American Minister Arthur Bliss Lane heard the shooting, rushed to the scene, and asked Gutiérrez what the trouble was. The captain said the Sandinistas had fired first. Lane realized that serious trouble was brewing and decided to waste no time with Gutiérrez; he hurried back to the legation to call Sacasa and do what he could to prevent a *coup d'état*. When Lane had gone, Gutiérrez loaded his troops and their prisoner aboard a truck and proceeded to the airfield.

Sócrates Sandino joined his brother and Generals Estrada and Umanzor at the Managua airfield at about eleven o'clock. They stood in the glare of truck headlights while Major Delgadillo's Guardsmen began setting up a machine gun. The major, who did not want to witness the death of a brother Mason, walked away and sat down behind a small knoll; he would give the signal for the execution by firing his pistol into the air. Sandino, the eternal optimist, hoped that his father would be able to contact Somoza and persuade him to call off these proceedings before it was too late. When the machine gun was ready, Sandino tried to stall for time. He asked the commander of the gun crew, Second Lieutenant Carlos Eddy Monterrey, for a drink of water and was refused. He asked for permission to urinate and again was refused. "Don't ask anything of them, General," Francisco Estrada said; "let them kill us." Juan Pablo Umanzor approached a National Guard sergeant saying, "I give you this package of cigarettes and this neckerchief for you to keep as souvenirs." [31]

Sandino also wanted to pass out some souvenirs, but when he put his hands in his pockets he found nothing in them. "*Jodido!*" the general exclaimed, "*Mis líderes políticos me embrocaron*"—"Screwed! My political leaders [already] emptied me of my contents." [32] Major Delgadillo fired his pistol into the air and the machine gun mowed down the four prisoners.

The next morning Somoza's troops moved against the Sandinista cooperative at Guiguili. Without Sandino there could be no Sandinismo, and within a matter of weeks the movement was crushed.[33] General Somoza allowed President Sacasa to continue in office until 1936, when the President was finally deposed by the commander of the "non-partisan" National Guard. From then until 1956, when Somoza was cut down by an assassin's bullets, the burly general was dictator in Nicaragua. The country then passed into the hands of his sons—Luís, the President, and Anastasio, the Chief Director of the National Guard.

Postscript
The Ghost of Sandino

A

Although the United States was not directly involved in the assassination of Sandino, it was, and is, widely believed in Latin America that the crime was instigated by "Yankee Imperialists." The United States was in fact guilty to the extent of supplying the murder weapon—the American-trained and -equipped Nicaraguan National Guard. If the United States government did not intend that the National Guard be used for such a purpose, it did little to prevent the perversion of the role of this "non-partisan constabulary."

To many, American duplicity seemed clear: with one hand the Americans supervised honest elections in Nicaragua, fully realizing that the winner was likely to be Dr. Sacasa—whose possible ascension to the presidency six years before had provoked the landing of the Marines. But with the other hand the United States arranged for the incoming President to be placed in the custody of a military force whose chief was hand-picked by the Yankees. Knowing that Sacasa would come to terms with Sandino, the United States depended upon Somoza to eliminate the elusive guerrilla by means that would have been unbecoming of straight-shooting North Americans. Having done the Yankees' dirty work, Somoza met no opposition from Washington when he deposed Sacasa in 1936 and made himself dictator of Nicaragua. It was all part of a deal between Somoza and the Yankees, many Latin

Americans contend, and twenty years of extravagant American praise for the Nicaraguan dictator proved that the "imperialists" never regretted the bargain. Thus the United States gained a satellite in Central America—and confirmed the worst suspicions of Latin Americans from California to Cape Horn.

There is, however, no evidence of a formal "deal" between Somoza and American officials for the murder of Sandino and the establishment of the Nicaraguan dictatorship. But Somoza was in effect a time bomb, planted in Managua by the Hoover administration, and Franklin Roosevelt allowed it to explode. Given the "Good Neighbor Policy" announced in 1933, Roosevelt could hardly have done otherwise. The United States was pledged not to intervene in the internal affairs of its neighbors under any circumstances— not even to prevent the establishment of military dictatorships. After 1936, when Nazi infiltration in Central America became a real problem, U.S. relations with the pro-American Nicaraguan dictator became quite cordial. "He's a sonofabitch," Roosevelt is reported to have said of Somoza, "but he's ours." [1] After World War II American fear of Nazism was replaced by fear of communism, and United States friendship for the anti-communist Somoza continued.

Nicaragua made progress of a sort under the rule of Anastasio Somoza. Private enterprise was encouraged, and foreign capital was welcomed in Somoza's fief. He paid special attention to the development of agriculture and himself acquired ownership of an estimated one-tenth of his country's productive land. During World War II and the Korean War world cotton and coffee prices boomed, and Nicaragua began showing a healthy trade surplus. Of course, much of the Nicaraguan produce sold on world markets came from the dictator's farms. Somoza's interest in agriculture did not cause him to ignore commerce and industry. His personal holdings included rum distilleries, textile, soap, and cement factories, sugar mills, cotton gins, and a steamship line. At the time of Somoza's death in 1956, Nicaragua's gross national product had risen to a respectable $310 million. A good share of this accrued to the dictator himself, whose personal fortune amounted to some $60 million. Nevertheless, the standard of living of the average Nicaraguan did rise appreciably under Somoza, especially during the prosperous 1950's when many schools, hospitals, and roads were built—with the help of American foreign aid.

Nicaraguan economic progress has continued under the regime of Somoza's sons, who also have permitted some political advances. The more obnoxious practices of police state control have been discontinued, and a measure of freedom of the press has been tolerated. Luís Somoza stepped down as President in 1963—after elections that were preceded by spirited debate, violence, and the withdrawal and imprisonment of the principal opposition candidate. The presidency devolved upon Luís Somoza's hand-picked successor, René Schick, who has continued his predecessor's liberalization program. But the all-important Nicaraguan National Guard remains in the hands of Chief Director Major General Anastasio Somoza, Jr.—better known as "Tachito." Should President Schick carry liberalization too far, or threaten the vast Somoza economic interests, or try to obstruct Tachito's own presidential ambitions, the National Guard commander would be in a position to deliver a military coup.

Thus the current Nicaraguan political situation is somewhat similar to that of early 1936. But a military coup in Nicaragua today would provoke a much stronger popular reaction than did the coup of 1936. Today Nicaraguans are experiencing a rising standard of living and rising democratic expectations after a long period of oppression. The situation is like that of the Dominican Republic in 1963. If this "revolution of rising expectations" is suddenly cut short by a military coup, or the fraudulent election of a military President, the resulting discontent could lead to violent social upheaval. Revolutions are seldom bred in abject poverty or under the oppression of an iron dictatorship. Revolutions usually come when things are getting better, when the dictatorship begins to weaken—when people are conscious of the improvement but consider it "too slow." Any attempt to arrest Nicaragua's current progress toward democracy would be dangerous indeed.

The spirit of Sandino has reappeared in Nicaragua since the death of Anastasio Somoza. In 1958 Tachito had to put down a minuscule guerrilla movement led by Ramón Raudales, a veteran of Sandino's army. The next year the National Guard disposed of a much larger band of guerrillas, many of whom had been armed and trained in Fidel Castro's Cuba. Rumors of guerrilla activity in the mountains of Nicaragua persist to this day, despite the denials of the National Guard, which is undoubtedly the most efficient military organization in Central America.

What the recent guerrilla movements in Nicaragua have lacked is a charismatic leader of the Sandino type—a "respected leader fighting for the salvation of his people," as "Che" Guevara put it, around whom a guerrilla conspiracy should center.[2] In the popular reaction to a future coup in Nicaragua, such a leader might arise—as Sandino emerged in the reaction to the Chamorro coup of 1925, and as Fidel Castro arose in the reaction to the Batista coup of 1952.

Retaliating for a 1966 offer by President Schick of military training bases in Nicaragua to anti-Castro Cubans, Fidel Castro's government has openly proclaimed its support for armed revolution in the land of Sandino. Cuban support for a neo-Sandinista movement in Nicaragua could also be considered the repayment of a debt; in the matter of guerrilla organization and tactics, Fidel Castro owes much to Sandino, although the Cuban revolutionary was not at first attracted by Sandino's style of fighting. Castro had associated with Sandinistas as early as 1947 on Cayo Confites, the Cuban-owned island on which Latin American revolutionaries of various nationalities formed an expeditionary force to invade Trujillo's Dominican Republic. (The expeditionary force, including the Nicaraguan "Sandino Brigade," was dispersed by Cuban government forces after Washington brought pressure on the liberal regime in Havana.) On July 26, 1953, when Castro attacked Moncada barracks in Santiago de Cuba, he demonstrated that he had profited little from his association with Sandinistas. This assault on a well-fortified enemy was a greater fiasco than Sandino's attack at Ocotal; Castro's entire force was killed or captured. It was three years later, when he came under the influence of Alberto Bayo and Ernesto "Che" Guevara in Mexico, that Castro came fully to appreciate the Sandinista concept of guerrilla warfare.

Spanish Colonel Alberto Bayo, originally an air force officer, directed guerrilla operations for the Loyalists during the Spanish Civil War. After the Franco victory he emigrated to Cuba and later settled in Mexico. In Bayo the thorough professional soldier merged with the revolutionary dreamer. His goal was to liberate his homeland from fascism, and, to prepare himself for this undertaking, he carefully studied post–World War II military developments, especially those in China. He further sharpened his talents by dabbling in Caribbean revolutions.

Colonel Bayo became a military adviser to some of the various armed groups of liberal and radical revolutionaries collectively known as the "Caribbean Legion." The Legion, which took vague shape after World War II, was dedicated to the overthrow of Latin American dictators, but it was in fact more a state of mind than a formal organization. Legionnaires took part in the ill-fated Cayo Confites expeditionary force, and they fought in the successful revolution of 1948 in Costa Rica. At various times they enjoyed the support of democratic governments in Venezuela, Cuba, Guatemala, and Costa Rica. The Somoza dictatorship in Nicaragua was one of the prime targets of the Legion, some of whose members had served with Sandino. It was a group of Nicaraguan Legionnaires that promoted Bayo to the rank of "general" in 1948. Like all good teachers, Bayo learned something from his students. He came to believe that Sandino's style of warfare was ideal for Caribbean revolutionaries facing vastly superior government forces. "Always remember Sandino,"[3] he wrote in a handbook for the Caribbean Legion first published in the 1940's. He gave the same advice to Fidel Castro when he came to him for training in 1956.

Among the men he trained in Mexico for Castro's invasion of Cuba, Bayo considered Ernesto "Che" Guevara his star pupil. It had taken Guevara three years to travel from his native Argentina to Mexico, where he had his fateful rendezvous with Bayo and Castro in 1956. Guevara took the revolutionary trail after graduating from medical school in Buenos Aires; his odyssey began as a flight to avoid being drafted into the Argentine Army medical corps. From Argentina the impoverished young physician drifted northward, taking odd jobs along the way. He tarried awhile in revolutionary Bolivia, then pushed on to San José, Costa Rica, arriving in the fall of 1953. San José at that time was a favorite meeting place for Caribbean Legionnaires, who enjoyed the patronage of Costa Rican President José Figueres.

Among the Legionnaires in San José when Guevara arrived were some aging Sandinista veterans who still dreamed of overthrowing the Somoza dictatorship of neighboring Nicaragua. Most of the important Sandinista officers who had survived the massacres of 1934 were dead or definitely retired by 1953. Juan Gregorio Colindres had been mysteriously murdered in Nicaragua the year before, and Pedrón had been treacherously assassinated by National Guardsmen in 1937. But some minor Sandinista officers, including Ramón Raudales, continued to plot against Somoza from exile in Costa Rica. After a brief association with these rather disorganized and demoralized emigrés, Guevara was not impressed by their chances of overthrowing the Nicaraguan dictator. But he was impressed by their stories of Sandino. From them Guevara discerned the reasons for Sandino's success in resisting the Marines: the inspirational quality of his leadership and his guerrilla tactics.

From San José Guevara traveled overland to Guatemala. Along the way he got a look at the jungle-clad Segovia mountains of northern Nicaragua, where Sandino got his start—terrain very similar to the Cuban Sierras. Arriving in Guatemala in December 1953, Guevara soon landed a job with that country's communist-infiltrated Agrarian Reform Institute. When an anti-communist revolution broke out in July 1954 Guevara was organizing peasant militia outfits to defend the government. President Jacobo Arbenz, however, gave up almost without a fight, and Guevara went into hiding. Eventually he crossed the border into Mexico where he met Fidel Castro.

In Castro Guevara found a revolutionary who seemed to have all the qualities that were lacking in Arbenz and the Sandinistas of San José. Guevara recognized Castro as a leader of vast imagination and determination, limitless self-confidence, and great personal magnetism—qualities he shared with Sandino. Like Sandino, Castro gave an impression of sincere patriotism and absolute integrity. Here was the "respected leader" around whom to center a guerrilla conspiracy. After completing General Bayo's guerrilla course, Castro, Guevara, and eighty others sailed from Mexico for Cuba in November 1956. Only twelve of the eighty-two, including Castro and Guevara, eluded the Cuban government forces that were waiting for them when they landed on the coast of Oriente province. These twelve brought Sandino-style guerrilla warfare to Cuba. Within a year the band of twelve had grown to a force of several hundred.

Castro's rebel army, like Sandino's, was organized into self-supporting columns. As in Nicaragua, each rebel column in Cuba was assigned an area of operations and normally operated independently of the other columns—although joint operations were sometimes undertaken, especially in the later stages of the rebellion. Column commanders—majors rather than generals in Castro's army—were responsible directly to Maximum Leader Castro, who, like Sandino, acquired symbolic value early in the campaign and thereafter remained remote from combat.

Like Sandino's larger units, Castro's columns were broken

down into units of fifteen to fifty men, called "patrols" in
Cuba. These patrols were sometimes further broken down
into squads. Flexibility in organization was valued equally by
Sandino and Castro. The existence of subunits depended upon
the tactical situation or upon the weapons or leaders available.

Communications in both guerrilla armies were maintained
almost exclusively by runners. Radio was not understood by
Castro or Guevara and was not available to Sandino. Nevertheless, Castro, like Sandino, had a most effective intelligence
and security system. Fidelista sympathizers in the towns, villages, and throughout the countryside lost no time in reporting government troop movements to the guerrillas.

Castro's supply service functioned like Sandino's. Food,
clothing, and work animals were requisitioned from the local
peasantry and, when possible, were paid for with money collected from the rich in "taxes" or voluntary gifts. When
Castro's troops took property without payment, they usually
followed Sandino's practice of leaving I.O.U.'s. These pieces
of paper, as Guevara was later to write, "bind old and new
owner to a common hope for success of the cause." [4] Castro,
like Sandino, proscribed indiscriminate pillaging as harmful
to the revolutionary cause, but the Cuban leader was much
more successful in enforcing the prohibition.

The Cuban rebels, like their Nicaraguan counterparts, depended partly on the enemy for arms, ammunition, medicine,
and combat equipment. But in both cases more of these items
were bought from foreign suppliers than were captured or
stolen from the enemy. As Sandino's supply lines crossed the
Honduran border, Castro's supply lines spanned the Florida
Straits. In both cases the ultimate source of supply was the
United States.

Sandino's "hit-and-run" tactics were successfully employed by the Cuban rebels. Like the Sandinistas, the Fidelistas sometimes concentrated as many as two hundred guerrillas against ten- to forty-man garrisons and patrols. Sieges
of Cuban Army outposts often lasted hours or even days,
until the garrison surrendered or the approach of a relief

column forced the guerrillas to withdraw. Guerrilla ambushes, on the other hand, seldom lasted more than a few minutes; if the ambushed enemy survived the initial shock of the attack and managed to launch a counter-attack, the Fidelistas, like the Sandinistas, would withdraw. As in Nicaragua, guerrilla ambushes in Cuba usually were not set up with the idea of destroying the enemy; they were conceived as a means of inflicting upon him as much damage as possible with minimum risk to the guerrillas. The line of withdrawal was always an important feature of any position occupied by Fidel Castro's guerrillas. Like the Sandinistas, the Fidelistas could foil pursuers by scattering after an action and reassembling later at a prearranged rendezvous.

Not only did the Fidelistas make meticulous preparations for their own withdrawal, but in most instances they followed the Sandinista practice of purposely leaving open a line of retreat for the enemy. They would position an ambush party in a "V" or horseshoe formation, with the open end serving as an escape hatch for the victims. Without this exit the ambushed patrol would have no choice but to try to smash out through the guerrilla lines. From the guerrillas' standpoint this would be undesirable, for they usually could inflict more casualties on the enemy at less cost to themselves by inducing the ambush victims to run a gantlet through the open end of the horseshoe or "V." This concept of leaving an exit for the enemy, however, was of neither Nicaraguan or Cuban origin. It had been advocated more than two thousand years ago in China by one of Mao Tse-tung's favorite authors, Sun Tzu.[5]

In its later phases the Castro rebellion was more like that of the Chinese communists than the Sandino insurrection, which never reached the final, victorious stage. And Sandino never had to contend with the massive government penetrations, or "sweeps," of his territory that confronted the Fidelistas and the Chinese communists. Castro's repelling of Batista's 1958 summer offensive in the Sierra Maestra was more like the Chinese communist resistance to Chiang Kai-shek's

"annihilation campaigns" of 1930–1932 than anything Sandino accomplished. And Sandino never attempted to strangle
his country's cities with the countryside, as Castro did late in
1958 in Oriente and Las Villas provinces, and as the Chinese
communists did in Manchuria in 1948. Sandino kept his
promise to lay down his arms when the Marines left Nicaragua in 1933 and did not attempt to carry his insurrection to
this advanced stage. Sandino lacked insight as a social revolutionary rather than resources for bringing the guerrilla struggle to a victorious conclusion. Before Sandino's death in 1934
guerrilla warfare had become the instrument of social revolutionaries more astute than the Nicaraguan rebel.

In 1895, the year Sandino was born, Friedrich Engels discussed the futility of revolutionary warfare in his introduc-
tion to that year's edition of Karl Marx's *The Class Struggle
in France*. The old-style urban uprising, "the street fight behind barricades," Engels declared, "has become antiquated." [6]
Modern weapons and communications had made the old
means of revolution obsolete. A "people's" victory over regular military forces in a street battle had become all but
impossible. Railroads and telegraphs facilitated the rapid concentration of government forces against any insurrectionary
center. Modern artillery could systematically reduce work-
ing-class suburbs to rubble. There could be no revolution
against the army; the soldiers would have to be converted to
the revolutionary cause before victory would be possible.
Engels urged the workingmen of Europe not to attempt
armed rebellions but instead to organize, propagandize, and
participate in non-violent political activity. Then, when the
capitalist system would inevitably begin to crumble because
of its "inner contradictions," the proletariat would be ready
to seize power.

But Marx and Engels overlooked the revolutionary possibilities of the underdeveloped countries—where the lack of
an industrial society, they believed, precluded a true proletarian revolution—and of the peasant classes, whom they
considered "unreliable." Lenin and Stalin, who contradicted

the prophets of communism by establishing socialism in a semi-developed country, were more concerned with the underdeveloped world and recognized some revolutionary potential in the peasant class. But even the Soviet leaders believed that the revolution in the underdeveloped countries would have to center in the cities—that the rural masses would play only a secondary role, with urban workers assuming the leadership and bearing the brunt of the struggle. It was Mao Tse-tung and his followers—"margarine communists" in Stalin's phrase [7]—who first brought communism to power in an underdeveloped country. They achieved this by practically ignoring China's urban workers (who remained loyal to Chiang until the very last days of his regime), by relying on the peasantry for mass support, and by resorting to revolutionary warfare—which Engels had declared obsolete in 1895.

While Chinese communist guerrillas were winning their first victories over the troops of Chiang Kai-shek, Sandino was demonstrating that a "people's army" could successfully resist the military forces of a modern industrial power. Instead of massing his forces behind city barricades, Sandino dispersed them in highly mobile bands throughout the countryside, where slow-moving concentrations of enemy troops—with their artillery, airpower, and the other appurtenances of modern warfare—were of little use. Most important, Sandino's guerrillas enjoyed the support of the rural population. The Sandinistas were, borrowing a metaphor from Mao Tse-tung, fish moving through friendly waters; as long as the waters—i.e., the peasants—were friendly, the fish would survive.

A government, therefore, must draw peasant support away from the guerrillas before it can dominate a guerrilla insurrection. But once the countryside has been lost to a well-organized guerrilla movement, it is not easy to regain. Guerrilla control cannot be broken by good intentions and good deeds alone; the government must also establish a permanent military presence in the guerrilla-infested areas. This is not done by massive "sweeps," which may temporarily clear the guerrillas from a region but allow them to move back in as soon as the troops have returned to their bases. Nor can it be done by dotting the area with defensive garrisons which the guerrillas can isolate and pick off, one by one. And a permanent military presence cannot be established by aerial bombardment, which kills relatively few guerrillas, reveals the impotence of the government, and incurs the hatred of the non-combatants inevitably victimized by the bombings.

For a government on the verge of collapse, however, aerial bombardment of guerrilla-controlled areas might provide a temporary reprieve—especially if the bombing is accompanied by the massive intervention of friendly foreign troops. Such measures would hardly endear the government to its people, but in this situation it would already be at the nadir of its popularity and have little to lose. Guerrillas concentrating for a final offensive could be seriously hampered by the bombing, and the large-scale commitment of fresh troops to the government would certainly force the guerrillas to revise their schedule for conquest. The guerrilla war of moral attrition would now have to be waged against a new enemy: the intervening foreign power.

Any first- or second-rank power can prevent the guerrilla conquest of a smaller country—as long as it is willing to maintain a large military force in the field against the guerrillas. The French Army was not driven out of Indochina or Algeria by guerrillas; it was withdrawn by a nation that no longer had the will to continue the war effort. The guerrillas won these wars *in France:* year after year the human casualties and the damage to the nation's economic and political structure mounted until France lost its will to continue the confrontation in the colonies. Patience is the guerrilla's cardinal virtue; he must be willing to wait long years until his war of attrition has its effect upon the morale of the enemy. It took Mao Tse-tung twenty-two years to topple Chiang Kai-shek, Ho Chi Minh nine years to make the French withdraw from Indochina. The guerrilla's will to outlast the enemy should enable him to accept setbacks and revise his schedules when necessary. Under pressure from massive conventional military forces, he must be willing to disband his concentrations and revert to small-unit hit-and-run actions (as did Ho in 1946 and Mao in 1934 and 1947). In the case of foreign intervention, the guerrilla must maintain enough pressure on the enemy—inflict upon him enough casualties and material damage—to make the people of the intervening nation question the price they are paying to prevent a guerrilla victory in another country.

If the massive commitment of foreign conventional forces can forestall a guerrilla takeover, it may not, however, necessarily lead to a government victory. If the guerrillas miscalculate and expose too many men in an effort to maintain pressure on the enemy, the conventional forces might conceivably win. But if the guerrillas disperse properly and refuse combat when victory is not assured, the war could continue indefinitely. The problem of the intervening foreign troops is to destroy the guerrillas before their war of attrition can sap morale on the home front.

To anyone who has served with guerrillas, the solution should be obvious. General Bayo recognized it when he wrote: "We are in greater danger if our guerrilla unit of 15 men is pursued by 25 soldiers than 5,000." [8] Nothing upsets a guerrilla band more than to be chased by a compact, fast-moving patrol of soldiers who are familiar with the people and terrain of the area of operations, and are willing to stay in the field until decisive contact is made. Wars against guerrillas are won by de-escalating them into wars of patrol actions. Instead of deploying a division to "clear" an area of a regiment of guerrillas, a regiment of soldiers should be sent in to hunt down and destroy the guerrillas. Each component unit of the anti-guerrilla regiment, down to the squad level, should be capable of sustained independent patrol action; when the guerrilla regiment breaks down into its component units and disperses, the anti-guerrilla regiment breaks down into independent patrols, each of which pursues a specific guerrilla unit. A patrol stays in the field until it has destroyed its assigned quarry or has been relieved by another patrol which takes up the same pursuit.

This kind of warfare is not popular with conservative American military men, because it denies the classic infantry role of seizing and holding terrain, from which are derived the roles of all the supporting arms and services—artillery, armor, airpower, supply, and so on. Oblivious to the fact that guerrillas are seldom willing to defend terrain, Americans are still intent on seizing—or "clearing"—it. This causes the evicted guerrillas some inconvenience, but usually not enough for them to attempt a counterattack and give their enemy an opportunity to "hold" the terrain he has "seized." The guerrillas merely wait until the soldiers have completed their exercises and have moved on—then they reinfiltrate the area. The American soldier realizes that his job is to close with and destroy the enemy, but he is made to believe that, even in guerrilla war, this is done by moving great masses of men and machines across a stretch of land.

In Nicaragua the American command did designate one unit as a perpetual anti-guerrilla patrol, and it effectively neutralized one of Sandino's columns. According to a post-intervention Marine staff study, seven more such patrols—one for each of the remaining Sandinista columns—could have dominated the guerrilla situation.[9] This model patrol, however, was composed of two extraordinary Marine officers and some thirty Nicaraguans. Company "M"'s success was due as much to the native background of the Nicaraguan enlisted men as to the leadership of Captain Puller and Lieutenant Lee. The participation of native troops is essential to final victory over guerrillas.

Ideally, combat operations against guerrillas should be carried out exclusively by native troops. Their proper employment in the earlier stages of a guerrilla conflict can prevent a situation in which foreign forces must be called in to shore up a crumbling regime. Natives, rather than foreigners, are best able to move swiftly and silently through the countryside, talk with the people and discern their moods, and win their confidence—or at least their respect. Guerrilla warfare is a very human business; it must be dealt with on a man-to-man basis. Government troops must be able and willing to compete with the guerrillas personally on the village level. The soldier must be able to convince the average citizen that his side offers the best hope for future peace and prosperity. He does this not only by exemplary conduct and good deeds, but by pursuing the guerrilla on foot into the jungles, the cane fields, or the rice paddies, and by destroying him where he finds him. He does not win the people's confidence or their respect by dropping bombs from an airplane, by riding down a road in an armored personnel carrier, or by fluttering above the treetops in a helicopter. The government soldier must show his mettle by coming out and fighting the guerrilla. He must be as tough and as highly motivated as his enemy.

The American tragedy in Vietnam is that successive South Vietnamese governments have too readily accepted American military advice. Instead of insisting that the Vietnamese soldier live with the people and slug it out with the guerrilla on the village level, the United States convinced the Saigon authorities that victory could be achieved by modern technology and American-style military organization. The American passion for machines and high-level organization was disastrous. The initiative passed to the Viet Cong who dealt very humanly—if not always humanely—with the aspirations and fears of the Vietnamese peasantry. This initial failure of American advice led to the United States' fourth major war in less than half a century.

In Latin America the U.S. may well be headed for a similar catastrophe. Guerrilla movements are already under way in several Latin American countries, although they have not yet won the popular support necessary for success. If the military of these countries continue to bomb nonexistent concentrations and supply lines, the guerrillas may well gain this popular support. Latin American leaders must be made to realize that in the early stages of conflict the normal guerrilla practice is dispersal rather than concentration, that guerrillas live off the land, and that what supply lines they have are usually so thin and irregular as to be invulnerable from the air. Most important, Latin American leaders must realize that no one wins the respect of his people by dropping bombs on them.

Latin America has always been weak militarily in relation to the United States. And the peoples of Latin America have been weak in relation to their own military—often supported and supplied by the United States government—and they have resented this weakness. They have a natural antipathy for the man in the tank or the warplane, and a natural affection for the man with the rifle and the *bandoliers* who challenges the man in the machine. Latin Americans prefer the human to the mechanical, the passionate revolutionary to the military martinet. And, like people everywhere, Latin Americans tend to prefer their own kind—no matter how perverse—to the interfering foreigner—no matter how upright or well intentioned. They sided with Pancho Villa against General Pershing, with Sandino against the Marines.

The traditions of Latin America and its social and political conditions are as conducive to large-scale guerrilla operations as those of any other region of the world. Hatred of "Yankee Imperialism," rekindled by the Dominican episode in the mid-1960's, is stronger in Latin America than anywhere else—excepting, perhaps, China and her satellites. The interventionist policy of the United States government and its open support for repressive regimes have convinced many Latin Americans that eventually they will have to fight Yankee soldiers if they take the path of social revolution. There are those who are willing to risk such a conflict, and they are capable of sparking a guerrilla conflagration that could drain the resources of the United States for years to come. The return of American troops to Latin America in 1965 awak-

ened a hemisphere-wide spirit of popular resistance to
"Yankee Imperialism"—the spirit of Sandino. More than the
"International Communist Conspiracy," the ghost of Sandino
confronts the United States in Latin America today. Like
Banquo's, it can provoke the beholder to self-destructive
reaction.

Notes

◘

Chapter One: Land of Lakes and Volcanos

1. Quoted in Anastasio Somoza, *El verdadero Sandino, o el calvario de las Segovias* (Managua: Tipografía Robelo, 1936), p. 506.

2. Thomas L. Karnes, *The Failure of Union: Central America, 1824–1960* (Chapel Hill: University of North Carolina Press, 1961), p. 34.

3. Quoted in Henry F. Pringle, *The Life and Times of William Howard Taft* (New York: Farrar & Rinehart, 1939), II, 678–679.

4. Isaac Joslin Cox, *Nicaragua and the United States* (Boston: World Peace Foundation, 1927), pp. 847–848; Robert W. Dunn, *American Foreign Investments* (New York: Viking, 1926), pp. 112–114.

5. Officials of the Zelaya regime had good reason to fear the dictator's "purges": Zelaya was the ruler "who instituted enemas as a political punishment." Gustavo Alemán Bolaños, *Sandino, el libertador; la epopeya, la paz, el invasor, la muerte* (Mexico: Ediciones del Caribe, 1952), p. 216.

6. The Secretary of State (Knox) to the Nicaraguan Chargé, December 1, 1909, *Foreign Relations, 1909*, pp. 455–457.

7. Roscoe R. Hill, *Fiscal Intervention in Nicaragua* (New York: Paul Maisel, 1933), pp. 12–16; U.S. Department of State, *A Brief History of the Relations Between the United States and Nicaragua, 1909–1928* (Washington: U.S. Government Printing Office, 1928), pp. 12–13.

8. U.S. Department of State, *Brief History . . . 1909–1928*, pp. 28–33.

9. Charles E. Frazier, Jr., "The Dawn of Nationalism and Its Consequences in Nicaragua" (University of Texas Doctoral Dissertation, 1958), p. 338; Calvin B. Carter, "The Kentucky Feud in Nicaragua," *The World's Work*, LIV (July 1927), 312–321.

10. *La Prensa* (Managua), August 20, 1926.

11. Bryce Wood, *The Making of the Good Neighbor Policy* (New York: Columbia University Press, 1961), p. 15.

12. Arthur M. Schlesinger, Jr., *The Age of Roosevelt: The Politics of Upheaval* (Boston: Houghton Mifflin, 1960), p. 74.

13. Arthur Derounian (John Roy Carlson, pseud.) *Under-Cover: My Four Years in the Nazi Underground of America* (New York: Dutton, 1943), p. 462. The minutes of the *Denver* conference are in J. Barcenas Meneses, *Las conferencias del "Denver"; actas auténticas de las sesiones con introducción y ligeros comentarios* (Managua: Tipografía y Encuadernación Nacional, 1926).

14. U.S. Department of State, *Brief History* . . . *1909–1928*, pp. 34–40.

15. The Minister in Nicaragua (Eberhardt) to the Secretary of State, December 13, 1926, in Foreign Service Section, National Archives, Washington, D.C., Records of the U.S. Department of State (hereafter cited as DS), 817.00/4243.

16. Lt. Col. James J. Meade to Maj. Gen. John A. Lejeune, January 21, 1927, in U.S. Marine Corps Historical Archives, Arlington, Va. (hereafter cited as MCHA), Records pertaining to Nicaragua (13 boxes and 23 reels of 16 mm. microfilm), Reel 1. Military operations in Nicaragua during the winter of 1926–1927 are described in U.S. Marine Corps, *The United States Marines in Nicaragua* (Washington: Historical Branch, G-3 Division, Headquarters, U.S. Marine Corps, 1961), pp. 21–22, and in Robert D. Heinl, Jr., *Soldiers of the Sea: The United States Marine Corps, 1775–1962* (Annapolis: United States Naval Institute, 1962), p. 263.

17. Third Battalion, Fifth Regiment, Bn-2 Report, April 9, 1927, MCHA, Nicaragua: Reel 6.

18. Maj. M. E. Shearer, Proclamation of Neutral Zone, April 17, 1927, MCHA, Nicaragua: Reel 6.

19. Brig. Gen. Logan Feland to Maj. Gen. John A. Lejeune, April 4, 1927, MCHA, Nicaragua: Reel 1.

20. Maj. M. S. Berry to the Commanding Officer, Third Battalion, Fifth Regiment, April 23, 1927, MCHA, Nicaragua: Reel 6.

21. Bryce Wood, *op. cit.*, pp. 23–24.

Chapter Two: The Peace of Tipitapa

1. Quoted in Alexander DeConde, *Herbert Hoover's Latin American Policy* (Stanford: Stanford University Press, 1951), p. 7.

2. Quoted in Lejeune Cummins, *Quijote on a Burro; Sandino and the Marines, a Study in the Formulation of Foreign Policy* (Mexico: Impresora Azteca, 1958), p. 114.

3. *Ibid.*, p. 115. Cf. Harold Norman Denny, *Dollars for Bullets: The Story of American Rule in Nicaragua* (New York: Dial Press, 1929), pp. 250–251.

4. Stimson describes his mission to Nicaragua in his book, *American Policy in Nicaragua* (New York: Scribner's, 1927). Other phases of Stimson's career are discussed in Henry L. Stimson and McGeorge Bundy, *On Active Service in Peace and War* (New York: Harper, 1948) and Richard N. Current, *Secretary Stimson: A Study in Statecraft* (New Brunswick: Rutgers University Press, 1954).

5. *New York Times*, February 13, 1927, p. 7. Other sources of information on the Chinandega bombing are Francis D. White, Memorandum, May 11, 1931, DS, 817.00/7153, *¿Quién incendió Chinandega?* (Managua: Editorial, *La Prensa*, 1946), and Rafael de Nogales, *The Looting of Nicaragua* (New York: McBride, 1928), pp. 158–161, photographs opposite p. 177.

6. Rubén Darío, "Momotombo," *Poesías completas* (Madrid: Aguilar, S.A., 1954), p. 801.

7. Message from Stimson, in The Minister in Nicaragua (Eberhardt) to the Secretary of State, April 29, 1927, DS, 817.00/4736.

8. Denny, *op. cit.*, pp. 66–72.

9. Stimson Diary, May 3, 1927, Stimson Papers, Yale University.

10. Quotations from Ramón Romero, *Somoza, asesino de Sandino* (Mexico: Ediciones Patria y Libertad, 1959), pp. 41–44. Moncada's *Lo porvenir* (2nd ed; Managua: Tipografía Alemana, 1929) is an exposition of classical liberalism; his *El gran ideal* (Managua: Imprenta Nacional, 1929) is a paean to "daughters, mothers, and wives" (p. 5). Moncada's military and political career is described in Ronald Hilton, ed., *Who's Who in Latin America, Part II: Central America and Panama* (Stanford: Stanford University Press, 1945), p. 76; Denny, *op. cit.*, pp. 266–269, 291–293; Nogales, *op. cit.*, pp. 134-136, 148-158, 168-171.

11. Stimson, *op. cit.*, pp. 75–76.

12. *Ibid.*, p. 76.

13. Gen. José María Moncada, *Estados Unidos en Nicaragua* (Managua: Tipografía Atenas, 1942), pp. 7–9.

14. Stimson, *op. cit.*, pp. 76–79.

15. *Ibid.*, pp. 79–80.

16. Stimson Diary, May 10, 1927.

17. Nogales, *op. cit.*, p. 244.

18. Dom Albert Pagano, *Bluejackets* (Boston: Meador Publishing Co., 1932), p. 82.

19. *New York Times*, August 21, 1927, VIII, 5.

20. Rear Adm. Julian L. Latimer, *Aviso*, May 10, 1927, MCHA, Nicaragua: Reel 11.

21. Stimson, *op. cit.*, pp. 79–84.

22. Capt. Julian P. Brown, Final Report of the Arms Commission, June 10, 1927, MCHA, Nicaragua: Reel 23.

23. The Legation in Costa Rica (Davis) to the Secretary of State, May 22, 1927, DS, 817.00/4860; Cox, *op. cit.*, pp. 803-804; Denny, *op. cit.*, pp. 306–307.

24. Feland to Maj. Gen. John A. Lejeune, May 15, 1927, MCHA, Nicaragua: Reel 1; Bryce Wood, *op. cit.*, p. 27.

25. Quotations from Second Brigade, B-2 Report for May 15, 1927, MCHA, Nicaragua: Reel 4. Capt. Hart's negotiations with Gen. Cabulla are reported in Daily Log of Commander, Chinandega Detachment, May 14, 1927, MCHA, Nicaragua: Reel 11.

26. The action at La Paz Centro is described in 2nd Lt. C. J. Chappell to the Commanding Officer, May 18, 1927, and Sgt. Glendell L. Fitzgerald, Report on the Engagement at La Paz Centro, in "Combat Operations in Nicaragua," *Marine Corps Gazette*, XIII, 4 (December 1928), 243-247.

27. Quoted in William W. Savage, Jr., "They Were Called 'Banana Wars,'" *The State* (Columbia, S.C.), September 8, 1963, sect. C, 1.

28. Pagano, *op. cit.*, p. 90.

29. *Ibid.,* pp. 90–91.

30. Second Brigade, B-2 Report for May 17, 1927, MCHA, Nicaragua: Box 2.

31. Pagano, *op. cit.,* pp. 99–100.

32. *Ibid.,* p. 57.

33. Gregorio Selser, *Sandino, general de hombres libres* (Buenos Aires: Editorial Triángulo, 1959), I, 291.

34. Landing Force Order Number 17, June 3, 1927, MCHA, Nicaragua: Reel 11.

35. Second Brigade, B-2 Report for May 18, 1927, MCHA, Nicaragua: Reel 4. See also *ibid.,* May 16, 1927, and Naval Forces Ashore, F-3 Reports for May 16 and May 17, 1927, MCHA, Nicaragua: Box 1.

36. U.S. Department of State, Press Release, May 19, 1927, Harvard University.

37. Second Brigade, B-2 Report for May 26, 1927, MCHA, Nicaragua: Reel 4.

38. "Official Report Received from Brigadier General Feland," *New York Times,* May 29, 1927, II, 20; Second Brigade, B-2 Report for May 26, 1927, MCHA, Nicaragua: Reel 4; Second Battalion, Eleventh Regiment, Bn-2 Report for May 26, 1927, MCHA, Nicaragua: Reel 8.

Chapter Three: Sandino

1. Sandino to Froylán Turcios, April 10, 1928, in Alberto Ghiraldo, *Yanquilandia bárbara; la lucha contra el imperialismo; historia nueva* (Madrid: Imprenta Argis, 1929), pp. 67–68; Augusto C. Sandino, "Para la historia de Nicaragua," in Xavier Campos Ponce, *Los Yanquis y Sandino* (Mexico: Ediciones X.C.P., 1961), p. 126; Gustavo Alemán Bolaños, *Sandino, el Libertador; la epopeya, la paz, el invasor, la muerte* (Mexico: Ediciones del Caribe, 1952), p. 19; Selser, *Sandino,* I, 159. Somoza, *op. cit.,* p. 5; Denny, *op. cit.,* p. 333; and Carlton Beals, *Banana Gold* (Philadelphia: Lippincott, 1932), p. 262, give different dates. Another name for Niquinohomo was La Victoria. Other sources of information on Sandino's life prior to 1927 are Ramón de Belausteguigoitia, *Con Sandino en Nicaragua: la hora de la paz* (Madrid: Espasa-Calpe, 1934), pp. 86–90, 135, 174; Gustavo Alemán Bolaños, *¡Sandino! Estudio completo del héroe de las Segovias* (Mexico: Imprenta La República, 1932), pp. 3–8, 23, 53; Solomón de la Selva, "Sandino," *Nation,* CXXVI (January 18, 1928), 63–64; William Krehm, *Democracia y tiranías en el Caribe* (Mexico: Union Democrática Centroamericana, 1949), pp. 157–158.

2. Ghiraldo, *op. cit.,* p. 68. In 1930 Don Gregorio's age was reported to be fifty-eight, making him twenty-three at Sandino's birth. Roy T. Davis (Panama) to the Secretary of State, May 5, 1930, DS, 312.1722/folder 2.

3. De la Selva, *op. cit.,* p. 63. Margarita Calderón's hut, as pictured in Somoza, *op. cit.,* p. 6, had a run-down tile roof.

4. De la Selva, *op. cit.,* p. 64. De la Selva also claims that U.S. intervention ruined Sandino's grain business (p. 63).

5. Krehm, *op. cit.*, pp. 157–158.

6. Somoza, *op. cit.*, p. 6.

7. Quotations from Willard Beaulac, *Career Ambassador* (New York: Macmillan, 1951), pp. 44–45. Cf. Charles David Kepner, Jr., and Jay Henry Soothill, *The Banana Empire: A Case Study of Economic Imperialism* (New York: Vanguard Press, 1935), p. 112.

8. Augusto C. Sandino, Application for Employment with the Huasteca Petroleum Company, August 15, 1925 (photostat), DS, 312.1722/folder 1. On this application form Sandino listed previous employment with what appears to be the "Penn-Mex. Inc." and with the "New York Eng. Co. (Guatemala)." Sandino's bold and flowing handwriting is not always legible.

9. Sandino "diría más tarde que de México pasó a los Estados Unidos y que de allí retornó a su punto de partida para volver a emplearse en la Huasteca." Selser, *Sandino*, I, 162. Sandino wrote to Abraham Rivera, February 22, 1930, "recorrí todo nuestro istmo centro-americano, México y los Estados Unidos." Selser, *Sandino*, II, 125–126.

10. Quotations from Beaulac, *op. cit.*, pp. 12–35. Willard Beaulac was an American consular official in Tampico in 1922 and 1923. See also Carlton Beals's novel, *Black River* (Philadelphia: Lippincott, 1934). Other sources for developments in Mexico while Sandino was there are John W. F. Dulles, *Yesterday in Mexico: A Chronicle of the Revolution, 1919–1936* (Austin: University of Texas Press, 1961), pp. 229–246; Marjorie Clark, *Organized Labor in Mexico* (Chapel Hill: University of North Carolina Press, 1934), pp. 58–82, 118–119, 169–170, 289; Robert J. Alexander, *Communism in Latin America* (New Brunswick: Rutgers University Press, 1957), pp. 324–325; Rosendo Salazar and José G. Escobeda, *Las pugnas de la gleba* (Mexico: Editorial Avante, 1923), pp. 237–246; Rosendo Salazar, *Historia de las luchas proletarias de México* (Mexico: Editorial Avante, 1938), pp. 17–250.

11. Sandino, Application for Employment with the Huasteca Petroleum Company, August 15, 1925 (photostat), DS, 312.1722/folder 1.

12. Villa was killed in 1923, the year Sandino arrived in Mexico, but his "bandit" activities had ceased several years before. There is little to support the story Stimson "heard" (Stimson, *op. cit.*, p. 85) about Sandino's gaining "bandit experience" with Pancho Villa in Mexico.

13. Clark, *op. cit.*, pp. 58–82.

14. William Green, Vice President and General Manager of Huasteca Petroleum Company, to Harold Walker, March 15, 1928, DS, 312.1722/folder 1.

15. Selser, *op. cit.*, II, 113.

16. William Green, to Harold Walker, March 15, 1928, DS, 312.1722/folder 1.

17. Philip R. Gleason to Frank B. Kellogg, July 25, 1927, DS, 312.1722/folder 1.

18. Charles Butters, Statement, June 21, 1927, cited in Edwin C. Godbold, Nicaragua, MCHA, Personal Papers files: Edwin C. Godbold.

19. Philip R. Gleason to Frank B. Kellogg, July 25, 1927, DS, 312.1722/folder 1.

20. Sandino's attack at Jícaro and his subsequent role in the Constitutionalist Revolution are described in J. B. Pate, "Information Furnished by Humberto Torres . . . Who Served as an Officer in Sandino's Army," November 6, 1928, MCHA, Nicaragua: Box 10, folder 3; Maj. M. E. Shearer, to Commanding Officer, Fifth Regiment, March 28, 1927, Third Battalion, Fifth Regiment, Bn-3 Report for April 8, 1927, MCHA, Nicaragua: Reel 6; Augusto C. Sandino, Circular to All the Authorities of the Segovias, May 18, 1927, MCHA, Nicaragua: Box 10, folder 3; Augusto C. Sandino, "Para la historia de Nicaragua," August 4, 1932, in Campos Ponce, *op. cit.*, pp. 127–133; Selser, *Sandino*, I, 172–184, 219–225; Bolaños, *¡Sandino!* pp. 3, 7–8, 11–16; Belaustignigoitia, *op. cit.*, pp. 89–93; José María Moncada, "Nicaragua and American Intervention," *Outlook*, CXLVII, 15 (December 14, 1927), 461; Moncada, *Estados Unidos en Nicaragua*, pp. 23–25; De la Selva, *op. cit.*, pp. 63–64; Nogales, *op. cit.*, p. 158.

21. Moncada, *Estados Unidos en Nicaragua*, pp. 23–24.

22. Augusto C. Sandino, "Para la historia de Nicaragua," August 4, 1932, in Campos Ponce, *op. cit.*, pp. 127–128.

23. Sandino, quoted in Selser, *Sandino*, I, 230.

24. J. B. Pate, "Information Furnished by Humberto Torres . . . Who Served as an Officer in Sandino's Army," November 6, 1928, MCHA, Nicaragua: Box 10, folder 3.

25. De la Selva, *op. cit.*, p. 63.

26. Quoted in Belausteguigoitia, *op. cit.*, pp. 89–90.

27. In *Foreign Relations, 1927*, III, 344. A Spanish version is in Selser, *Sandino*, I, 226.

28. Sandino, quoted in Belausteguigoitia, *op. cit.*, p. 91.

Chapter Four: The Battle of Ocotal

1. In Selser, *Sandino*, I, 227–230.

2. Sandino's activities in Jinotega and San Rafael del Norte are reported in Alemán Bolaños, *Sandino, el Libertador*, p. 29; Belausteguigoitia, *op. cit.*, pp. 92–93; Selser, *Sandino*, I, 219, 227–231; J. B. Pate, "Information Furnished by Humberto Torres . . . Who Served as an Officer in Sandino's Army," November 6, 1928, MCHA, Nicaragua: Box 10, folder 3.

3. Quoted in Selser, *Sandino*, I, 230–231.

4. English translation in MCHA, Nicaragua: Box 10, folder 3.

5. J. B. Pate, "Information Furnished by Humberto Torres . . . Who Served as an Officer in Sandino's Army," November 6, 1928, MCHA, Nicaragua: Box 10, folder 3.

6. Belausteguigoitia, *op. cit.*, p. 92.

7. Quotations from Selser, *Sandino*, I, 231–232.

8. Sandino to Brig. Gen. Logan Feland, May 21, 1927, MCHA, Subject File: Augusto C. Sandino. Cf. Selser, *Sandino*, I, 232; Bolaños, *¡Sandino!*, pp. 17–18.

9. Col. L. M. Gulick to the Commanding General, May 30, 1927, MCHA, Nicaragua: Box 10, folder 3.

10. *Ibid.*

11. Sandino to Señor Jefe del Destacamento de Marinos, Jinotega, May 24, 1927, in Somoza, *op. cit.*, p. 36.

12. Don Gregorio Sandino to Santiago Sandino, December 18, 1927, MCHA, Nicaragua: Box 10, folder 2.

13. Accounts of this expedition are found in Maj. Pierce's Report to the Commanding General, June 10, 1927, MCHA, Nicaragua: Reel 10, and in Maj. Edwin North McClellan, "He Remembered His Mission," *Marine Corps Gazette*, XV, 3 (November 1930), 30–31.

14. McClellan, "He Remembered His Mission," pp. 31–32.

15. Quoted in McClellan, "He Remembered His Mission," p. 32.

16. Second Brigade, B-2 Report, June 17, 1927, MCHA, Nicaragua: Reel 4. Compare this evaluation of Sandino's military ability with the observations of Maj. M. S. Berry, who visited Sandino's outfit prior to the Tipitapa truce. *Supra*, p. 28.

17. Brig. Gen. Logan Feland to Maj. Gen. John A. Lejeune, June 6, 1927, MCHA, Nicaragua: Reel 1.

18. Feland to Lejeune, June 30, 1927, MCHA, Nicaragua: Reel 1. See also Heinl, *Soldiers of the Sea*, pp. 265–266.

19. Sandino to Arnoldo Ramírez Abaunza, June 14, 1927, in Selser, *Sandino*, I, 245–246.

20. Sandino to Lt. Col. D. Francisco Estrada, June 18, 1927, in Selser, *Sandino*, I, 246.

21. Copies of these telegrams and the subsequent ones are found in MCHA, Subject File: Augusto C. Sandino.

22. Feland to Lejeune, June 30, 1927, MCHA, Nicaragua: Reel 1.

23. Maj. Julian C. Smith, *et al.*, *A Review of the Organization and Operations of the Guardia Nacional de Nicaragua* (n.p., n.d.), pp. 9–27.

24. U.S. Department of State, Press Release, July 1, 1927, Harvard University. See also The Minister in Nicaragua (Eberhardt) to the Secretary of State, June 30, 1927, *Foreign Relations, 1927*, III, 439–440.

25. Maj. Floyd's operations are discussed in his Summary of Operations and Final Report of Commanding Officer, Nueva Segovia Expedition, August 21, 1927, MCHA, Nicaragua: Reel 2, in his Report to the Commanding Officer, Fifth Regiment, July 24, 1927, and in his field messages, MCHA, Nicaragua: Reel 10; in Maj. Edwin North McClellan, "The Nueva Segovia Expedition," Part One, *Marine Corps Gazette*, XV, 5 (May 1931), 21–25, and Part Two, *Marine Corps Gazette*, XVI, 2 (August 1931), 8–11, 59; in Maj. John A. Gray, "The Second Nicaraguan Campaign," *Marine Corps Gazette*, XVII, 4 (February 1933), 38; in Heinl, *Soldiers of the Sea*, p. 273; and in Beals, *Banana Gold*, pp. 232–233.

26. Feland to Lejeune, June 30, 1927, MCHA, Nicaragua: Reel 1.

27. Beals, *Banana Gold*, p. 344.

28. In Selser, *Sandino*, I, 248-251.

29. Feland to Lejeune, July 8, 1927, MCHA, Nicaragua: Reel 1; McClellan, "The Nueva Segovia Expedition," p. 25.

30. Francisco Estrada to Manuel Echeverría, July 7, 1927, MCHA, Nicaragua: Box 10, folder 2.

31. Second Brigade, Intelligence Report, July 12, 1927, MCHA, Nicaragua: Reel 4.

32. Telegrams in MCHA, Subject File: Augusto C. Sandino.

33. Maj. Oliver Floyd to the Commanding Officer, Fifth Regiment, July 24, 1927, MCHA, Nicaragua: Reel 10.

34. Capt. Hatfield gives his account of the events of July 15–16 in his Report to the Commanding General, Second Brigade, July 20, 1927, MCHA, Nicaragua: Reel 10. A slightly altered version of this report, with a diagram of the battle, is in "Combat Operations in Nicaragua," *Marine Corps Gazette*, XIV, 1 (March 1929), 18–20. Other Marine sources include Maj. Ross E. Rowell, Report of Engagement, July 16, 1927, MCHA, Nicaragua: Reel 11; Aircraft Squadrons, Second Brigade, Record of Events for the Week Ending July 16, 1927, MCHA, Nicaragua: Reel 10; Gen. Vernon E. Megee, "United States Military Intervention in Nicaragua, 1909–1932," University of Texas Master's Thesis, 1963, pp. 102–103; James W. Wright, "No Surrender," *Leatherneck*, XXIII, 10 (October 1940), 10–14; Peard, "Tactics of Bush Warfare," p. 28; Maj. E. H. Brainard, "Marine Corps Aviation," *Marine Corps Gazette*, XIII, 1 (March 1928), 27–30; Heinl, *Soldiers of the Sea*, pp. 268–269; Lynn Montross, *Cavalry of the Sky* (New York: Harper, 1954), p. 22.

35. In MCHA, Nicaragua: Reel 10. The attack is described from the Sandinista side in Selser, *Sandino*, I, 254–255, and Bolaños, *¡Sandino!*, p. 19. Another valuable account is the report of Arnoldo Ramírez Abaunza to President Adolfo Díaz, published in the *New York Times*, July 19, 1927. Both Governor Ramírez and Gen. Telles, Ramírez's aide and chief of police at Ocotal, were probably in league with Sandino. After the battle Ramírez claimed that he and Telles had fought off the Sandinistas from the barricaded police station. Ramírez, however, admitted having had conversations with several Sandinista officers during the fighting. Telles was later expelled from Nicaragua for complicity in the attack. The Minister in Nicaragua (Eberhardt) to the Secretary of State, September 11, 1927, DS, 817.00/5027.

36. Sandino, Attack Order, in MCHA, Nicaragua: Reel 10.

37. Hatfield to the Commanding General, Second Brigade, July 20, 1927, MCHA, Nicaragua: Reel 10.

38. *Ibid.*

Chapter Five: El Chipote: The Illusive Fortress

1. Sandino, Proclamation, July 20, 1927, quoted in *New York Times*, July 21, 1927, p. 5. The exiled Dr. Sacasa did little to encourage Sandino's insurrection. He remained publicly silent on Sandino until early in 1928, when he expressed the belief that the general was mistaken, although his motives were good. *New York Times*, January 7, 1928, p. 2.

2. Quoted in *New York Times*, July 19, 1927, p. 10.

3. Selser, *Sandino*, I, 272.

4. *New York Times*, January 5, 1928, p. 2.

5. *Ibid.,* January 18, 1928, p. 3.

6. Aircraft Squadrons, Second Brigade, Record of Events for the Week Ending July 23, 1927, MCHA, Nicaragua: Reel 10.

7. This account of Maj. Floyd's operations is drawn from the sources listed in note 25, Chapter Four.

8. Bolaños, *¡Sandino!,* p. 20.

9. Floyd, Field Message Number 4, July 26, 1927, MCHA, Nicaragua: Reel 10.

10. Aircraft Squadrons, Second Brigade, Record of Events for the Week Ending July 30, 1927, MCHA, Nicaragua: Reel 10.

11. Quoted in Bolaños, *¡Sandino!,* pp. 20–21. Although Bolaños calls this engagement the "Battle of Los Flores" and gives September 9, 1927, as its date, it is obvious that Sandino in his statement was referring to the events of July 27, 1927.

12. Smith, *et al., op. cit.,* pp. 23–24.

13. Floyd to the Commanding Officer, Fifth Regiment, Summary of Operations and Final Report of Commanding Officer, Nueva Segovia Expedition, August 21, 1927, MCHA, Nicaragua: Reel 2.

14. Heinl, *Soldiers of the Sea,* p. 273.

15. Second Brigade, B-2 Report, August 8, 1927, MCHA, Nicaragua: Reel 4.

16. Midshipman David Brant McGuigan, "A Case Study in Civil Military Relations: Nicaragua, 1926–1929; An Essay Submitted to the Head of the Department of English, History, and Government" (United States Naval Academy, February 1957), pp. 19–20; Heinl, *Soldiers of the Sea,* p. 266.

17. 1st Lt. George J. O'Shea to the Commanding Officer, Fifth Regiment, September 4, 1927, MCHA, Nicaragua: Box 6.

18. In Selser, *Sandino,* I, 288–290. Selser says this document was signed by "more than a thousand persons." Ten of the fourteen articles are cited in Carlton Beals, "With Sandino in Nicaragua," Part 6, *The Nation,* CXXVI (March 28, 1928), 340.

19. Peard, "Tactics of Bush Warfare," p. 28.

20. *Ibid.,* p. 29. Other sources of information on the Telpaneca attack are 1st Lt. H. S. Keimling, Account of the Engagement at Telpaneca, and Pvt. L. C. Handzlik, Statement, in "Combat Operations in Nicaragua," *Marine Corps Gazette,* XIV, 1 (March 1929), 23–26; and Bolaños, *¡Sandino!,* pp. 21–22.

21. Keimling, in "Combat Operations in Nicaragua," *Marine Corps Gazette,* XIV, 1 (March 1929), 23–25.

22. Augusto C. Sandino, Communiqué, October 8, 1927, and photograph of the body of Lt. Thomas with comments by Maj. Ross E. Rowell, MCHA, Nicaragua: Box 10, folder 2; Guardia Nacional de Nicaragua, Summary of Intelligence Reports, January 20, 1928, in *History of the Guardia Nacional, 23 January 1927 – 24 October 1929* (mimeograph), MCHA, Nicaragua: Box 11; Heinl, *Soldiers of the Sea,* p. 271.

23. Lieutenant O'Shea's patrol report is in "Combat Operations in Nicaragua," *Marine Corps Gazette,* XIV, 1 (March 1929), 26–30.

24. *Ibid.*, pp. 28–30.

25. 1st Lt. Moses J. Gould to the Commanding Officer, Fifth Regiment, November 2, 1927, MCHA, Nicaragua: Reel 22.

26. Bolaños, *¡Sandino!*, p. 28.

27. Will Rogers told the American military attaché in Costa Rica in 1931 that Zepeda had been his "good friend" for "some years." Maj. Fred T. Cruse, Military Attaché to Central America, Report, April 11, 1931, DS, 817.00/7115.

28. Beals, *Banana Gold*, pp. 189, 193.

29. Megee, "United States Military Intervention in Nicaragua," pp. 116, 129. The initial air actions against El Chipote are also discussed in Brainard, "Marine Corps Aviation," p. 32. See also Second Brigade, Summary of Operations in Nicaragua, February 9, 1928, MCHA, Nicaragua: Reel 11.

30. In MCHA, Subject File: Augusto C. Sandino.

31. Sandino to Gen. Echeverría, December 6, 1927, MCHA, Subject File: Augusto C. Sandino.

32. Sandino to Roy A. Johnson, December 6, 1927, MCHA, Subject File: Augusto C. Sandino. Portions of this correspondence were printed in the *New York Times*, March 4, 1928, p. 13, but the dates given for the letters are incorrect.

33. *New York Times*, January 13, 1928, p. 2.

34. Sandino to Jones and Sayre, January 1, 1928, MCHA, Nicaragua: Box 10, folder 2; John Nevin Sayre, "A Try at Peace and Justice with Sandino," *World Tomorrow*, XI (March 1928), 113–117; Cummins, *op. cit.*, pp. 117–118; The Chargé in Nicaragua (Munro) to the Secretary of State, December 20, 1927, DS, 817.00/5193.

35. Col. Louis M. Gulick to Maj. Gen. John A. Lejeune, December 3, 1927, MCHA, Nicaragua: Reel 1.

36. The operations of the Livingston and Richal columns are described in "Combat Operations in Nicaragua," *Marine Corps Gazette*, XIV, 2 (June 1929), 84–89; 1st Lt. Moses J. Gould to the Brigade Commander, December 31, 1927, and Gunnery Sgt. Edward G. Brown to the Brigade Commander, January 4, 1928, MCHA, Nicaragua: Reel 22; Evans F. Carlson, "The Guardia Nacional de Nicaragua," *Marine Corps Gazette*, XXXI, 3 (August 1937), 9; Clyde H. Metcalf, *A History of the United States Marine Corps* (New York: Putnam, 1939), pp. 429–430; Heinl, *Soldiers of the Sea*, pp. 275–276; Bolaños, *¡Sandino!*, pp. 27–28.

37. Second Brigade, B-2 Report, December 20, 1927, MCHA, Nicaragua: Box 2, folder 6.

38. *New York Times*, January 7, 1928, p. 1. Marine headquarters admitted that the two were still missing and had been dropped from the rolls of the corps.

39. Heinl, *Soldiers of the Sea*, p. 276.

40. Megee, "United States Military Intervention in Nicaragua," p. 120. See also Aircraft Squadrons, Second Brigade, Record of Events for the Weeks ending January 7 and 14, 1928, MCHA, Nicaragua: Reel 10; Frederick R. Neely, "Schilt, 'Corsair' and 'Wasp' in Nicaragua," *U.S. Air Services*, XIII (February 1928), 35–36.

41. Smith, *et al.*, *op. cit.*, pp. 110–111; Second Brigade, B-1 Journal, January 11, 1928, MCHA, Nicaragua: Reel 4.

42. Second Brigade, B-1 Journal, January 15, 1928, MCHA, Nicaragua: Reel 4; *Army and Navy Journal*, LXV, 19 (January 7, 1928), 1.

43. Sellers to Sandino, January 20, 1928, Sellers Papers, Library of Congress, Box 250, Special Service Squadron Commander's Correspondence, I.

44. The renewed air-ground operations against El Chipote are discussed in Maj. Ross E. Rowell, Annual Report of Aircraft Squadrons, Second Brigade, July 1, 1927 to June 20, 1928, in "Professional Notes," *Marine Corps Gazette*, XIII, 4 (December 1928), 258; Rowell, Report of Engagement, January 14, 1928, and 1st Lt. Howard N. Kenyon, Report, in "Combat Operations in Nicaragua," *Marine Corps Gazette*, XIV, 2 (June 1929), 91–94; Second Brigade, B-1 Journal, January 19–21, 1928, MCHA, Nicaragua: Reel 4; Second Brigade, B-2 Report, January 13, 1928, MCHA, Nicaragua: Box 2, folder 7; Peard, "Tactics of Bush Warfare," p. 33; Megee, "United States Military Intervention in Nicaragua," p. 115; Heinl, *Soldiers of the Sea*, p. 279; Bolaños, *¡Sandino!*, p. 30.

45. Bolaños, *Sandino, el Libertador*, p. 100; Beals, *Banana Gold*, p. 246; Second Brigade, B-2 Report for the Period 2–15 December, 1928, MCHA, Nicaragua: Box 2, folder 14.

46. In MCHA, Nicaragua: Reel 22.

47. Second Brigade, B-2 Report, January 13, 1928, MCHA, Nicaragua: Box 2, folder 7.

48. *New York Times*, January 26, 1928, p. 3.

Chapter Six: 1928: The Survival of Sandinismo

1. Second Brigade, B-1 Journal, February 3, 1928, MCHA, Nicaragua: Reel 4; The Minister in Nicaragua (Eberhardt) to the Secretary of State, February 8, 1928, *Foreign Relations, 1928*, III, 564.

2. Second Brigade, B-2 Reports, January 13 and 30, 1928, MCHA, Nicaragua: Reel 4.

3. Carleton Beals, "With Sandino in Nicaragua," *The Nation*, CXXVI (February 22–April 11, 1928). The substance of these articles was later incorporated in Beals' book, *Banana Gold, op. cit.* Quotations are from *The Nation*.

4. Second Brigade, B-1 Journal, February 3, 1928, MCHA, Nicaragua: Reel 4; Maj. Ross E. Rowell, Annual Report of Aircraft Squadrons, 1 July 1927 to 20 June 1928, in "Professional Notes," *Marine Corps Gazette*, XIV, 2 (June 1929), 254; Beals, *Banana Gold*, pp. 266–267.

5. In *Foreign Relations, 1928*, III, 569. A Sandinista who joined Beals in San Salvador in January 1928 later told the Marines an interesting story. Julio César Rivas, whom Beals considered "a man without principles of any kind" (*Banana Gold*, p. 180), was detained by Honduran authorities at Amapala and threatened with deportation to Nicaragua, while Beals was allowed to proceed to Tegucigalpa. In Amapala, Rivas claimed, he de-

stroyed a treaty signed by him, as General Sandino's representative, and President Plutarco Elías Calles of Mexico, dated January 5, 1928. In May of that year, when he was questioned by American authorities in Nicaragua, Rivas revealed the provisions of the alleged treaty: Mexico would give Sandino a million rounds of ammunition in various shipments "as the opportunity permits"; upon the withdrawal of the Marines from Nicaragua, Mexico would recognize a Sandinista government and supply it with heavy military equipment and Mexican Army personnel; the new Nicaraguan government would disavow the Bryan-Chamorro Treaty and sell "Nicaraguan Canal Stocks to all the Nations of the world but the United States"; $25,000,000 in stocks would be reserved for the Japanese Empire and $15,000,000 for Mexico; no other nation would be allowed to buy more canal stock than Japan; Japan would be allowed to fortify the canal; the Bluff Fortress at Bluefields would become a coaling station for the Mexican and Japanese navies; Japanese immigration would be promoted and a minimum of 25 percent of the construction workers on the canal would be Japanese (another 25 percent had to be Mexican); fifty hectares of uncultivated land along the canal would be given to each Japanese immigrant and to every Mexican veteran of Sandino's army; the Nicaraguan Army would be supervised by Mexican officers for five years; Nicaragua would "accept the regulations prepared by the nations holding the stocks for the construction of the canal"; "in case of any disagreement between Mexico and Nicaragua," the contracting parties agreed "to accept the Emperor of Japan as Arbitrator." Textual Copy of the Treaty Celebrated between Sandino and Calles as Rewritten in his Own Words by Julio César Rivas, and Sworn Declaration Made by Julio César Rivas, May 2–15, 1928, U.S. Navy Department, Naval Records Sections, National Archives, Washington, D.C., Record Group 127, Entry 129, Nicaragua: Records of Marine Detachments, 1928–1932, tray 131, Case Files, Natives: Rivas, Julio César. This collection in the National Archives consists of records of the Guardia Nacional de Nicaragua and is hereafter cited as GN.

6. Denny, *op. cit.*, pp. 277, 328. Other sources of information for the Sandinista incursions into the coffee region are the *New York Times*, February 11 and 20, 1928; S. Stadhagen to the editor, *La Noticia* (Managua), February 12, 1928; Second Brigade, B-2 Report, February 19, 1928, MCHA, Nicaragua: Reel 4.

7. Smith, *et al.*, *op. cit.*, p. 69. See also Somoza, *op. cit.*, pp. 11, 233. Ortez's name is sometimes spelled "Orthés."

8. Eleventh Regiment, R-3 Report, January 22, 1928, MCHA, Nicaragua: Reel 8.

9. Megee, "United States Military Intervention in Nicaragua," p. 137; "Combat Operations in Nicaragua," *Marine Corps Gazette*, XIV, 3 (September 1929), 171–172.

10. 1st Lt. Edward F. O'Day to the Battalion Commander, Second Battalion, Eleventh Regiment, March 1, 1928, MCHA, Nicaragua: Reel 22. See also Capt. William K. MacNulty to the Battalion Commander, Second Battalion, Eleventh Regiment, March 5, 1928, MCHA, Nicaragua: Reel 22.

A Sandinista version of the Bromaderos engagement is in Bolaños, *¡Sandino!*, 34–35.

11. Smith, *et al., op. cit.*, p. 25.

12. The Chargé in Nicaragua (Munro) to the Secretary of State, January 11, 1928, *Foreign Relations, 1928*, III, 560.

13. The Secretary of State (Kellogg) to the Chargé in Nicaragua, January 13, 1928, *Foreign Relations, 1928*, III, 561.

14. U. S. Department of State, Memorandum, May 21, 1928, DS, 817.00/5676.

15. Smith, *et al., op. cit.*, p. 23.

16. U.S. Senate, *Use of the United States Navy in Nicaragua: Hearings before the Committee on Foreign Relations* (Washington: U.S. Government Printing Office, 1928), p. 64. See also *New York Times*, March 3, 1928, p. 1.

17. Beals, *Banana Gold*, p. 307.

18. Víctor Alba, *Historia del comunismo en América Latina* (Mexico: Ediciones Occidentales, 1954), p. 86. See also Robert J. Alexander, *op. cit.*, pp. 35, 139.

19. "Sandino of Nicaragua: Bandit or Patriot?", *Literary Digest*, XCVL, 5 (February 4, 1928), 46.

20. Campos Ponce, *op. cit.*, pp. 156–158; various undated clippings from Mexican and Guatemalan newspapers, MCHA, Nicaragua: Box 10, folder 2; the Ambassador in Mexico (Morrow) to the Secretary of State, April 12, 1928, *Foreign Relations, 1928*, III, 571.

21. Sandino to Colonels Fernando Quinteras and Juan Gregorio Colindres, October 15, 1928, MCHA, Nicaragua: Box 10, folder 2.

22. Gabriela Mistral, "Sandino," *Repertorio Americano*, XVI (April 14, 1928), 216.

23. *Repertorio Americano*, XVI (March 24, 1928), 178–179.

24. Alexander, *op. cit.*, p. 378.

25. Sandino to Henri Barbusse, July 31, 1928, in Selser, *Sandino*, II, 32–33. For the Frankfurt Congress, see Campos Ponce, *op. cit.*, p. 162, and Alba, *op. cit.*, p. 86.

26. Heinl, *Soldiers of the Sea*, p. 288; Selser, *Sandino*, I, 272.

27. John Foster Dulles, "Conceptions and Misconceptions Regarding Intervention," *Annals of the American Academy of Political and Social Science*, CXLIV (July 1929), 103–104.

28. Quotations from Megee, "United States Military Intervention in Nicaragua," pp. 123, 142–143. See also Heinl, *Soldiers of the Sea*, p. 278.

29. Sandino to Señores jefes de las fuerzas norteamericanas encampomentadas en Jinotega y Matagalpa, March 22, 1928, MCHA, Nicaragua: Reel 22.

30. Maj. Ross E. Rowell, Resumé of Air Operations Against Hostile Outlaws in Vicinity of Murra, 18, 19, and 20 March 1928, MCHA, Nicaragua: Reel 11.

31. Second Brigade, Principal Engagements, May 15, 1927 to May 18, 1928, MCHA, Nicaragua: Reel 1.

32. Aircraft Squadrons, Second Brigade, Record of Events for the Week Ending April 7, 1928, MCHA, Nicaragua: Reel 10.

33. Second Brigade, Principal Engagements, May 15, 1927 to May 18, 1928, MCHA, Nicaragua: Reel 1.

34. Aircraft Squadrons, Second Brigade, Record of Events for the Week Ending April 14, 1928, MCHA, Nicaragua: Reel 10.

35. Aircraft Squadrons, Second Brigade, Record of Events for the Week Ending June 16, 1928, MCHA, Nicaragua: Reel 10.

36. Maj. Ross E. Rowell, "Aircraft in Bush Warfare," *Marine Corps Gazette*, XIV, 3 (September 1929), 181.

37. Quotations from Maj. Ross E. Rowell, Annual Report of Aircraft Squadrons, Second Brigade, July 1, 1927 to June 20, 1928, in "Professional Notes," *Marine Corps Gazette*, XIII, 4 (December 1928), 248-257. Other sources of information on Marine air operations in 1928 are Rowell, "Aircraft in Bush Warfare," p. 196; Lt. Col. Charles R. Sanderson, "The Supply Service in Western Nicaragua," *Marine Corps Gazette*, XVII, 1 (May 1932), 42-43; Midshipman John J. Kilday, "Air Support to the Marine Corps Expeditionary Force in Eastern Nicaragua, 1927-1929; An Essay Submitted to the Head of the Department of English, History, and Government" (United States Naval Academy, February 1959), p. 36.

38. Capt. Victor F. Bleasdale, "La Flor Engagement," *Marine Corps Gazette*, XVI, 4 (February 1932), 30; Beals, *Banana Gold*, p. 262. The activities of the Sandinistas in the mining region are discussed in Bolaños, *¡Sandino!*, p. 33; Belausteguigoitia, *op. cit.*, pp. 120-121; Somoza, *op. cit.*, p. 87; Denny, *op. cit.*, p. 73; *New York Times*, April 24, 1928, p. 1.

39. The Minister in Nicaragua (Eberhardt) to the Secretary of State, October 2, 1928, DS, 817.00/6010; *New York Times*, October 3, 1928, p. 37.

40. In *Foreign Relations, 1928*, III, 575-576.

41. Beaulac, *op. cit.*, p. 123.

42. Second Battalion, Eleventh Regiment, Bn-2 Report, September 7, 1928, MCHA, Nicaragua: Reel 12.

43. Maj. Harold H. Utley to Maj. Gen. John A. Lejeune, May 13, 1928, MCHA, Nicaragua: Reel 1; *New York Times*, April 24, 1928, p. 1.

44. Bleasdale, *op. cit.*, pp. 29, 33; Metcalf, *op. cit.*, p. 436; Smith, *et al.*, *op. cit.*, pp. 29-30.

45. Information from a Deserter . . . Who Has Been with Sandino's Forces for Almost a Year, in Second Brigade, B-2 Report, February 12, 1929, MCHA, Nicaragua: Reel 14.

46. Bleasdale, *op. cit.*, pp. 29-33, 38.

47. *Ibid.*, pp. 33-40. See also Brig. Gen. Dion Williams, "Captain Stuart Hunter, U.S. Marine Corps," *Marine Corps Gazette*, XIV, 1 (March 1929), 4-5.

48. Second Brigade, B-3 Journal, June 4, 1929, MCHA, Nicaragua: Reel 10.

49. Heinl, *op. cit.*, p. 281. Other sources of information on Edson's patrol are Capt. Merritt A. Edson to the Commanding Officer, Eastern Area, August 7, 1928, MCHA, Nicaragua: Reel 12; Edson, "The Coco Patrol," *Marine Corps Gazette*, XXI, 1 (February 1936), 41-43, 57-63;

Maj. Edwin North McClellan, "The Saga of the Coco," *Marine Corps Gazette*, XV, 3 (November 1930), 79; Campos Ponce, *op. cit.*, pp. 56–57, 80.

50. Metcalf, *op. cit.*, p. 436.

51. Second Brigade, B-2 Report, December 13, 1927, MCHA, Nicaragua: Reel 4.

52. Statements of Miguel A. Arauz, J. Francisco Barrios, and Ester Viuda de Arauz, in MCHA, Nicaragua: Box 10, folder 2; Second Brigade, B-2 Report, February 7, 1928, MCHA, Nicaragua: Reel 4.

53. Lejeune to Feland, March 20, 1928, MCHA, Nicaragua: Reel 11.

54. Testimonials in MCHA, Nicaragua: Reel 11.

55. Second Brigade, B-2 Report, January 23, 1928, MCHA, Nicaragua: Reel 4.

56. Bryce Wood, *op. cit.*, pp. 30–31; Marvin Goldwert, *The Constabulary in the Dominican Republic and Nicaragua: Progeny and Legacy of United States Intervention* (Gainesville: University of Florida Press, 1962), pp. 33–34; Second Brigade, B-2 Report, February 7, 1928, MCHA, Nicaragua: Reel 4.

57. Capt. Victor F. Bleasdale to Maj. Gen. John A. Lejeune, July 1, 1928, MCHA, Nicaragua: Reel 1.

58. Beals, *Banana Gold*, p. 293.

59. McCoy, quoted by Feland in Midshipman David Brant McGuigan, "A Case Study in Civil-Military Relations: Nicaragua, 1926–1929; An Essay Submitted to the Head of the Department of English, History and Government" (U.S. Naval Academy, 1957), p. 27.

60. Maj. Fred T. Cruse to Brig. Gen. Logan Feland, April 21, 1928, MCHA, Nicaragua: Box 5, folder 2; Belausteguigoitia, *op. cit.*, p. 189; Bolaños, *¡Sandino!*, p. 32.

61. Gen. Matthew B. Ridgway, *The Memoirs of Matthew B. Ridgway*, as told to Harold H. Martin (New York: Harper, 1956), p. 38.

62. Capt. Roger W. Peard, Brief Survey of Bandit Operations in the Northern Area, November 14, 1928, and Maj. J. B. Pate to Capt. M. B. Ridgway, November 14, 1928, MCHA, Nicaragua: Reel 13.

63. Ridgway, *op. cit.*, p. 39.

64. Fifth Regiment, R-2 Report, October 7, 1928, MCHA, Nicaragua: Reel 9; *New York Times*, July 20, 1928, p. 1, and September 4, 1928, p. 8; "Events in Nicaragua," *Marine Corps Gazette*, XIII, 3 (September 1928), 204–205.

65. Belausteguigoitia, *op. cit.*, pp. 78–79; Somoza, *op. cit.*, pp. 16, 339; Smith, *et al.*, *op. cit.*, pp. 69–70; Beals, *Banana Gold*, p. 251; Bolaños, *Sandino, el Libertador*, p. 182.

66. Brig. Gen. Logan Feland to Maj. Gen. John A. Lejeune, February 2, 1929, MCHA, Biography File: Norman M. Shaw; Capt. Norman M. Shaw to the Commanding Officer, Fifth Regiment, October 9, 1928, MCHA, Nicaragua: Reel 3.

67. Harold W. Dodds, "American Supervision of the Nicaraguan Elections," *Foreign Affairs*, VII, 3 (April 1929), 488–496; Maj. Edwin North McClellan, "Supervising Nicaraguan Elections: 1928," *United States Naval Institute Proceedings*, LIX (January 1933), 35–44; The Minister in Nicara-

gua (Eberhardt) to the Secretary of State, November 1, 1928, DS, 817.00/ 6097.

68. Sellers to Maj. E. M. McClellan, April 23, 1929, Sellers Papers, Box 250. See also the *New York Times*, February 14, 1931, p. 1; Capt. Russell E. Jamison, "United States Supervision of the Nicaraguan Elections (1928–1930–1932)," MS 153 (University of Maryland, January 1961), p. 10.

69. Ridgway, *op. cit.*, pp. 40–41.

70. Second Brigade, Intelligence Memorandum to All Officers, October 9, 1928, MCHA, Nicaragua: Reel 11.

71. Second Battalion, Eleventh Regiment, Bn-2 Report, November 12, 1928, MCHA, Nicaragua: Reel 8.

72. Gregorio Sandino to Augusto C. Sandino, November 16, 1928, and Gregorio Sandino to Blanca Arauz de Sandino, November 14, 1928, MCHA, Nicaragua: Reel 23; Gregorio Sandino to Alcibiades Alvarado, September 25, 1928, MCHA, Nicaragua: Box 10, folder 2; Somoza, *op. cit.*, pp. 104–105.

73. Margarita Calderón to Blanca Arauz de Sandino, November 11, 1928, MCHA, Nicaragua: Reel 23.

74. *El Comercio* (Managua), December 20, 1928.

75. Sellers to Sandino, November 1928 (no day); Feland to Sandino, December 4, 1928; Sandino to Sellers and Feland, January 1, 1929; MCHA, Nicaragua: Reel 14. Spanish versions of these letters are in Selser, *Sandino*, II, 45–48.

76. Sandino to Moncada, January 1, 1929, in Selser, *Sandino*, II, 49.

77. "Professional Notes," *Marine Corps Gazette*, XIV, 1 (March 1929), 54.

78. *New York Times*, December 30, 1928, p. 10.

Chapter Seven: A Stalemate and a Trip to Mexico

1. Metcalf, *op. cit.*, p. 439.

2. U.S. Congress, *Congressional Record*, LXX, part 4 (70th Congress, 2nd Session), 4046–4067, 4118–4119. See also Herbert Hoover, *The Memoirs of Herbert Hoover* (New York: Macmillan, 1952), II, 211–212, 333–334; Eberhardt to the Secretary of State, January 3, 1929, *Foreign Relations, 1929*, III, 549.

3. Eberhardt to the Secretary of State, January 22, 1929, DS, 817.1051/ 238; Metcalf, *op. cit.*, p. 438; Megee, "United States Military Intervention in Nicaragua," p. 167; Heinl, *Soldiers of the Sea*, pp. 266, 271.

4. Eberhardt to the Secretary of State, January 23, 1929, *Foreign Relations, 1929*, III, 606–607; Eberhardt to the Secretary of State, January 22, 1929, DS, 817.1051/238; Eberhardt to the Secretary of State, March 30, 1929, *Foreign Relations, 1929*, III, 624; McGuigan, *op. cit.*, p. 22.

5. Eberhardt to the Secretary of State, February 28, 1929, DS, 817.00/ 6222. See also Rear Adm. David F. Sellers to Adm. Charles F. Hughes,

February 16, 1929, Sellers Papers, *op. cit.*, box 247; Dana G. Munro to Francis D. White, September 10, 1929, DS, 817.00/6413; Goldwert, *op. cit.*, p. 34.

6. Eberhardt to the Secretary of State, February 28, 1929, DS, 817.00/6222.

7. Eberhardt to the Secretary of State, March 16, 1929, DS, 817.00/6286. For subsequent developments in the Eberhardt-Feland feud, see Eberhardt to the Secretary of State, April 4, 1929, DS, 817.77/212.

8. Guardia Nacional de Nicaragua, *Bulletin* (mimeograph), number 7, 1 July 1928 to 31 March 1929, MCHA, Nicaragua: Box 10, folder 20.

9. Capt. James Snedeker to the Commander, Third Battalion, Fifth Regiment, January 24, 1929; 1st Lt. Alexander Galt to the Commander, Third Battalion, Fifth Regiment, February 8, 1929, and 2nd Lt. Marshall C. Levie to the Commander, Northern Area, January 23, 1929, MCHA, Nicaragua: Box 8.

10. 1st Lt. Herman H. Hanneken, extract from Patrol Report, February 11, 1929, MCHA, Biography File: Herman H. Hanneken.

11. Feland to Lejeune, January 18, 1929, MCHA, Nicaragua: Reel 1. See also *New York Times*, January 29, 1929, p. 20.

12. Ejército Voluntario, Record of Events, January 16 to February 16, 1929, MCHA, Nicaragua: Reel 22.

13. Capt. Herman H. Hanneken, A Discussion of the Voluntario Troops in Nicaragua, c. May 1939, MCHA, Nicaragua: Reel 22. A heavily censored version of this account is in the *Marine Corps Gazette*, XXVI, 4 (November 1942), 120, 247-266. See also Maj. Gen. Douglas C. McDougal, Memorandum, January 18, 1930, *Foreign Relations, 1931*, II, 864. All quotations in the following account of the Escamilla-Hanneken column are from the uncensored version of Hanneken's article.

14. Beaulac. *op. cit.*, p. 117.

15. Frazier, *op. cit.*, p. 521; Cummins, *op. cit.*, p. 37.

16. Raymond L. Buell, "Reconstruction in Nicaragua," *Foreign Policy Reports*, VI, 18 (November 12, 1930), 338.

17. The Chargé in Nicaragua (Hanna) to the Secretary of State, May 24, 1929, *Foreign Relations, 1929*, III, 567-568.

18. *La Prensa* (Managua), July 24, 1929.

19. The Secretary of State (Stimson) to the Chargé in Nicaragua, June 19, 1929, *Foreign Relations, 1929*, III, 574; Guardia Nacional de Nicaragua, GN-3, Annual Report, December 2, 1929, MCHA, Nicaragua: Reel 20; Guardia Nacional de Nicaragua, Articles for the Government of the Guardia Nacional de Nicaragua, July 5, 1929, MCHA, Nicaragua: Reel 21; The Chargé in Nicaragua (Hanna) to the Secretary of State, June 19, 1929, *Foreign Relations, 1929*, III, 575; Smith, *et. al.*, *op. cit.*, p. 62.

20. GN-3, case files: H. Samuelson, GN, tray 128.

21. H. Samuelson to General D. C. McDougal, December 2, 1929, GN 94.0.

22. J. A. Willey to Capt. D. A. Stafford, November 10, 1931, GN 43.0.

23. W. G. Mosher, to E. E. Morris, January 20, 1931, DS, 817.00/7066.

24. Lt. W. W. Benson to the Commander, Eastern Area, October 15, 1929, MCHA, Nicaragua: Reel 15. See also Buell, "Reconstruction in Nicaragua," p. 337.

25. Benjamin C. Warnick to Dana G. Munro, April 18, 1930, DS, 817.00/6588.

26. David Castrillo to Maj. C. H. Metcalf, February 14, 1930, MCHA, Nicaragua: Reel 20.

27. Brig. Gen. Dion Williams to Maj. Gen. W. C. Neville, June 11, 1929, MCHA, Nicaragua: Reel 1.

28. Bolaños, *Sandino, el Libertador,* p. 16.

29. Walter C. Thurston to J. R. Beker, February 26, 1931, DS, 817.00/7030.

30. Second Brigade, B-2 Report, January 29, 1929, MCHA, Nicaragua: Reel 14.

31. Augusto C. Sandino to Froylán Turcios, June 10, 1928, in Selser, *Sandino,* II, 27-28.

32. Selser, *Sandino,* II, 24-25, 57-59. See also Second Brigade, B-2 Report, January 29, 1929, MCHA, Nicaragua: Reel 14.

33. Augusto C. Sandino to Emilio Portes Gil, January 6, 1929, in Selser, *Sandino,* II, 59-60.

34. Example: "U.S. Marines: You have always kissed our ass at El Bromadero, Las Cruces, El Zapote, El Chipón and in many other places. It would be better for you to go back to your own country where you are needed to finish the Chicago's gangsters. /s/ Capt. José de Paredes (of General Sandino's Staff)." MCHA, Nicaragua: Box 10, folder 16. See also Campos Ponce, *op. cit.,* 77-78.

35. Augusto C. Sandino to Herbert Hoover, March 6, 1929, in Selser, *Sandino,* II, 64-67.

36. The Minister in Honduras (Summerlin) to the Secretary of State, April 8, 1929, DS, 817.00/6271.

37. Selser, *Sandino,* II, 68-71. Includes text of letter.

38. Somoza, *op. cit.,* p. 244; Selser, *Sandino,* II, 75.

39. The American Ambassador to Mexico (Morrow) to the Secretary of State, March 1, 1929 and April 30, 1929, *Foreign Relations, 1929,* III, 584-586; Maj. Fred T. Cruse, Report of Military Attaché, July 9, 1929, DS, 312.1722, folder 2; Emilio Portes Gil, *Quince años de política mexicana* (Mexico: Ediciones Botas, 1941), pp. 342-344, 349-355.

40. Selser, *Sandino,* II, 75; Northern Area, R-2 Report, July 28, 1929, MCHA, Nicaragua: Reel 7; The Minister in the Dominican Republic (Frost) to the Secretary of State, September 14, 1928, DS, 817.00/6000; Somoza, *op. cit.,* p. 134; Bolaños, *¡Sandino!,* p. 43.

41. Maj. Fred T. Cruse, Report of Military Attaché, July 9, 1929, DS, 312.1722, folder 2. Other sources of information on Sandino's journey from Nicaragua to Mérida, Mexico, are Selser, *Sandino,* II, 73-75; Bolaños, *¡Sandino!,* p. 43; *Diario de El Salvador,* July 22, 1929; Campos Ponce, *op. cit.,* p. 114; Portes Gil, *op. cit.,* pp. 351-355; *New York Times,* June 30, 1929, p. 7, and July 12, 1929, p. 4.

42. Northern Area, R-2 Reports, June 30 and July 28, 1929, MCHA,

Nicaragua: Reel 7; Augusto C. Sandino to Generales Pedro Altamirano, Ismael Peralta, y Carlos Quesada, July 1, 1929, in Selser, *Sandino*, II, 75.

43. Northern Area, R-2 Report, July 28, 1929, MCHA, Nicaragua: Reel 7.

44. Sandino to Gustavo Alemán Bolaños, August 4, 1929, in *Bolaños, Sandino, el Libertador*, p. 81. See also The Chargé in Nicaragua (Hanna) to the Secretary of State, August 8, 1929, DS, 817.00/6398.

45. The Commander of the Second Brigade (Williams) to the Minister in Nicaragua, May 6, 1929, *Foreign Relations, 1929*, III, 564–566.

46. Commanding Officer, "H" Company, Second Battalion (Lt. Neel) to the Jefe Director, July 8, 1929, and Capt. Howard H. Stent to the Area Commander, Ocotal, August 4, 1929, GN, 51.o.

47. Metcalf, *op. cit.*, p. 438.

48. The Chargé in Nicaragua (Hanna) to the Secretary of State, July 23, and August 22, 1929, *Foreign Relations, 1929*, III, 578–579.

49. The Chargé in Nicaragua (Hanna) to the Secretary of State, August 22, 1929, *Foreign Relations, 1929*, III, 579; Smith, *et al., op. cit.,* pp. 30–31.

50. Sandino's wife Blanca kept her job as telegraph operator in San Rafael del Norte until early in 1929. On March 2 of that year she was reported to have been suspected of "passing information" to her husband's forces and was taken to Managua where she could be "watched." (*New York Times*, March 3, 1929, p. 10.) Later in the year she was apparently allowed to go to Mexico and join her husband in Mérida. (Eli Taylor to Herschel V. Johnson, December 17, 1929, DS, 312.1722, folder 2.) Teresa Villatoro, the general's mistress, was tending to Sandinista business in Comayaguela, Honduras, in mid-July 1929. Agustín Farabundo Martí and Toribio Pérez to Teresa Villatoro, July 17 and 18, 1929, GN, tray 84, folder A.

51. Smith, *et al., op. cit.,* pp. 90–93.

52. *Ibid.*, p. 41.

53. "Professional Notes: Care and Feeding of Native Animals," *Marine Corps Gazette*, XIV, 4 (December 1929), 298–299; Sanderson, *op. cit.*, p. 44; Bolaños, *Sandino, el Libertador*, pp. 114–115.

54. Smith, *et al., op. cit.*, p. 62; Beaulac, *op. cit.*, pp. 122–123; Cummins, *op. cit.*, pp. 81–82.

55. Capt. H. N. Stent to the Area Commander, August 13, 1929, and Col. Tom E. Thrasher, Jr., to the Jefe Director, August 31, 1929, GN, 51.o; Smith, *et al., op. cit.*, pp. 312–315.

56. Goldwert, *op. cit.*, p. 37; Smith, *et al., op. cit.*, pp. 111–115.

57. In Bolaños, *¡Sandino!*, pp. 48–51.

58. Second Brigade, B-2 Report, November 11, 1929, MCHA, Nicaragua: Reel 15.

59. Capt. H. H. Hanneken to the Jefe Director, November 29, 1929, GN, 51.o.

60. H. Samuelson to the Jefe Director, March 22, 1930, GN, 94.o.

61. Campos Ponce, *op. cit.*, pp. 116–117. See also Somoza, *op. cit.*, p. 244; Eli Taylor to Herschel V. Johnson, December 17, 1929, DS, 312.1722, folder 2.

62. Sandino to Gustavo Alemán Bolaños, September 9, 1929, in Selser, *Sandino*, II, 86. See also Alba, *op. cit.*, pp. 85–86.
63. Alba, *op. cit.*, pp. 86–87; Robert J. Alexander, *op. cit.*, pp. 378–379; *New York Times*, January 8, 1930, p. 6; *El Universal* (Mexico City), December 25, 1929.
64. Alba, *op. cit.*, pp. 86–87; Selser, *Sandino*, II, 95–96. The hostility toward Zepeda felt by Martí, Pavletich, *et al.*, is revealed in Ernesto Carrera and José Constantino González to Augusto C. Sandino, June 18, 1930, in Somoza, *op. cit.*, pp. 156–162.
65. The Chargé in Mexico (Johnson) to the Secretary of State, January 31, 1930, DS, 312.1722/folder 2; Campos Ponce, *op. cit.*, p. 116.
66. César Falcón, quoted in Selser, *Sandino*, II, 115–116.
67. Bolaños, *Sandino, el Libertador*, p. 98; Col. Gordon Johnston, Memorandum for the Chargé d'Affaires, DS, 312.1722/folder 2.
68. *New York Times*, May 30, 1930, p. 6.
69. Agustín Farabundo Martí, quoted in Selser, *Sandino*, II, 86–87.

Chapter Eight: The National Guard Offensive

1. Smith, *et al.*, *op. cit.*, p. 28.
2. Miguel Angel Orthés y Guillén, *El Ejército Defensor de la Autonomia de Nicaragua* (broadside), January 1, 1930, MCHA, Nicaragua: Box 10, folder 16.
3. Capt. N. E. Clauson to the Northern Area Commander, January 20, 1930, GN, tray 84, folder A. The principal source of information on the patrol from Quilali is 2nd Lt. Harold A. Uhrig to the Battalion Commander, Jícaro, January 13, 1930, GN, tray 84, folder A. The following quotations are from this report.
4. Miguel Angel Ortez to Pedro Altamirano, February 4, 1930, MCHA, Nicaragua: Reel 19.
5. Fifth Regiment, R-2 Report, February 20, 1930, MCHA, Nicaragua: Reel 13.
6. 2nd Lt. F. Anderton to the Northern Area Commander, April 3, 1930, GN, 52.0; Smith, *et al.*, *op. cit.*, pp. 318–320.
7. 2nd Lt. Edward L. Livermore to the Jefe Director, May 10, 1930, GN, 52.0.
8. Northern Area, Intelligence Report, May 11, 1930, MCHA, Nicaragua: Reel 17.
9. H. Samuelson to the Jefe Director, March 22, 1930, GN, 94.0.
10. L. S. McWhinney to Maj. Charles F. B. Prince, September 9, 1930, GN, tray 12, Case Files: Salvador Ortez; Evans F. Carlson, "The Guardia Nacional de Nicaragua," *Marine Corps Gazette*, XXI, 3 (August 1937), 10.
11. The Minister in Nicaragua (Hanna) to the Secretary of State, June 6, 1930, DS, 817.00/6673. Other sources of information on the resettlement program are Matthew Hanna to Francis White, June 7, 1930, DS, 817.00/6890; Hanna to the Secretary of State, July 8, 1930, DS, 817.00/6709; L. S.

McWhinney to Maj. Charles F. B. Price, September 9, 1930, GN, tray 122, Case Files: Salvador Ortez.

12. Northern Area, Intelligence Report, September 21, 1930, MCHA, Nicaragua: Reel 18.

13. Augusto C. Sandino to Pedro Altamirano, May 24, 1930, MCHA, Nicaragua: Reel 19. See also Bolaños, *Sandino, el Libertador,* p. 98; Northern Area, Intelligence Report, September 21, 1930, MCHA, Nicaragua: Reel 18.

14. Northern Area, Intelligence Report, June 8, 1930, MCHA, Nicaragua: Reel 17.

15. Augusto C. Sandino, Communiqué, in Northern Area, Intelligence Report, September 7, 1930, MCHA, Nicaragua: Reel 19.

16. Miguel Angel Ortez to Coronel Don Pilar Oseguerra, June 29, 1929, MCHA, Nicaragua: Box 10, folder 16.

17. Moisés Castro, quoted in Northern Area, Intelligence Report, September 21, 1930, MCHA, Nicaragua: Reel 18. Other sources of information on the El Saraguazca action are Bolaños, *¡Sandino!,* pp. 63–64; Megee, "United States Military Intervention in Nicaragua," pp. 179–181; Second Brigade, B-2 Report, July 1, 1930, MCHA, Nicaragua: Reel 16; Northern Area, Intelligence Report, September 7, 1930, MCHA, Nicaragua: Reel 19.

18. Northern Area, List of Thompson Submachine Guns in the Northern Area, GN, 31.0; *Excelsior* (Mexico City), March 29, 1931; Campos Ponce, *op. cit.,* p. 154; Bolaños, *¡Sandino!,* p. 28; Central Area Order, August 6, 1931, GN, 32.0; Gen. Vernon E. Megee to Neill Macaulay, undated (1963).

19. Northern Area, Reorganization Order, June 31, 1930, GN, 42.0. For the Schwerin ambush see Fifth Regiment, First Battalion, Bn-2 Report, July 25, 1930, MCHA, Nicaragua: Reel 16; Capt. R. A. Johnson to the Northern Area Commander, June 29, 1930, GN, 52.0.

20. Somoza, *op. cit.,* p. 15.

21. Augusto C. Sandino to Coronel Abraham Rivera, November 21, 1930, in Somoza, *op. cit.,* pp. 185–186.

22. Capt. Evans F. Carlson to the Northern Area Commander, July 10, 1930, GN, 52.0. Carlson's operations against González are also described in Michael Blankfort, *The Big Yankee: The Life of Carlson of the Raiders* (Boston: Little, Brown, 1947), pp. 161–162.

23. Capt. William P. Kelly to the Northern Area Commander, August 4, 1930, GN, 52.0.

24. Carlson, "Guardia Nacional," p. 11. Capt. Good discusses his patrol in his report to the Northern Area Commander, August 26, 1930, GN, 52.0.

25. Carlson, "Guardia Nacional," p. 11.

26. Good to the Northern Area Commander, August 26, 1930, GN, 52.0.

27. Guardia Nacional, GN-2 Intelligence Summary for August, 1930, MCHA, Nicaragua: Box 10, folder 1; Northern Area, Operations Report, September 15, 1930, GN, 37.3; Capt. Lewis B. Puller to the Central Area Commander, August 22, 1930, GN, 52.0.

28. Capt. Lewis B. Puller to the Central Area Commander, August 22, 1930, GN, 52.0.

29. Quotations from Carlson, "Guardia Nacional," pp. 15–16. Puller and Lee are also discussed in Smith, *et al., op. cit.,* p. 37, and Burke Davis, *Marine! The Life of Chesty Puller* (Boston: Little, Brown, 1962), pp. 61, 69–70, 81.

30. Carlson, "Guardia Nacional," p. 11.

31. Smith, *et al., op. cit.,* pp. 110–122.

32. Col. H. S. Reisinger, "La Palabra del Gringo, Leadership of the Nicaraguan National Guard," *United States Naval Institute Proceedings,* LXI, 2 (February 1935), 215–220.

33. Donald L. Truesdale, quoted in *The State* (Columbia, S.C.), September 8, 1963, sect. C, 1. See also Peard, "Tactics of Bush Warfare," pp. 32–33.

34. *The State* (Columbia, S.C.), September 8, 1963, sect. C, 1; Reisinger, "La Palabra del Gringo," pp. 215–220; Peard, "Tactics of Bush Warfare," p. 33; Lt. J. C. Walraven, "Typical Combat Patrols in Nicaragua," *Marine Corps Gazette,* XIV, 4 (December 1929), 243–253; Lt. W. T. Minnick, "Medical Difficulties Encountered by Combat Forces Operating in Nicaragua," *United States Naval Medical Bulletin,* XXVI, 4 (October 1928), 884–888.

35. Lt. Robert L. Denig, "Native Officer Corps, Guardia Nacional de Nicaragua," *Marine Corps Gazette,* XVII, 3 (November 1932), 76–77. See also The Minister in Nicaragua (Eberhardt) to the Secretary of State, February 14, 1929, *Foreign Relations, 1929,* III, 614–615.

36. Brig. Gen. Logan Feland to Maj. Gen. John A. Lejeune, May 24, 1927, MCHA, Nicaragua: Reel 1; Smith, *et al., op. cit.,* p. 84.

37. Blankfort, *op. cit.,* p. 160.

38. Capt. Evans F. Carlson, "The Guardia as a Police Force," *Leatherneck,* XV, 10 (October 1932), 21, 61.

39. Capt. G. C. Darnall to the Jefe Director, February 16, 1929, MCHA, Nicaragua: Box 12, folder 19.

40. Francis White to the Chargé in Nicaragua, November 9, 1929, *Foreign Relations, 1929,* III, 605. See also The Chargé in Nicaragua to the Secretary of State, October 1 and 9, 1929, *Foreign Relations, 1929,* III, 599–602.

41. The Secretary of State (Stimson) to the Minister in Nicaragua, January 3, 1931, *Foreign Relations, 1930,* III, 708. See also The Minister in Nicaragua (Hanna) to the Secretary of State, January 14, 1931, *Foreign Relations, 1931,* II, 836–838.

42. Guardia Nacional de Nicaragua, Money Accountability and Pay Regulations, May 1, 1930, MCHA, Nicaragua: Reel 21; Smith, *et al., op. cit.,* pp. 27, 84–85; Denig, *op. cit.,* p. 76.

43. The Minister in Nicaragua (Hanna) to the Secretary of State, October 10, 1930, DS, 817.00/6926.

44. Charles A. Thomson, "The Caribbean Situation: Nicaragua and Salvador," *Foreign Policy Reports,* IX, 13 (August 30, 1933), 144; Henry L. Stimson, Diary, October 21, 1930, Yale University.

45. Jamison, *op. cit.,* pp. 15–17.

46. Extracts from Pastoral Letter, signed by the Archbishop of Managua

and the Bishops of Granada, León, and Matagalpa, in The Minister in Nicaragua (Hanna) to the Secretary of State, November 18, 1930, DS, 817.00/6894.

47. Smith, *et al., op. cit.*, pp. 29-30; U.S. Department of State, Memorandum for U.S. Marine Corps, December 7, 1929, DS, 817.00/6481.

48. Smith, *et al., op. cit.*, p. 30.

49. Second Brigade, B-2 Report, December 1, 1930, MCHA, Nicaragua: Reel 14; 2nd Lt. Paul Kerns to the Department Commander, November 16, 1930, GN, 52.0.

50. 2nd Lt. W. W. Stevens to the Jefe Director, November 20, 1930, GN, improperly filed in tray 108; Smith, *et al., op. cit.*, p. 3.

51. Midence's encounter with Ortez is related in W. C. Bales, Memo for Area Commander, November 19, 1930, GN, tray 121, Case Files: W. C. Bales. All quotations are from this memo.

52. Second Brigade, B-2 Report, January 1, 1931, MCHA, Nicaragua: Reel 14; 2nd Lt. F. M. McCorkle to the Commanding Officer, January 21, 1931, in Smith, *et al., op. cit.*, pp. 267-269.

53. *New York Times*, January 3, 1931, p. 5; January 7, 1931, p. 2.

54. Henry L. Stimson, *et al.*, Statement of Policy in Nicaragua, undated, DS, 817.1051/501.

55. Quoted in *New York Herald Tribune*, February 10, 1931.

56. Metcalf, *op. cit.*, p. 448.

Chapter Nine: Guerrilla Offensives

1. Second Brigade, B-2 Report, April 2, 1931, MCHA, Nicaragua: Reel 16; Charles David Kepner, Jr., and Jay Henry Soothill, *The Banana Empire: A Case Study in Economic Imperialism* (New York: Vanguard, 1935), p. 286.

2. Augusto C. Sandino, Credentials of Gen. Pedro Blandón as Expeditionary Chief to the Atlantic Coast, March 16, 1931, GN, tray 122, Case Files: Pedro Blandón; Augusto C. Sandino to Gen. Pedro Altamirano, March 30, 1931, in Somoza, *op. cit.*, pp. 215-216. Contrary to the claims of Marine and State Department sources, these attacks were ordered prior to the March 31 earthquake.

3. Archie Fairly Carr, *High Jungles and Low* (Gainesville: University of Florida Press, 1953), p. 139. See also Eduard Conzemius, *Ethnological Survey of the Miskito and Sumu Indians of Honduras and Nicaragua* (Smithsonian Institution Bureau of American Ethnology Bulletin 106; Washington: U.S. Government Printing Office, 1932), pp. 215-216.

4. Conzemius, *op. cit.*, p. 104.

5. Quotations from Carr, *op. cit.*, pp. 210-216.

6. Second Brigade, B-2 Report, March 2, 1931, MCHA, Nicaragua: Reel 16. See also Somoza, *op. cit.*, p. 13 (photograph, p. 187).

7. Somoza, *op. cit.*, pp. 275-276. See also Augusto C. Sandino, Headquarters Bulletin, July 26, 1930, in Guardia Nacional de Nicaragua, GN-2 Report, October 1, 1931, MCHA, Nicaragua: Reel 20.

8. Smith, *et al.*, *op. cit.*, p. 70; Somoza, *op. cit.*, p. 14.

9. Pedro Blandón to Augusto C. Sandino, April 7, 1931, extracts in Somoza, *op. cit.*, pp. 220–221.

10. Augusto C. Sandino to Gen. Pedro Altamirano, March 30, 1931, in Somoza, *op. cit.*, pp. 215–216.

11. Beaulac, *op. cit.*, pp. 128–130.

12. *Ibid.*, pp. 130–133. See also Brig. Gen. Dion Williams, "Managua Disaster," *Marine Corps Gazette*, XVI, 2 (August 1931), 12–17, 35.

13. Augusto C. Sandino, Circular, April 15, 1931, in Selser, *Sandino*, II, 123.

14. Blandón's raid and National Guard counter-operations are described in Capt. John C. Wood, Memorandum, April 17, 1931, GN, tray 122, Case Files: Pedro Blandón; Capt. John C. Wood to the Area Commander, April 22, 1931, GN, 53.0; Second Brigade, B-2 Report, May 1, 1931, MCHA, Nicaragua: Reel 16; Capt. John C. Wood and 1st Lt. J. D. Wilmeth, "Sandino Strikes Again," *Leatherneck*, XXII, 2 (February 1939), 8, 55–57; Beaulac, *op. cit.*, 125–126.

15. Beaulac, *op. cit.*, pp. 125–126.

16. Capt. John C. Wood to the Area Commander, April 22, 1931, GN, 53.0.

17. Second Brigade, B-2 Report, March 2, 1931, MCHA, Nicaragua: Reel 16. Rivera's Cabo Gracias a Dios raid is reported in Maj. Gen. Calvin Matthews to the Minister of Governación, March 6, 1931, GN, 60.0; Somoza, *op. cit.*, p. 274; Lisandro Salazar to the Collector General of Customs, April 28, 1931, GN, 70.0; Second Brigade, B-2 Report, May 1, 1931, MCHA, Nicaragua: Reel 16.

18. Lisandro Salazar to the Collector General of Customs, April 28, 1931, GN, 70.0.

19. *Ibid.*

20. *Ibid.*

21. Henry L. Stimson, Diary, April 15, 1931, quoted in Stimson and Bundy, *op. cit.*, p. 182.

22. Henry L. Stimson, Diary, April 16, 1931, Yale University.

23. The Secretary of State (Stimson) to the Minister in Nicaragua, April 16, 1931, *Foreign Relations, 1931*, II, 808.

24. Walter C. Thurston, quoted in Bryce Wood, *op. cit.*, p. 35.

25. Henry L. Stimson to Calvin Coolidge, April 29, 1931, DS, 817.00/7111A. See also Bryce Wood, *op. cit.*, pp. 41–44; Second Brigade, B-2 Report, May 1, 1931, MCHA, Nicaragua: Reel 16.

26. Beaulac, *op. cit.*, pp. 115, 123–124; Lawrence Dennis, "Revolution, Recognition, and Intervention," *Foreign Affairs*, IX (January 1931), 204–221, and "Nicaragua: In Again, Out Again," *Foreign Affairs*, IX (April 1931), 496–500.

27. Lawrence Dennis, "Revolution, Recognition, and Intervention," p. 219. Cf. Lawrence Dennis, *Is Capitalism Doomed?* (New York and London: Harper and Brothers, 1932), and *The Coming American Fascism* (New York and London: Harper and Brothers, 1936), *passim*.

28. Deconde, *op. cit.*, p. 82. See also Bryce Wood, *op. cit.*, p. 45.

29. Augusto C. Sandino, Circular, May 10, 1931, in Guardia Nacional de Nicaragua, GN-2 Report, July 1, 1931, MCHA, Nicaragua: Reel 20.

30. Smith, *et al.*, *op. cit.*, pp. 70, 349-350.

31. Ortez, Umanzor, and the Palacaguina attack are discussed in Somoza, *op. cit.*, pp. 15, 233-235; 1st Lt. J. Ogden Brauer to the Area Commander, May 18, 1931, GN, 53.0.

32. Somoza, *op. cit.*, pp. 234-235.

33. Smith, *et al.*, *op. cit.*, p. 69.

34. Maj. Julian C. Smith to the Jefe Director, June 18, 1931, in Smith, *et al.*, *op. cit.*, pp. 260-263.

35. Augusto C. Sandino, Comunicado, July 28, 1931, in Bolaños, *¡Sandino!*, pp. 53-54. See also Smith, *et al.*, *op. cit.*, p. 25.

36. Capt. John C. McQueen to the Department Commander, July 4, 1931, in Smith, *et al.*, *op. cit.*, pp. 264-266; Lt. W. F. Bryson to the Area Commander, July 25, 1931, GN, 53.0.

37. Quotations from W. Pfaeffle, Statement, August 2, 1931, GN, tray 122, Case Files: W. Pfaeffle.

38. Smith, *et al.*, *op. cit.*, pp. 31, 280-283.

39. Lt. Fred Riewe to the Area Commander, July 21, 1931, GN, 53.0.

40. The adventures of Heritage and Simmons are described in Staff Sgt. Gordon W. Heritage, "Forced Down in the Jungles of Nicaragua," *Leatherneck*, XV, 5 (May 1932), 13-15. All quotations are from this article.

41. Suprenant's encounter with Cockburn is discussed in Somoza, *op. cit.*, pp. 274-275; The Chargé in Nicaragua (Beaulac) to the Secretary of State, October 19, 1931, DS, 817.1051/570. For the incriminating headquarters bulletin, see Guardia Nacional de Nicaragua, GN-2 Report, October 1, 1931, MCHA, Nicaragua: Reel 20.

42. Lt. Francisco Gaitán to the Department Commander, October 27, 1931, Synopsis, GN, 44.0.

43. Augusto C. Sandino, quoted in Bolaños, *¡Sandino!*, pp. 70-71. See also Enrique Sánchez F., Statement of Enrique Sánchez F., Who Was Captured by Bandits, July 15, 1932, GN, 35.0; Somoza, *op. cit.*, pp. 230-231, 306; Gen. Pedro Antonio Irías, Receipt for Goods, GN, tray 130, Case Files: Pedro Antonio Irías.

44. Somoza, *op. cit.*, pp. 230-231; Bolaños, *¡Sandino!*, p. 70; Augusto C. Sandino to Pedro José Zepeda, August 20, 1930, in Selser, *Sandino*, II, 153; Sandino, Circular a los jefes de nuestro ejército, October 16, 1930, in Somoza, *op. cit.*, p. 179.

45. Augusto C. Sandino, Manifiesto, November 15, 1931, in Somoza, *op. cit.*, pp. 280-286. Other sources of information on Sandinista justice are Somoza, *op. cit.*, pp. 152-153, 279-280; Bolaños, *¡Sandino!*, p. 72; Gen. Pedro Altamirano, Notice, March 3, 1930, in Northern Area Intelligence Report, September 7, 1930, MCHA, Nicaragua: Reel 19; Belausteguigoitia, *op. cit.*, p. 80; James L. Price, *The Autobiography of James L. Price, Jungle Jim*, in collaboration with Samuel Duff McCoy (New York: Doubleday, Doran, 1941), pp. 116-133; Frazier, "The Dawn of Nationalism," p. 466.

46. Kepner and Soothill, *op. cit.*, pp. 134-135; Second Brigade, B-2 Re-

port, March 2, 1931, MCHA, Nicaragua: Reel 16; Statement of Bandit Prisoner Captured by Lt. Broderick, January 26, 1931, MCHA, Nicaragua: Box 10, folder 13; Selser, *Sandino*, I, 310; Belausteguigoitia, *op. cit.*, pp. 112–114; Fred Walker, *Destination Unknown: The Autobiography of a Wandering Boy* (London: Harrap, 1934), pp. 255–256.

47. Belausteguigoitia, *op. cit.*, p. 133.

48. Belausteguigoitia, *op. cit.*, pp. 131, 191; see also Somoza, *op. cit.*, 93–94; Bolaños, *¡Sandino!*, pp. 32–33, 70; Augusto C. Sandino, Boletín de Información, November, 1931, in Somoza, *op. cit.*, p. 260.

49. Selser, *Sandino*, II, 103; Bolaños, *¡Sandino!*, p. 58.

50. Augusto C. Sandino, Luz y verdad: manifiesto a los miembros de nuestro ejército, February 15, 1931, in Somoza, *op. cit.*, pp. 206–208.

51. Belausteguigoitia, *op. cit.*, p. 145.

52. Sandino to Rivera, February 21, 1931, in Somoza, *op. cit.*, p. 202.

53. Alejandro Cerda to José María Moncada, February 16, 1931, GN, tray 121, Case Files: Alejandro Cerda. For Sócrates Sandino's return to Nicaragua, see GN, tray 128, Case Files: Sócrates Sandino.

54. Frazier, "The Dawn of Nationalism," pp. 444, 497–498; Alberto Rivera, Statement, in Guardia Nacional de Nicaragua, GN-2 Report, July 1, 1931, MCHA, Nicaragua: Reel 20; Alejandro Cerda to Col. Hunt, August 21, 1931, GN, tray 121, Case Files: Alejandro Cerda; Guardia Nacional de Nicaragua, GN-2 Report, September 1, 1931, MCHA, Nicaragua: Reel 20; Ladislao Palacios to Augusto C. Sandino, December 1, 1931, GN, 35.o.

55. Sandino to Rivera, undated, in Somoza, *op. cit.*, p. 205.

56. Quoted in Somoza, *op. cit.*, pp. 278–279.

57. Smith, *et al.*, *op. cit.*, pp. 29, 31–32; Carlson, "Guardia Nacional," p. 13; The Secretary of State (Stimson) to the Chargé in Nicaragua, November 25, 1931, *Foreign Relations, 1931*, II, 826–827; The Chargé in Nicaragua (Beaulac) to the Secretary of State, November 23, 1931, *Foreign Relations, 1931*, II, 825; 2nd Lt. H. D. Hutchcroft to the Department Commander, November 7, 1931, GN 53.o.

58. Capt. R. G. Griffin, Jr., to Col. T. E. Watson, November 26 (27), 1931, GN, 53.o. Other sources of information on the pursuit of Umanzor and Colindres are 2nd Lt. H. E. Dumas to the Jefe Director, November 23, 1931, GN, 53.o.; 2nd Lt. Charles Henrich to Col. T. E. Watson, November 26, 1931, GN, 53.o; 2nd Lt. George E. Gardner to the Department Commander, December 6, 1931, GN, 53.o.

59. Guardia Nacional de Nicaragua, GN-2 Report, December 1, 1931, MCHA, Nicaragua: Reel 20.

60. The Chargé in Nicaragua (Beaulac) to the Secretary of State, November 25, 1931, *Foreign Relations, 1931*, II, 828.

61. Herbert Hoover, Message to Congress, December 10, 1931, in William Starr Myers, ed., *The State Papers and Other Public Writings of Herbert Hoover* (New York: Doubleday, Doran, 1934), II, 78.

Chapter Ten: The End of a Banana War

1. Lt. Chandler W. Johnson to the Department Commander, December 24, 1931, GN, 53.0.

2. Capt. Granville K. Frisbie to the Area Commander, January 5, 1932, in GN, 53.0.

3. 2nd Lt. Earl T. Gray to the Department Commander, February 4, 1932, in Smith, *et al., op. cit.,* pp. 270–272; 1st Lt. M. S. Cramer to the Area Commander, February 10, 1932, GN, 54.0; Capt. J. P Schwerin to the Area Commander, February 15, 1932, GN, 54.0; 2nd Lt. C. H. Clark to the Director of Operations, February 26, 1932, GN, 54.0.

4. Beaulac, *op. cit.,* p. 126; see also U.S. Department of State, *The United States and Nicaragua: A Survey of the Relations from 1909 to 1932* (Washington: U.S. Government Printing Office, 1932), pp. 117–124.

5. Beaulac, *op. cit.,* pp. 126–127. Other sources of information on the Moncada-Chamorro entente are Willard Beaulac to the Secretary of State, January 13, 1932, DS, 817.00/7295; Jamison, *op. cit.,* pp. 19–20; Bryce Wood, *op. cit.,* pp. 33–34.

6. For the León and Rivas fighting see 1st Lt. Stanley D. Atha to the Department Commander, March 21, 1931, and Col. T. E. Watson to the Jefe Director, March 23, 1931, GN, 54.0; Somoza, *op. cit.,* pp. 310–311; Guardia Nacional de Nicaragua, Department of Rivas, Account of the Fight at El Carmen, April 5, 1932, GN, 8.0. Sources of information on the mutiny are Somoza, *op. cit.,* p. 319; Smith, *et al., op. cit.,* pp. 119–120; Augusto C. Sandino, Boletín de Noticias, May 18, 1932, in Campos Ponce, *op. cit.,* pp. 137–138.

7. Smith, *et al., op. cit.,* pp. 120–121; Augusto C. Sandino, Boletín de Noticias, May 18, 1932, in Campos Ponce, *op. cit.,* p. 138; Somoza, *op. cit.,* p. 315; *New York Times,* April 13, 1932, p. 22.

8. 1st Lt. C. W. Johnson to the District Commander, April 26, 1932, GN, 54.0; Augusto C. Sandino, Boletín de Noticias, May 18, 1932, in Campos Ponce, *op. cit.,* pp. 139–140.

9. Smith, *et al., op. cit.,* p. 68. Colindres, Salgado, *et al.,* are also discussed in Peard, "Tactics of Bush Warfare," p. 28; Somoza, *op. cit.,* pp. 13–14, 201; Belausteguigoitia, *op. cit.,* p. 82; Beals, *Banana Gold,* p. 247.

10. Smith, *et al., op. cit.,* pp. 121–122, 175–198; Carlson, "Guardia Nacional," p. 11; Francisco Gaitán to the Area Commander, April 22, 1932, GN, 54.0; 2nd Lt. Earl T. Gray to the Department Commander, May 27, 1932, in Smith, *et al., op. cit.,* pp. 277–279; Guardia Nacional de Nicaragua, GN-3 Memorandum, June 30, 1932, GN, 35.0; 2nd Lt. Francisco Gaitán to the Area Commander, July 5, 1932 and 1st Lt. R. L. Peterson to the Area Commander, July 9, 1932, GN, 54.0.

11. Bolaños, *¡Sandino!,* p. 75.

12. Capt. Evans F. Carlson to the Jefe Director, February 22, 1932, GN, 73.0.

13. J. Edgar Hoover to Pierre de L. Boal, June 25, 1932, DS, 817.00/7474.

14. Quoted in Belausteguigoitia, *op. cit.*, p. 181. See also Augusto C. Sandino to José Idiaquez, August 10, 1931, in Somoza, *op. cit.*, p. 254.

15. Sandino to Gustavo Alemán Bolaños, August 9, 1932, in Selser, *Sandino*, II, 150–151.

16. Quoted in an unidentified newspaper clipping, GN, tray 129, Case Files: Ramiro Molla Sanz.

17. Belausteguigoitia, *op. cit.*, pp. 199–200.

18. Guardia Nacional de Nicaragua, GN-2 Reports, 1932, *passim*, MCHA, Nicaragua: Box 9, folders 17 and 18.

19. This and the following quotations about the autogiro are from Montross, *Cavalry of the Sky*, pp. 19–24. See also Lynn Montross, "The Marine Autogiro in Nicaragua," *Marine Corps Gazette*, XXXVII, 2 (February 1953), 56–61.

20. "Marine Aviators in Nicaragua Furnish Proof of the Practicability of Aviation and Make Lasting Contributions to Its Development," *Leatherneck*, XV, 10 (October 1932), 14.

21. All these stories were included in an article by C. Hernández Salinas in *La Prensa* (Managua), March 2, 1933, entitled "Ocho días con el General A. C. Sandino." This article was evidently a source for more recent writers and anti-American propagandists. Cf. Bolaños, *Sandino, el Libertador*, pp. 183–190; Selser, *Sandino*, I, 311–312; Frente unitario nicaraguense, *Intervención sangrienta: Nicaragua y su pueblo* (Caracas: n.p., 1961), cover and page 1.

22. Gustavo Alemán Bolaños to Benjamin Cohen, Assistant to the Secretary General of the United Nations, September 24, 1950, extract in Selser, *Sandino*, I, 311; Frazier, "The Dawn of Nationalism," p. 502; Walker, *op. cit.*, pp. 256–259. Fred Walker was an Englishman who claimed to have served briefly with Sandino. The story of his adventures in Nicaragua was either wholly or partly fabricated, but Walker seems to have had little anti-American bias, and his account of Marine brutality in handling prisoners could have been based on truthful second-hand information, if not on personal experience as claimed.

23. *La Prensa* (Managua), January 26, 1933. The "water treatment" consisted of forcing water down the throat of a prostrate prisoner to make him "talk." It has since been used on captured guerrillas in South Vietnam in the presence of American advisers. *Time*, LXXX (July 20, 1962), 27.

24. The Ambassador in Mexico (Clark) to the Secretary of State, April 18, 1932, DS, 817.00/7394; The Consul in Matamoros (Haller) to the Secretary of State, March 29, 1932, DS, 817.00/7381; *El Popular* (Matamoros, Mexico), March 22, 1932.

25. The Consul in Matamoros (Haller) to the Secretary of State, March 29, 1932, DS, 817.00/7381; *El Popular* (Matamoros, Mexico), March 22, 1932.

26. Megee, "United States Military Intervention in Nicaragua," p. 184.

27. For example, the charge that Lt. Lee stabbed prisoners to death and then forced his own men to eat bloody bread he cut with the fatal knife. Bolaños, *Sandino, el Libertador*, p. 187.

28. Guardia Nacional de Nicaragua, GN-2 Report, July 1, 1931, MCHA, Nicaragua: Reel 20.

Notes to Chapter Ten 303

29. Denig, *op. cit.*, pp. 76–77. See also the Jefe Director of the Guardia Nacional de Nicaragua (Matthews) to the American Minister in Nicaragua, August 8, 1932, *Foreign Relations, 1932*, V, 869; Megee, "United States Military Intervention in Nicaragua," p. 207.

30. Bryce Wood, *op. cit.*, p. 46.

31. Cummins, *op. cit.*, pp. 136–137; Jamison, *op. cit.*, pp. 21–24; Bryce Wood, *op. cit.*, p. 45.

32. The Liberal-Conservative negotiations are reported in The Minister in Nicaragua (Hanna) to the Secretary of State, October 8 and 20, 1932, *Foreign Relations, 1932*, V, 834–838.

33. Belausteguigoitia, *op. cit.*, p. 37. See also *New York Times*, July 6, 1932, p. 7, and July 13, 1932, p. 7; Guardia Nacional de Nicaragua, GN-2, Confidential Files, Baladares Case, GN, tray 133, folder 33.

34. DeConde, *op. cit.*, p. 83.

35. Guardia Nacional de Nicaragua, GN-2 Report, October 1, 1932, MCHA, Nicaragua, Box 9, folder 18; Bolaños, *¡Sandino!*, p. 76.

36. Capt. Lewis B. Puller to the Jefe Director, October 3, 1932, in Smith, *et al., op. cit.*, pp. 273–275; Guardia Nacional de Nicaragua, Intelligence Summary for the Week Ending 26 September 1932, MCHA, Nicaragua: Box 10, folder 1.

37. 2nd Lt. James F. Atwell to the Department Commander, October 25, 1932, GN, 54.0; Smith, *et al., op. cit.*, p. 39; *New York Times*, October 3, 1932, p. 7.

38. The commander of this guard patrol, 2nd Lt. Frederico Davidson Blanco, describes his operations in his report to the Jefe Director, November 4, 1932, GN, 54.0. See also Capt. Willett Elmore to the Jefe Director, October 29, 1932, GN, 54.0.

39. Quotations from Capt. W. P. Kelly to the Area Commander, November 10, 1932, first endorsement to 2nd Lt. Jacob G. Keller to the District Commander, November 7, 1932, GN, 54.0.

40. Quotations from The Minister in Nicaragua (Hanna) to the Secretary of State, November 4, 1932, *Foreign Relations, 1932*, V, 876–877.

41. Dana G. Munro, *The United States in the Caribbean Area* (Boston: World Peace Foundation, 1934), p. 268.

42. Augusto C. Sandino to Pedro Altamirano, November 9, 1932, and Sandino to Francisco Estrada and Tomás Blandón, November 17, 1932, in Selser, *Sandino*, II, 181–184; Sandino to Pedro Altamirano, December 12, 1932, in Somoza, *op. cit.*, p. 383; *New York Times*, November 8, 1932, p. 25.

43. Augusto C. Sandino to Juan Pablo Umanzor and Juan Santos Morales, November 18, 1932, in Selser, *Sandino*, II, 178, 184–185.

44. *New York Times*, November 16, 1932, p. 4; Metcalf, *op. cit.*, p. 446; The Jefe Director of the Guardia Nacional de Nicaragua (Matthews) to the Nicaraguan Conservative Candidate for the Vice Presidency, October 20, 1932, *Foreign Relations, 1932*, V, 874–875; The Minister in Nicaragua (Hanna) to the Secretary of State, November 21, 1932, *Foreign Relations, 1932*, V, 899–900. Biographical information on Somoza is provided by Krehm, *op. cit.*, pp. 159–161; Hilton, *Who's Who in Latin America*, II, 81; Partido Liberal, *Un hombre de estado ante la historia: Datos biográficos*

del General Anastasio Somoza (Managua: Talleres Nacionales, 1944), *passim;* Romero, *Somoza,* pp. 57–73; Gustavo Alemán Bolaños, *Un lombrosiano: Somoza* (Guatemala: Editorial Hispania, 1945), pp. 9–19, 124; "I'm the Champ," *Time,* LII, 46 (November 15, 1948), 38–43; Selser, *Sandino,* II, 133, 338–339.

45. Sofonías Salvatierra to Augusto C. Sandino, November 23, 1932, in Selser, *Sandino,* II, 190–191.

46. Guardia Nacional de Nicaragua, GN-2 Report, December 1, 1932, MCHA, Nicaragua: Reel 20.

47. The Minister in Nicaragua (Hanna) to the Secretary of State, December 19, 1932, DS, 817.00/7671; Sofonías Salvatierra, *Sandino: O, la tragedia de un pueblo* (Madrid: Europa, 1934), pp. 105–107.

48. The action at El Sauce is described in Carlson, "Guardia Nacional," p. 19; Smith, *et al., op. cit.,* p. 407; Guardia Nacional de Nicaragua, Recommendation for Navy Cross: Lt. Bennie M. Bunn, December 31, 1932, GN, 83.0.

49. Smith, *et al., op. cit.,* p. 408; U.S. Marine Corps, Marine Corps Casualties in Nicaragua, January 1, 1927, to January 2, 1933, MCHA, Nicaragua: Reel 21; "Marines Return from Nicaragua," *Marine Corps Gazette,* XVII, 4 (February 1933), 23–27.

50. Stimson and Bundy, *op. cit.,* p. 115.

51. Beaulac, *op. cit.,* p. 123.

52. Dana G. Munro, "The Establishment of Peace in Nicaragua," *Foreign Affairs,* XI (July 1933), 699.

53. Dana G. Munro, *The Latin American Republics: A History* (New York: Appleton-Century-Crofts, 1950), p. 476.

54. Heinl, *Soldiers of the Sea,* p. 288.

55. Megee, "United States Military Intervention in Nicaragua," p. 225.

56. Quotations from Heinl, *Soldiers of the Sea,* pp. 288–289.

Chapter Eleven: The Death of Caesar

1. Quoted in Selser, *Sandino,* II, 196.

2. Augusto C. Sandino, Interrogatorios, January 1, 1933, and Bases de paz, January 3, 1933, in Somoza, *op. cit.,* pp. 396–399; *New York Times,* January 7, 1933, p. 4.

3. Ildefonso Solórzano (pseud. Ildo Sol), *La Guardia Nacional de Nicaragua: su trayectoria incognita, 1927-1944* (Granada, Nicaragua: El Centroamericano, 1944), pp. 9–10; Partido Liberal, *Un hombre de estado,* pp. 23–26; Somoza, *op. cit.,* pp. 408–409.

4. Blanca de Sandino to Augusto C. Sandino, January 13, 1933, in Somoza, *op. cit.,* pp. 411–413.

5. The Minister in Nicaragua (Hanna) to the Secretary of State, January 16, 1933, DS, 817.00/7713; Somoza, *op. cit.,* pp. 412–413.

6. Blanca de Sandino to Augusto C. Sandino, January 25, 1933, in Somoza, *op. cit.,* pp. 426–427. See also Salvatierra, *op. cit.,* pp. 124–127; Somoza, *op. cit.,* pp. 419–428; *New York Times,* January 25, 1933, p. 3.

7. Quoted in Salvatierra, *op. cit.*, pp. 169–175. Other sources of information on the peace talks and Sandino's trip to Managua are Bolaños, *Sandino, el Libertador*, pp. 175–176; Somoza, *op. cit.*, pp. 432–454; The Minister in Nicaragua (Hanna) to the Secretary of State, February 3, 1933, DS, 817.00/7750; Campos Ponce, *op. cit.*, p. 177; Augusto C. Sandino, *Manifiesto a los pueblos de la tierra y en particular al de Nicaragua* (Managua: La Prensa, 1933), pp. 21–23; "Sandino Calls Off His Gadfly War," *Literary Digest*, CXV, 7 (February 18, 1933), 8.

8. Quoted in Somoza, *op. cit.*, p. 450.

9. The Minister in Nicaragua (Lane) to the Secretary of State, January 3, 1934, DS, 817.00/7922.

10. Convenio de paz, February 2, 1933, in Somoza, *op. cit.*, pp. 451–454; also in Sandino, *Manifiesto a los pueblos de la tierra*, pp. 21–23.

11. Quoted in Campos Ponce, *op. cit.*, p. 177.

12. The Minister in Nicaragua (Hanna) to the Secretary of State, April 13, 1933, DS, 817.00/7782. See also Acta de cumplimiento, February 22, 1933, in Sandino, *Manifiesto a los pueblos de la tierra*, pp. 24–27; *New York Times*, February 24, 1933, p. 9; Somoza, *op. cit.*, p. 497. The number of automatic weapons accounted for was two less than the minimum number National Guard intelligence estimated Sandino to have in April 1932; Smith, *et al.*, *op. cit.*, p. 295.

13. *Op. cit.* (*Manifiesto a los pueblos de la tierra e en particular al de Nicaragua*).

14. Carlos Castillo Ibarra, *Los Judas de Sandino* (Mexico: n.p., 1945), p. 24. See also Belausteguigoitia, *op. cit.*, pp. 183–185.

15. Quotations from Somoza, *op. cit.*, pp. 9–10, 449–450. See also Castillo Ibarra, *op. cit.*, p. 44.

16. The Minister in Nicaragua (Hanna) to the Secretary of State, April 13, 1933, DS, 817.00/7782; Bolaños, *Sandino, el Libertador*, p. 153.

17. The Chargé in Nicaragua (Daniels) to the Secretary of State, November 1, 1933, DS, 817.00/7901.

18. The Chargé in Nicaragua (Daniels) to the Secretary of State, November 29, 1933, DS, 817.00/7910. See also Maj. A. R. Harris, Military Attaché to Central America, G-2 Report, November 29, 1933, DS, 817.00/7920; The Minister in Nicaragua (Hanna) to the Secretary of State, May 29, 1933, DS, 817.00/7829; Hanna to the Secretary of State, August 16, 1933, DS, 817.00/7867; The Chargé in Nicaragua (Daniels) to the Secretary of State, December 2, 1933, DS, 817.00/7911.

19. The Chargé in Nicaragua (Daniels) to the Secretary of State, January 3, 1934, DS, 817.00/7922; The Minister in Nicaragua (Lane) to the Secretary of State, January 2, 1934, DS, 817.00/7919.

20. Quotations from The Minister in Nicaragua (Lane) to the Secretary of State, January 3, 1934, DS, 817.00/7922.

21. The Minister in Nicaragua (Lane) to the Secretary of State, February 5, 1934, DS, 817.00/7932.

22. The Minister in Nicaragua (Lane) to the Secretary of State, February 14, 1934, DS, 817.00/7935.

23. The Minister in Nicaragua (Lane) to the Secretary of State, Feb-

ruary 20, 1934, DS, 817.00/7968; Salvador Calderón Ramírez, *Últimos días de Sandino* (Mexico: Ediciones Botas, 1934), pp. 94–95.

24. Quotations from the Minister in Nicaragua (Lane) to the Secretary of State, February 20, 1934, DS, 817.00/7968. See also Campos Ponce, *op. cit.*, pp. 201–202.

25. Salvatierra, *op. cit.*, pp. 239–244. See also Calderón Ramírez, *op. cit.*, pp. 120–124.

26. Quotations from The Minister in Nicaragua (Lane) to the Secretary of State, February 22, 1934, DS, 817.00/7939.

27. *Ibid.*

28. Quoted in Selser, *Sandino*, II, 293–298. The meeting of National Guard officers is also described in Enrique Rodríguez Loeche, "Como fué asesinado el General Augusto César Sandino," *Bohemia* (Havana), XLI, 7 (February 13, 1949), 20–21, 106, and *Diario de Costa Rica*, February 21, 1936. These accounts are based on the testimony of Abelardo Cuadra, one of the officers at the meeting who later defected to Costa Rica. Other accounts—Somoza, *op. cit.*, pp. 564–565, and Alberto Medina, *Efemerides Nicaraguenses, 1502-1941* (Managua: La Nueva Prensa, 1945), pp. 64–65— tend to support Cuadra, although they omit many of the details. Subsequent events on the night of February 21, 1934, are related in the above works and in The Minister in Nicaragua (Lane) to the Secretary of State, February 22, 1934, DS, 817.00/7939; Lane to the Secretary of State, March 7, 1934, DS, 817.00/7983; Salvatierra, *op. cit.*, pp. 246–249; and Calderón Ramírez, *op. cit.*, pp. 152–157.

29. Quoted in Salvatierra, *op. cit.*, pp. 247–248.

30. *Ibid.*, p. 249.

31. Quotations from Rodríguez Loeche, *op. cit.*, p. 106.

32. *Diario de Costa Rica*, February 21, 1936.

33. *Ibid.*; *New York Times*, March 4, 1934, p. 5; The Minister in Nicaragua (Lane) to the Secretary of State, March 7, 1934, DS, 817.00/7983.

Postscript: The Ghost of Sandino

1. Quoted in *Time*, LIII, 46 (November 15, 1948), 43.

2. Ernesto Guevara, *On Guerrilla Warfare* (New York: Praeger, 1961), p. 66.

3. Alberto Bayo, *150 Questions for a Guerrilla* (Boulder, Colo.: Panther Publications, 1962), p. 31.

4. Guevara, *op. cit.*, p. 31.

5. Sun Tzu, *The Art of War* (New York: Oxford University Press, 1963), p. 109.

6. Engels, in Karl Marx, *The Class Struggles in France, 1848-1850* (New York: New York Labor News Co., 1928), pp. 3–23.

7. Conrad Brandt, *Stalin's Failure in China, 1924-1927* (Cambridge: Harvard University Press, 1958), p. 174.

8. Bayo, *op. cit.*, p. 31.

9. Smith, *et al.*, *op. cit.*, p. 38.

Bibliographical Note

⊂≣

The four principal sources for this book are the writings of General Sandino and his collaborators, the records of the United States Marine Corps, the records of the Guardia Nacional de Nicaragua, and the records of the United States Department of State. The archives of Sandino's army were seized by the Guardia Nacional when General Somoza's troops overran the Sandinista colony at Guiguili in March 1932; many documents captured at this time were subsequently published in Somoza's book, *El verdadero Sandino* (Managua, 1936), but the originals, together with most of the records of the Guardia Nacional since 1932, are not available to researchers. Somoza's book, generally believed to have been ghost-written, is a major source of Sandinista material. Although the nominal author's intention was to show Sandino in an unfavorable light, some of the documents published in the book reflect favorably upon the guerrilla chieftain. The present author has found little reason to doubt the authenticity of the Sandinista documents in *El verdadero Sandino*, some of which are printed in facsimile. Another important source of Sandinista material is Gregorio Selser's eulogistic, two-volume *Sandino, general de hombres libres* (Buenos Aires, 1959). Gustavo Alemán Bolaños, another admirer of Sandino, has published many Sandinista documents in his book *Sandino, el Libertador* (Mexico, 1952) and in other works, but most of this material can also be found in Selser. The works of Somoza, Selser, and Alemán Bolaños are, in fact, more compilations of raw documents than true historical studies.

Some original Sandinista material is available for study in the archives of the U. S. Marine Corps, of the Department of State, and of the Guardia Nacional de Nicaragua for the period 1927–1932. Most of the Sandinista documents in these archives were addressed to American officials or were captured by Marines or Nicaraguan Guardsmen under Marine command during the years 1927–1932. Unfortunately, many Sandinista documents once in Marine Corps possession have since been lost (or retained by individuals as souvenirs) and are available only in the form of Spanish copies or poor English translations.

The records of the Guardia Nacional de Nicaragua for the 1927–1932 period were withdrawn to the United States when the Marines evacuated Nicaragua in January 1933, and have since been deposited in the Naval Records Section of the National Archives in Washington. The records of the Department of State for this period are also in the National Archives, in the Foreign Service Section. Another important source for diplomatic developments is Henry L. Stimson's diary, deposited with the Stimson Papers at Yale University. The records of the U. S. Marine Corps for the 1927–1933 period are available for study at Marine Corps Headquarters in Arlington, Virginia. Much of this Marine material has been microfilmed and may be obtained through inter-library loans. The author has examined both the original Marine records and the microfilm reels but, because the microfilm is more accessible, has chosen to give microfilm references for Marine records cited in the notes whenever possible. Some Marine documents have been printed in the semi-official *Marine Corps Gazette*, and some Department of State records have been published in the serial *Papers Relating to the Foreign Relations of the United States*. In most cases the author has found the published documents to be true copies or accurate translations of the originals and has cited the printed sources in the notes.

Most of the books, pamphlets, and articles that have been written about Sandino and the Marines are strongly partisan. Generally, those published in Latin America (except Nicaragua) are pro-Sandino. Some of these are the works of journalists who interviewed Sandino at one time or another; others, including many of the more recent publications, were produced by writers who never knew Sandino personally and whose primary interests apparently lay in exploiting the Nicaraguan affair for anti-American propaganda purposes. Almost all the books and pamphlets published in Latin America contain some source material: interviews with Sandinistas or complete Sandinista documents. Articles and books published by Marines in the 1920's and 1930's tend to be highly critical of Sandino. More recent Marine writers, although still critical of Sandino's politics, have come to recognize him as an able guerrilla strategist. Many American veterans of the Nicaraguan campaign have written articles for the *Marine Corps Gazette*, a journal edited on the Marine base at Quantico, Virginia, by Marine officers on active duty. Articles in the civilian-edited magazine *Leatherneck* are sometimes more revealing.

Nicaragua during the Sandino period has been the subject of some academic research in the United States. Joseph O. Baylen's scholarly article, "Sandino: Patriot or Bandit?" (*Hispanic American Historical Review*, August 1951), is a creditable pioneering work and is based on published sources. Charles E. Frazier, Jr.'s doctoral dissertation, "The Dawn of Nationalism and Its Consequences in Nicaragua" (University of Texas, 1958), is more extensive in its treatment of Sandino and is based largely on the records of the State Department. Portions of Frazier's dissertation have been published in the *Journal of the West*, January 1963 and October 1964. Frazier is more critical of Sandino than is Baylen, who tends to idealize his subject. Even more partial to the guerrilla chieftain is Lejeune Cummins, whose book, *Quijote on a Burro* (Mexico, 1958), takes into account much of the Marine literature overlooked by Baylen and Frazier. Better yet, from the military angle, is General Vernon E. Megee's extensive master's thesis, "United States Military Intervention in Nicaragua" (University of Texas, 1963), which combines scholarly research with the insight of a veteran of the Nicaraguan campaign. Excerpts from Megee's thesis have been published in the *Marine Corps Gazette*, June 1965. Other interesting studies have been produced by midshipmen at the United States Naval Academy. For a listing of these and other works on the Nicaraguan campaign, see Neill Macaulay, "Sandino and the Marines" (doctoral dissertation, University of Texas, 1965), pp. 313–326.

Index

Abaunza, Arnoldo Ramírez. *See* Ramírez Abaunza, Arnoldo.
Abaunza, Gustavo, 236, 253, 254
Accessory Transit Company, 21, 22
Acevedo, Señor, 182, 183
Achuapa, ambush of Marines at, 183
Agrarian Reform Institute, Guatemala, 263
Aguinaldo, Emilio, 75
Aircraft squadrons. *See* U.S. Marines, aircraft squadrons.
Alday, Concepcion, 46–47
Alexander, Irving, 130
Algeria, 10, 268
All American Anti-Imperialist League, 112
Altamirano, Pedro. *See* Pedrón.
Altamirano, Rafael, 219
Altamirano (Rafael), Señora de, 219
Amauta (Lima), 113
American Legion, 113
American Popular Revolutionary Alliance (APRA), 114, 157
Anti-Imperialist Congress, Frankfurt, Germany, 113–114
Anti-Imperialist League, 112–113
Arauz, Angelita González, 248, 249
Arauz, Blanca. *See* Sandino, Blanca Arauz de.
Arauz, Lucila, 63
Arauz, Luís Rubén, 214, 215
Arauz, Pablo, 56, 63, 215
Arauz, Pedro Antonio, 214, 215
Arbènz, Jacobo, 263
Ardila Gómez, Rubén, 124, 147, 148
Ariel (Tegucigalpa), 96, 113
Asheville (USS), 196, 198
Autogiro, 226, 227, 228
Auypini trail, 194

Avendaño, Francisco, 210, 223

Bálsamo, Marine ambush near, 163
Banana industry, 22, 23, 186, 192, 225. *See also* Standard Fruit Company; United Fruit Company.
Barbusse, Henri, 113
Batista, Fulgencio, 260
Bayo, Alberto, 261, 269
Beadle, Elias R.: policy of as Director of the National Guard, 135; friction with President Moncada, 136; removal from command, 137; replacement for, 142
Beals, Carleton, 112; interview with Sandino, 105–106; estimate of McCoy by, 127
Beardsley, Ralph, 195, 196
Beaulac, Willard, 190, 217, 218, 221–222; on futility of intervention, 120, 240; American warship ordered by, 192–193
Becker, Herbert P., 208
Benson, W. W., 145
Bernard, Adolfo, 128, 129
Bernheim, Jorge, 234
Berry, M. S., 29
Blanco, Frederico Davidson, 233–
Blandón, Pedro, 189–190; attack at Logtown, 192, 194, 195
Bleasdale, Victor F., 74, 85, 89, 126–127
Bluefields, 22, 23, 25, 28, 186, 193, 199, 207
Boaco, 56, 58, 59
Boaquito, 58
Bocay, 123, 188
Bocay River, 123
Bolívar, Simón, 53, 123

Bonanza gold mine, 119, 145
Borah, William E., opposition to intervention, 31, 183
Bosch, Juan, 12
Boyden, Hayne D. (Cukoo), 80
Bragman's Bluff Lumber Company, 192
Brauer, J. Ogden, 202, 203
Brazil, 9
Brezenger, Rev. Otto, 190
Bromaderos, ambush at, 109–110
Brown, Ruben, 215
Brown, Wilbur S. (Big Foot), 67
Bruce, Thomas G., 78, 81, 100, 113
Brunton, Laurence C., 224
Bryan-Chamorro Treaty, 24, 220
Buchanan, Richard B., 43–44
Buena Vista, 162
Bundy, McGeorge, 8, 240
Bunker, Ellsworth, 8
Bunn, Bennie M., 239
Bush warfare, 94, 173. See Guerrilla warfare.
Business interests, American, 21–24; U.S. protection of, 199–200. See also Bluefields; Bonanza gold mine; Bragman's Bluff Lumber Company; Louisiana Farm; Neptune mine; Pis Pis mining district; Standard Fruit Company; United Fruit Company; Wakiwas Farm.
Butters, Charles, 54, 73

Caamaño Deñó, Francisco, 8, 9
Cabo Gracias a Dios, 196, 197, 198, 208
Cabulla, General, 42, 46, 47
Caldera, Augusto, 139, 141
Calderón, Margarita, 48, 49, 131, 278n
Calderón Ramírez, Salvador, 245, 251, 252, 254
Calles, Plutarco Elías, 158, 286
Camino Real, 99, 169
Cárdenas, Zoila Rosa, 254
"Caribbean Legion," 261, 262
Carlson, Evans F., 168, 169–170, 176, 225, 241
Carranza, Venustiano, 51
Carter, Calvin B., 25, 33
Castro, Fidel, 10–11, 260–264
Cayo Confites, 260, 261
Central America, Federation of, 19

Cerro Azul, Mexico, 51
Challacombe, Arthur D., 137
Chamorro, Emiliano, 24, 25, 26, 57, 221
Chappell, C. J., 43, 44, 95
Chiang Kai-shek, 265, 267, 268
Chichigalpa, 216, 233
China, 9, 10, 70, 114, 265, 268
Chinandega, 21, 27, 33, 42, 161, 164, 206, 233
Choluteca, Honduras, 180
Chontales department, 206
Cierva, Juan de la, 227
Clark, C. H., 220
Class Struggle in France (Marx), 266
Cockburn, Adolfo, 197, 208, 209; influence on Indians, 189; death of, 210–211, 223
Coco River, 62, 91, 141, 208, 249
Coffee plantations, 23, 108, 155, 171, 182
Colindres, Juan Gregorio, 124, 206, 216, 217, 223, 224, 233, 235, 262
Colindres, Vicente Mejía, 142, 146
Communications, 152, 183, 196
Communist International (Comintern): defense of Sandino by, 112, 113; representative of on Sandino's staff, 157; support of American communist, 225; partial rejection of by Sandino, 226
Congressional Medal of Honor, awards of to Marine officers, 101, 175
Constancia, 138
Coolidge, Calvin, 30, 31, 142, 199; non-intervention policy of, 8, 12; at Pan American Conference, 102
Corinto, 21, 22, 28, 105
"Cortes," 212
Costa Rica, 113, 223, 261
Covington, Laurin T., 224
Cruz, Ignacio, 138
Cuba, 10, 11, 41, 102, 142, 260. See also Castro, Fidel.
Cuyu Tigne – Puerto Cabezas railroad, 211

Danlí, Honduras, 180
Danta, 233
Darío, Rubén, 19, 34
Darnall, G. C., 76

Darrah, Clyde, 192, 194
Davidson, James A., 145
Davidson Blanco, Frederico. *See* Blanco, Frederico Davidson.
Defending Army of Nicaraguan Autonomy, 161
Defending Army of the National Sovereignty of Nicaragua, 146, 206; Articles of Incorporation of, 90, 91. *See also* Sandinistas.
De la Huerta, Adolfo, 52
Delgadillo, Lisandro, 253, 255, 256; membership in Masonic Order, 254, 255
De Mille, Cecil B., 111
Denig, Robert L., 161, 162
Dennis, Lawrence, 26, 200
Denver (USS), 26
Díaz, Adolfo, 26–29, 35, 38, 41, 42, 111, 119, 126, 135, 136, 221, 232; requests Marines, 24; agreement with Stimson, 34
Díaz, José León, 50, 182, 206, 215, 233
Dodds, Harold W., 126
Dollar Diplomacy, 22, 119
Dominican Republic, 7, 8, 12, 41, 240, 259, 272
Dowdell, Frank E., 93
Duggan, Lawrence, 230
Dulles, John Foster, 114
Dunlap, Robert H., 102, 114, 115, 118, 139, 140

Eberhardt, Charles C., 32, 34; at Tipitapa, 36; National Guard controversy, 136–137; replaced by Hanna, 142
Edson, Merrit A. (Red Mike), 123, 141
El Chipote mountain, 69, 87, 88, 90, 140, 165, 219; Sandino's headquarters at, 96; aerial attacks on, 103–104
El Chipotón, 206
El Salvador, 19, 148, 149
El Saraguazca, 166–167, 243–244
El Sauce, 217, 238
Embocaderos, 204, 232
Engels, Friedrich, 266
Escamilla, Juan, 140–143, 154
Estelí, 151, 206, 216, 233

Estrada, Francisco, 71, 150, 224–225, 248–255 *passim;* death of, 256

Fagan, Richard, 145, 165
Fagot, Albert, 197, 198
Fagot, Hugo, 198
Falcón, César, 159
Feland, Logan, 46, 65, 70, 72, 73, 89, 102, 114, 125, 127, 137; assumes command of Marines, 29; attempts to reason with Sandino, 131–132; National Guard dispute, 136, 139; leaves Nicaragua, 142
Fellowship of Reconciliation, 97
Ferrara, General. *See* Ortez y Guillén, Miguel Angel.
Ferretti, Juan, 255
Fidelistas, 263, 264, 265. *See also* Castro, Fidel.
Figueres, José, 262
Fitzgerald, Glendall L., 43, 44
Floyd, Oliver, 73, 74, 84–89 *passim*
French, A. E., 137
Friends, Society of, American, 97
Frisbie, Granville K., 219
Fuller, Ben H., 184

Galeano, Antonio, 119
Galt, Alexander, 137, 138
García, José, 234
Gardner, George E., 217
Garrobo, 121, 125
Gilbert, Gregorio, 148
Girón Ruano, Manuel María, 118, 121–123; capture of, 138; trial and execution, 140–141
Gleason, Philip, 54
Gómez, Rubén Ardila. *See* Ardila Gómez, Rubén.
González, José Constantino, 114, 184
González, Simón, 168, 169, 224, 225
Good, George F., Jr., 170, 171
Good Neighbor Policy, 258
Gould, Moses J., 95, 99
Granada, 20, 22
Granada, Bishop of (José Canuto), 126
Granada-Managua-Corinto railroad, 28
Graves, Avery, 172
Gray, Earl T., 220
Great Britain, protectorate over mosquito coast, 21, 22, 187

Griffin, R. G., Jr., 217
Groves, Leslie R., 191
Guanacastillo, 100, 137
Guapinol, Mount, 163, 170
Guatemala, 19, 51, 148, 261
Guerrilla warfare: general characteristics of, 9, 10, 263–271. *See also* China; Cuba; Sandinistas.
Guerrillas. *See* Sandinistas.
Guevara, Ernesto (Che), 10, 262–264
Guiguili, colonization project, 248
Gulick, Louis M., 89, 98, 102
Gutiérrez, Perfecto, 220
Gutiérrez, Policarpo, 100, 229, 242, 253, 255

Haiti, 41, 135
Hanna, Matthew E., 142, 154, 184, 190, 221–222; on road-building, 178; on resettlement, 164; and Somoza, 237
Hanna, Mrs. Matthew E., 222, 237
Hanneken, Herman H., 138, 140, 141, 143, 241
Hart, Frank A., 42, 46
Hatfield, Gilbert D., 69, 73, 76, 81, 84; corresponds with Sandino, 71, 72, 75, 79
Haya de la Torre, Victor Raúl, 84, 105, 114
Henrich, Charles, 217
Heritage, Gordon B., 208, 209
Hernández, Daniel, 220
Ho Chi Minh, 268, 269
Honduras, 19, 87, 102, 103, 141, 142, 147; Sandino's trip across, 148–149; Sandinista arms procurement in, 55, 150, 180; communists in, 225
Hoover, Herbert, 142, 179, 221, 258; for withdrawal of Marines, 135, 184–185, 218
Hoover, J. Edgar, 225
Huasteca Petroleum Company, Mexico, 51, 52, 54
Huerta, Adolfo de la. *See* De la Huerta, Adolfo.
Hughes, Charles Evans, 31, 102
Hunter, Robert S., 122; awarded posthumous Navy Cross, 123
Hutchcroft, D. H., 216

Ililiquas, ambush at, 123–124

Indians, 34, 67, 68, 87, 187, 196, 197, 209, 210
Indochina, 268
Industrial Workers of the World, in Mexico, 52
Irías, López. *See* López Irías, General.
Irías, Pedro Antonio, 150, 206

Jabali gold mine, 207
Jackson, Marvin A., 44
Jalapa, 168, 169
Japan, 201
J. G. White Company, 137
Jicaral, 223
Jícaro, 55, 71, 88, 89, 95, 150, 154, 224, 234
Jiménez, Sebastian, 223, 225
Jinotega, 29, 57, 58, 62, 98, 163, 233, 244
Jinotega department, 128, 138, 152, 172, 220, 232
Johnson, Alfred W., 179
Johnson, C. W., 224
Johnson, Lyndon B., 8, 12
Johnson, Roy, 96, 97
Jones, Robert Cuba, 98

Katayama Sen, 114
Keimling, H. S., 92
Keller, Jacob G., 234
Kellogg, Frank B., 31, 83, 111, 142
Kellogg-Briand Peace Pact, 111
Kennedy, John F., 11
Kipp, Harry E., 202
Kisalaya, 197, 210, 225; meeting at, 223
Knox, Philander C., 23, 119

Laborde, Hernán, 158
La Ceiba, Honduras, 50
La Colonia, 155, 156
La Flor, 122
Lake Managua, 20, 21, 233
Lake Nicaragua, 20, 21
La Luz gold mine, 119, 122, 145
Lane, Arthur Bliss, 251, 252, 255
La Paloma mountain, 216
La Pavona, 206
La Paz Centro, 43, 44
La Pelona, 233
Larios, Fernando, 154, 155
Las Cruces hill, 100, 170

Las Perlas, 22; attack on, 55, 56
Las Puertas, ambush near, 224
Latimer, Julian L., 27, 32, 34, 40, 70, 73, 89
Latin America: U.S. image in, 7, 257; revolutionaries in, 260; guerrilla movements in, 271–273; U.S. intervention in, 272
La Tribuna (Managua), 143
Lee, William A., 229, 233, 238, 270
Lejeune, John A., 70, 73, 112, 125, 139
Lenin, Nikolai, 266–267
León, 20, 21, 45, 105
León department, 154, 206, 216, 232
León, University of, 44, 226
Levonski, Charles J., 223
Lewis, A. T., 154
Lindo Lugar, ambush at, 232–233
Livermore, Edward L., 163
Livingston, Richard, 98, 99, 100
Logtown, 192, 194, 195
Loma Fortress, 24
López, Irías, General, 56, 58
López, José, 203
Los Angeles gold mine, 119
Los Leones, 224
Louisiana Farm, 192, 211
Lumber, 23

"M" Company, National Guard, 173, 229, 232, 270
Machado, Gustavo, 113, 157, 158, 226
Madero, Francisco, 51
Malacate mountain, 172
Managua, 20, 21, 24, 46, 118, 216, 251; airfield, 255; earthquake, 190, 191
Managua-Corinto railway, 216
Mao Tse-tung, 9, 267, 268, 269
Mariátegui, José Carlos, 113
Marín, Rufo, 75, 78, 79
Marines. *See* U.S. Marines.
Marshall, George B., 119
Martí, Agustín Farabundo, 148, 157, 160, 226
Martínez, Juana, 202, 203
Masonic Fraternity (Ancient Free and Accepted Masons). *See* Delgadillo; Sandino; Somoza.
Matagalpa, 23, 29, 67, 98, 101, 105, 107, 108

Matagalpa department, 152, 155, 171, 206, 219
Matiguas, 181
Matthews, Calvin B., 192, 236, 238
Mayacundo, 217
McCoy, Frank R., 126, 130, 184
McCoy Election Law, 220
McDougal, Douglas C., 142, 144, 154, 184
McGhee, William H., 204
MacNulty, William K., 110
Megee, Vernon E.. 167, 229
Merida, Mexico, 149, 157
Metcalf, Clyde H., 134
Mexico, 9, 24, 25, 27, 52, 158; nationalism in, 53
Midence, Juan, 182, 183
Mistral, Gabriela, 113
Molony, Guy R. (Machine Gun), 127
Momotombo volcano, 34
Moncada, José Maria, 25, 38, 55, 59, 60, 128–129, 136, 175, 178, 216, 221–222, 239; description of, 37–38; at Tipitapa, 38; on resettlement program, 164; favors Somoza, 236–237
Monterrey, Carlos Eddy, 255
Moravian Church, 187, 188, 190
Morrow, Dwight, 148
Mosher, W. G., 144
Mosquito Coast, 152, 198, 206, 211, 224; British protectorate of, 21, 22, 187; Indians on, 186, 189, 215, 223; Moravian Church on, 187, 188; raids on, 191
Mount Yucapuca, 56, 243
Mules, 67, 72, 139, 153, 170–171, 173
Munro, Dana G., 98, 240
Murphy, Austin, 192
Murra, 115, 116, 118
Muy Muy, 29, 56, 58

Nation (New York), 106
National Guard, 73, 114, 135–137, 161, 236, 256; auxiliaries, 178, 216, 217, 223, 233, 234; casualties, 239–240; desertions, 168, 169, 170; legal status of, 136, 137, 144; Marine officers of, 73, 151, 155, 173–177; mutinies in, 102, 154, 173, 223, 225; Nicaraguan officers of, 175, 176, 230, 236; supervision of elec-

National Guard, (cont.)
tions by, 179, 180, 230; transportation, 153–154 (see also Mules);
Volunteer Army, 73, 74, 84, 85,
136–144 passim; at Balsamo, 163;
in Camino Real, 99; at Dante, 233;
at El Chipote, 139; at El Sauce,
238; at El Saraguazca, 244; at
Guapinol, 170; at Jinotega, 98,
232; at La Pelona, 233; at Las
Cruces, 100, 170; at Las Puertas,
166, 220, 224; at Logtown, 192,
195; at Malacate, 172; at Matigues,
181; at Nueva Segovia, 171, 220,
223; at Ocotal, 76, 81, 139, 224; at
Palacaguina, 202–204; at Peña
Blanca, 220; at Puerto Cabezas,
194, 195; at San Albino, 139; at
Snaki bridge, 192, 194; at Somoto,
183; at Telpaneca, 92, 98; at
Wakiwas Farm, 194, 195; on Zapotillo ridge, 94. See also "M"
Company, National Guard.
National Guard Law, 144, 220
Navy Cross, awarded to Hunter, 123
Nehru, Jawaharlal, 114
Neptune mine, 145, 190
Nicaragua: political parties, 19, 20,
126, 220; civil war in, 25–26, 30,
287; U.S.-supervised elections in,
24, 129, 230, 235
Nicaraguan canal, 20
Nicaraguan Military Academy, 175,
217, 230
Nicarao, Chief, 34
Niquinohomo, 48, 49, 54, 66
Norris, George, 31
North American Newspaper Alliance, 112
Nueva Segovia, 54, 70–74 passim,
89, 128, 151, 202, 206, 220, 223,
233, 234; expedition to, 66–69

Obregón, Alvaro, 51, 52
Ocotal, 67, 68, 78, 80, 115, 161; airfield, 68, 118
O'Day, Edward F., 109, 110
O'Neill, Dr. John B., 94
Ortez family, 164
Ortez y Guillén, Miguel Angel
(General Ferrara), 109, 110, 118,
120, 151, 156, 163, 168, 171, 172;

proclamations, 161, 165; at Bálsamo, 163; description of, 182,
202; death of, 203
O'Shea, George J., 89, 90, 93, 94

Palacaguina, 202, 203
Pan American Conference, Havana,
102
Paredes, José de, 147, 148, 156, 292n
Parajón, Francisco, 27, 29, 33, 58,
60
"Part-time bandits," 128
"Patriotic Group," 231, 237
Pavletich, Esteban, 157, 158
Peard, Roger W., 101, 127; Brief
Survey of Bandit Operations in
the Northern Area, 127
Pedrón (Pedro Altamirano), 150,
151, 162, 163, 181, 182, 201, 204,
206, 207, 220, 225, 232, 233, 262
Pefley, Harlan, 192
Peña Blanca, 182, 204, 220, 232
Pennington, O. E., 228, 229
Peralta, Ismael, 181, 206, 233, 235
Pfaeffle, W., captured at Jabali gold
mine, 207
Pierce, Harold Clifton, mission to
Nueva Segovia, 66–67
Pis Pis mining district, 118, 120, 123,
145, 186, 190, 201, 225
Portes Gil, Emilio, 158; offers Sandino political asylum, 148
Portocarrero, Horacio, 232, 235–236,
251–254
Power, Lester E., at Embocaderos,
204, 232
Prinzapolca, 56; sailors and marines
land at, 27
Provisional Guardsmen. See National Guard.
Puerto Cabezas, 55, 56, 118, 124, 186,
189, 194, 199, 209; sailors and Marines land at, 27; terrorized by
guerrillas, 196; air patrols, 208
Puller, Lewis B., 172–174, 229, 241,
270; "The Tiger of the Mountains," 173; at Lindo Lugar, 232–
233; at El Sauce, 238–239

Quakers, American. See Friends,
Society of, American.
Quilali, 97, 99, 100; airlift, 101;
desertions from garrison, 223

Rama, 207
Ramírez, Salvador Calderón. *See* Calderón Ramírez, Salvador.
Ramírez Abaunza, Arnoldo, 66, 67, 69, 80, 282*n*
Raudales, Ramón, 260, 262
Repertorio Americano (San José), 113
Reyes, Alberto, 243
Reyes, Carlos, 223
Reyes, Rigoberto, 247
Richal, Merton A., 98, 100, 101
Richards, William P., 46
Ridgway, Matthew B., 127, 128, 130
Riewe, Fred, 207
Río Grande, 27
Rivas, Dagoberto, 50
Rivas, Julio César, 285–286*n*
Rivera, Abraham, 188, 196–198, 206, 210, 214
Rockey, Keller, 109
Rogers, Will, 95, 284*n*
Roosevelt, Franklin D.: non-intervention tradition, 8; initiates Good Neighbor Policy, 258
Rowell, Ross E., 80–81, 103, 116
Russel, Elbert, 97

Sacasa, Antioco, 254
Sacasa, Federico, 254
Sacasa, Juan Bautista, 24, 25, 28, 35, 55, 232, 237, 238, 242–254 *passim*, 282*n*; elected president, 235; peace agreement with Sandino, 246–247
Sacklin, 188, 208
Salazar, Lisandro, 197
Salgado, Carlos, 91, 128, 171, 182, 206, 215, 223, 224, 233
Salvatierra, Alejandro, 243
Salvatierra, Sofonías, 231, 237, 243–247, 251–255 *passim*
Samuelson, H., 144, 164
San Albino, 101, 103, 138
San Albino gold mine, 54, 73, 88
San Antonio, 138, 220
Sánchez, Porfirio, 79
Sandinistas, 263–264; anti-election activities, 232; camps, 219; casualties, 92, 110, 239–240 (*see also* under place of action); Civic Guard, 128; defections, 128; desertions, 65; discipline of, 119, 213; Emergency Auxiliaries, 248, 250;

insignia of, 58, 198; looting by, 78, 79, 110, 119, 169, 211; officers of, 204, 224, 262; tactics, 99, 121 (*see also* under place of action); weapons, 247; procurement of, 55, 150, 167, 168, 180
Sandino, Asunción, 48
Sandino, Augusto César, 8, 40, 54, 102, 115, 273; birth, 48; youth, 49–53; marriage, 64; daughter, 248; death, 256; characterizations of, 57, 106, 111–112, 159, 241; and communists, 112–114, 157–158, 160, 247; on destruction of American-owned property, 119, 186, 211; manifestos of, 74, 96, 248; membership in Masonic orders, 53, 215; motto, 157; and press, 95, 102, 107, 247; proclamations of, 62–64, 83, 214; tactics of, 10, 99, 100, 121–122, 266–267; peace agreement with Sacasa, 246
Sandino, Blanca Arauz de, 98, 103, 131, 132, 167, 214, 215, 242–244, 248, 293*n*
Sandino, Blanca Segovia, 148–149
Sandino, Don Gregorio, 48, 49, 66, 131, 243, 254, 255
Sandino, Doña América, 48
Sandino, Santiago, 50
Sandino, Sócrates, 48, 212, 214, 223, 251, 255, 256; and communists, 112, 158
Sandino, Zoila América, 48
"Sandino City." *See* Jícaro.
Sandoval, Onofre, 56
San Fernando, 71, 83, 85
San Francisco de Cuajiniguilapa, 156
San Francisco del Carnicero, 233
San Isidro, meeting at, 225
San Juan de Telpaneca, 168
San Juan del Norte, 21
San Marcos, 25
San Rafael del Norte, 56, 57, 63, 65, 67, 98, 105, 243, 247
Santa Clara, ambush at, 86
Santa Isabela, 217
Santo Domingo, raid on, 207
Sayre, John Nevin, 98
Schick, René, 259
Schilt, Christian F.: Quilali airlift, 101; awarded Congressional Medal of Honor, 101

Schmierer, Edward H., 225
Schwerin, J. P., 168
Scott, Marvin, 165
Segovia Mountains, 63, 248
Sellers, David F., 89, 102, 130, 132, 135
Selser, Gregorio, 278
Sequeira, Antonio, 127
Sequeira, Francisco. *See* Cabulla, General.
Shaw, Norman M., 129
Simmons, Orville B., 208, 209
Snaki bridge, ambush at, 193, 194
Solano, Isaac, 141
Solórzano, Carlos, 24, 25
Somotillo, meeting at, 102
Somoto, 183
Somoza, Anastasio (Tacho), 25, 36, 126, 191, 243, 245, 249, 251, 256, 258, 260, 262; description of, 236–237; Chief Director of National Guard, 236; membership in Masonic orders, 254; dictator, 256; assassinated, 257
Somoza, Luís, 256, 259
Somoza, Señora Salvadora Debayle de, 237
Somoza Debayle, Anastasio (Tachito), 259, 260
South Penn Oil Company, Mexico, 51
Stalin, Joseph, 266, 267
Standard Fruit Company, 50, 152, 186, 189, 192, 200, 211, 225; Sandinista raids on, 197–198
Standard Oil Company of Indiana, 51
Stimson, Henry L., 31, 70, 142, 143, 179, 217, 230; and Moncada, 37–39; intervention policy of, 41, 198, 240; on withdrawal of Marines, 184, 185, 201, 218, 232
Stimson, Mrs. Henry L. (nee Mabel White), 32
Stimson-Díaz agreement, 34, 102, 126
Sultan, Dan I., 191
Sun Yat-sen, Madame, 114
Suprenant, Edward J., 210, 223

Taft, William Howard, 24, 32; Dollar Diplomacy of, 22
Tamarindo, 165
Tampico, Mexico, 51–53

Telica, looting of, 181, 182
Telles, Ramón, 67, 282*n*
Telpaneca, 69, 91, 92; mutinies at, 154–155
Teustepe, 59
Thomas, Earl A., 93, 103
Toro, Rafael, 85
Torre, Haya de la. *See* Haya de la Torre, Víctor Raul.
Truesdale, Donald L., 44, 219; awarded Congressional Medal of Honor, 175
Trujillo, Rafael, 260
Turcios, Froylán, 95, 96, 102, 105, 146

Uhrig, Harold A., 162
Umanzor, Juan Pablo, 202, 203, 206, 216, 217, 220, 223, 232, 234, 238, 239, 254–256; description of, 202; death of, 256
United Fruit Company, 186, 225
United States government: intervention policy of, 7–9, 26, 27, 199, 240, 257, 272; supervision of elections, 24, 129, 230, 235
U.S.–Latin American relations, 7, 8, 11, 12, 240, 257, 271–273
U.S. Marines, 7, 23–25, 28, 89, 41, 134, 151, 184, 235, 239–241; at La Paz Centro, 43; at Jinotega, 65; mission to Nueva Segovia, 67–73 *passim*; at San Fernando, 85; at Santa Clara, 86; at Telpaneca, 92; on Zapotillo ridge, 94; in Camino Real, 99; at Bromaderos, 109–110; at La Flor, 122; at Achupa, 183; Marine officers of National Guard, 73, 173–174, 183, 217; civic-military relations, 125, 145; paid informers, 130–131; transportation problems, 153–154; communications, 68, 153–154, 183; supply problems, 75, 115; desertions from, 75, 100, 146; charged with atrocities, 228, 229
U.S. Marines, aircraft squadrons, 33, 75, 89, 92, 103, 118, 131, 166, 172; at Ocotal, 20, 80; at El Chipote, 25, 96, 103; at Sacklin, 60; at Santa Clara, 86; at Zapotillo ridge, 95; at Camino Real, 99; at Las Cruces hill, 100; at San Rafael del

Norte, 106; at Murra, 115, 116; at Jinotega, 166; at El Saraguazca, 167, 206; at Snaki bridge, 194, 195; at Cabo Gracias a Dios, 198; dive bombing by, 81, 118; patrol duty, 29, 86, 208; communications, 68, 152, 196; evacuations by, 84, 101, 124; use of Curtis Falcons, 103, 118; of Fokkers, 118; of De Haviland planes, 68, 80, 103; of Loening aircraft, 118, 124, 193, 208; of Vought Corsairs, 103, 118; combat support by, 101, 153; reconnaissance by, 117, 118; alleged atrocities of, 116, 302n
U.S. Marines, Eleventh Regiment, 89, 102, 109, 114
U.S. Marines, Fifth Regiment, 65, 89, 114

Vaca, Dr. Arturo, 56
Vaccaro Brothers and Company. *See* Standard Fruit Company.
Valle de las Zepatas, 217, 223
Vanderbilt, Cornelius, 21, 22
Vasconcelos, José, 84
Vega, Dr. Arturo, 235
Venezuela, 9, 261
Veracruz, Mexico, 52, 149
Vietnam, 10, 240, 271
Villa, Pancho, 51, 52, 272, 279n

Villatoro, Teresa, 103, 124, 167, 214, 293n
Volcanos, 20
Volunteer Army. *See* National Guard.

Wakiwas Farm, 194-195
Walker, Fred, 302n
Walker, William, 21, 22
Wamblam, 121, 124
Welles, Sumner, 31
Wheeler, Burton K., 84
Whitehead, Finis L., 224
Willey, J. A., 144
Williams, Dion, 145, 151, 154, 155, 184; replaces Feland, 142
Williams, George, 88
Wodarczyk, Michael, 80, 115
Wood, John C., 194, 195, 196
Woodward, Clark K., 221

Yali, 65, 109, 143, 154
Young, Archibald, 104

Zapata, Emiliano, 51
Zapotillo ridge, 93-95
Zelaya, José Santos, 22, 23, 24, 37, 49, 275n
Zepeda, Pedro José, 95, 113, 157, 168, 212, 235, 236, 244, 245, 251, 284n
Zincer, Julio, 245

Books by Neill Macaulay

Dom Pedro: The Struggle for Liberty in Brazil and Portugal

The Prestes Column: Revolution in Brazil

A Rebel in Cuba: An American's Memoir*

The Sandino Affair*

With David Bushnell: *The Emergence of Latin American in the Nineteenth Century*

Writing as Kevin O'Kelly: *Richland Street: A Novel**

*Available from Wacahoota Press
14312 SE 11th Drive
Micanopy, Florida 32667

www.wacahootapress.com